7-19-73

DACIA

Danube

MOESIA

THRACE

MEDONIA

ASIA

ACHAEA

CRETA

BITHYNIA PONTUS

GALATIA

CAPPADOCIA

CILICIA

Orontes

CYPRUS

ARMENIA

Tigris

P A R T H I A

SYRIA

Euphrates

JUDAEA

ARABIA

CYRENE

EGYPT

Nile

M.Verity

TIBERIUS

TIB

RO

UNIVERSITY OF CALIFORNIA PRESS
Berkeley and Los Angeles 1972

UNIVERSITY OF CALIFORNIA PRESS
Berkeley and Los Angeles, California

ISBN 0–520–02212–2
Library of Congress Catalog Card Number: 74–185511

Printed in Great Britain

To my father and mother

To my father and mother.

CONTENTS

CONTENTS

CONTENTS

ILLUSTRATIONS

Acknowledgements and thanks for permission to reproduce plates 4, 10a, 12, 13 and 14 are due to the Trustees of the British Museum and Richard Du Cane.

Plates 1, 2a, 2b, 3, 5, 6, 8, 10b and 10d are taken from the *Cambridge Ancient History* Vol. IV; plate 7 from Kornemann's *Tiberius*; plates 9 and 15 from Polacco's *Il Volto di Tiberio;* plate 10c from Rogers' *Studies in the Reign of Tiberius;* plate 11 from Lovel and Turner's *Oxyrybchus Papyri;* and plate 16 from Gordon's *Album of Dated Latin Inscriptions.*

The maps were drawn by M. Verity.

PREFACE

It is the aim of this book to give an account of Tiberius' character and of his career that will be at the same time intelligible to the general reader and useful to scholars and students of the early principate. No serious book on Tiberius' reign as a whole has appeared in English since that of Marsh in 1931. Since that time there have been many new discoveries in the fields of epigraphy and papyrology, as well as a steady stream of books and articles on various aspects of Tiberius' life and work. Thus a new biography needs no justification, except perhaps against the charge that imperial biography as a genre is obsolete, if not actually pernicious. In reply it may fairly be said that under Tiberius the political and social development of the empire and the personal history of its ruler are more intricately and intimately dependent upon one another than at any other time, so that neither can be understood in isolation.

I am deeply indebted to my friends Ewen Bowie, Eric Marsden and Jeremy Paterson, all of whom read the entire book in manuscript and made many valuable criticisms and suggestions; they are not of course responsible for whatever faults remain. I should also like to express my gratitude to my publishers for a constant and ready co-operation that has made my task much lighter and pleasanter than it might have been.

Plymouth, April 1971   Robin Seager

CHRONOLOGICAL TABLE

Tiberius' Age

B.C.

20	Tiberius in Armenia. Birth of C. Caesar. ?Marriage of Tiberius and Vipsania.	22
19	Augustus' *imperium* made valid inside Rome.	23
18	Agrippa receives tribunician power.	24
17	Birth of L. Caesar. Adoption of Gaius and Lucius.	25
16	Tiberius praetor.	26
15	Tiberius and Drusus in Rhaetia and Vindelicia. Birth of Germanicus (May 24).	27
14	?Birth of Drusus (October 7).	28
13	Tiberius consul. Agrippa's tribunician power renewed.	29
12	Death of Agrippa (February). Birth of Agrippa Postumus. Betrothal of Tiberius and Julia. Tiberius to Illyricum.	30
11	Tiberius in Illyricum. Tiberius and Drusus receive proconsular *imperium*. Marriage of Tiberius and Julia.	31
10	Tiberius in Illyricum. Son born to Tiberius and Julia.	32
9	Drusus consul. Tiberius in Illyricum. Death of Drusus.	33
8	Tiberius in Germany.	34
7	Tiberius consul 11. Tiberius' triumph (January). Tiberius in Germany.	35
6	Tiberius receives tribunician power, retires to Rhodes.	36
5	Gaius and Lucius *principes iuuentutis*.	37
4		38
3		39
2	Divorce of Tiberius and Julia. Exile of Julia.	40
1	Gaius' mission to the East.	41

A.D.

1	Gaius consul.	42
2	Tiberius returns to Rome. Death of Lucius (August 20).	43
3		44
4	Death of Gaius (February 21). Tiberius receives tribunician power. Adoption of Germanicus by Tiberius. Adoption of Tiberius and Agrippa Postumus by Augustus (June 26). Tiberius to Germany.	45
5	Tiberius in Germany.	46

A.D.

28 Trial of Titius Sabinus. Marriage of younger Agrippina and   69
    Cn. Domitius Ahenobarbus. Revolt of Frisii.
29 Death of Livia. Exile of Agrippina and Nero.   70
30 Imprisonment of Asinius Gallus. Imprisonment of Drusus.   71
    Betrothal of Seianus and Livia Julia.
31 Tiberius consul v, Seianus consul. Seianus executed (October 72
    18). Macro praetorian prefect. Death of Livia Julia.
32   73
33 Death of Asinius Gallus. Death of Drusus. Death of Agrip-   74
    pina (October 18). Financial crisis. Marriages: Gaius and
    Junia Claudilla; Drusilla and L. Cassius Longinus; Julia
    Livilla and M. Vinicius; Julia and C. Rubellius Blandus.
34 Tiberius' province renewed. Suicide of Mam. Scaurus.   75
35 Suicide of Fulcinius Trio. L. Vitellius in the East.   76
36   77
37 Suicide of L. Arruntius. Death of Tiberius (March 16).
    Funeral of Tiberius (April 3).

B   xvii

ABBREVIATIONS

AC	L'antiquité classique.
AJP	American Journal of Philology
BSR	Papers of the British School at Rome.
CAH	Cambridge Ancient History.
CJ	Classical Journal.
CP	Classical Philology.
CQ	Classical Quarterly.
CR	Classical Review.
EJ	V. EHRENBERG and A. H. M. JONES, Documents illustrating the reigns of Augustus and Tiberius,[2] Oxford, 1955.
GR	Greece and Rome.
HSCP	Harvard Studies in Classical Philology.
JRS	Journal of Roman Studies.
MH	Museum Helveticum.
PdP	La parola del passato.
REL	Revue des études latines.
RhM	Rheinisches Museum.
TAPA	Transactions of the American Philological Association.
WS	Wiener Studien.

All other abbreviations and short titles used in the notes should be self-explanatory if reference is made to the bibliography.

TIBERIUS

I

TIBERIUS' CHILDHOOD:
THE POLITICAL BACKGROUND

I. THE END OF THE REPUBLIC

For a man with political ambitions in the late republic the way to eminence in the state was the *cursus honorum*, the succession of magistracies that made up a career in public office. Beginning as quaestor at the age of thirty, he would find himself assigned as paymaster and general aide to a provincial governor or perhaps allotted a financial post at Rome. The next step up was the aedileship or the tribunate of the plebs. As aedile he would be in charge of markets and public buildings and would be expected to ensure his future progress by the giving of lavish games. As tribune he could play a more prominent part, with the power to initiate legislation himself and to hamper public business by his veto. Then came the praetorship, during which he would be engaged in the administration of the civil law or in presiding over one of the standing criminal courts, the *quaestiones*. After his year of office he could, if he chose, serve for a year or sometimes longer as proconsular governor of a province. Finally, at a minimum age of forty-three, he might attain the consulship. In the last decades of the republic a consul's duties were few except in moments of crisis, usually involving nothing more arduous than presiding at the election of the consuls for the following year. To follow his consulship he could again, if he wished, govern a province as proconsul.

The path was steep and narrowed as it climbed: twenty quaestors were elected each year, but only two consuls – it was not until the principate that it became a rare honour for a *consul ordinarius* to hold office for the whole of his year without giving way after a few months to a suffect. Hence many were bound to fall by the wayside. A man's success depended on the influence he could bring to bear, and he stood or fell alone, for at Rome there were no groups that bore any resemblance to the modern political party. He could enhance his personal standing by acquiring military glory and distinction in the arts of peace, oratory and jurisprudence. But even more important was the position he inherited. Over the years every great Roman family built up an intricate nexus of relationships on which the power of its members was based: ties of friendship, marriage and adoption with other families, ties of patronage with individuals of lower rank, with cities, tribes and provinces all over the empire. For a 'new man', one who came of a family no member of which had previously held public office and so lacked these connections, there would normally be no hope of advancement beyond the praetorship, for the *nobiles*, descendants of men who had reached the consulate, jealously guarded the highest office for the scions of their own houses.

But once a man had attained the consulship, whether on merit or because his father had held it, he was at the centre of power, for the dominant force in Roman politics was the senate. All former magistrates were senators for life, but their seniority and long experience gave the opinion of the consulars a weight that would not often be challenged by the mass of senators or by individual magistrates. For although the senate was nominally an advisory body and its decrees had no binding legal force, its traditional authority was so great that for any magistrate to defy or ignore it was an act of rare temerity.

The power of the magistrates was limited in other ways. Their actions could be vetoed by a holder of equal or greater power and also by a tribune of the plebs, for the office of tribune had originally been conceived to protect the people against high-handed magistrates. Even a consul's hands could be tied by his colleague or by a tribune. Moreover a magistrate held office for only a year. When his term was over and he became a private citizen again, he might find himself on trial for any illegal acts he had committed. Praetors, consuls and proconsuls, who might command troops, held *imperium*, which in theory gave them the right to bind, beat and decapitate, symbolized in the *fasces* borne by their attendant lictors. But this right had long been limited by that of *prouocatio*, appeal to the people against the arbitrary exercise of *imperium*. Only a dictator, who might be appointed in a crisis for a term of six months, was not subject to the checks of veto or appeal.

Nor were the various assemblies of the people, which met to pass laws and elect magistrates, able to offer any sustained and consistent challenge to the predominance of the senate. The people met only when summoned by a magistrate and could only say yea or nay to the proposals put before it by him. Moreover, the voting was weighted in various ways to favour the views of the right-thinking rich. The senate provided the only element of corporate continuity in the Roman constitution, and it was this above all that established its authority and gave it the advantage in any contest with an individual magistrate or with the people.

This brief sketch represents an oligarchic ideal. The senate was by no means always unanimous. But in its great days men contended for supremacy within it; they did not attempt to overthrow its power. Only in the last century of the republic was that power subjected to repeated attacks.

First it was the turn of the tribunes of the plebs. Between 133 and 100 the brothers Ti. and C. Sempronius Gracchus and L. Appuleius Saturninus all tried to circumvent the opposition of the senate by taking reforming legislation straight to the people, riding roughshod over the veto of their colleagues and seeking immediate re-election to office. When the customary constitutional checks proved ineffective, the senate did not hesitate to resort to violence: all three tribunes were murdered.

But among his other reforms C. Gracchus had transferred the right to serve on juries from the senate to the equestrian order. The measure, intended to check senatorial corruption, gave a political identity to the *equites*, whose only other unifying feature was the possession of a minimum census qualification, and control of the courts remained a bone of contention for fifty years. The most vocal and politically effective group within the order was formed by the *publicani*, whose interest lay in tax-farming and other state contracts: they were often able to influence the actions of provincial governors and the senate. The efforts of reformers to exploit the *equites* were shortlived and unsuccessful, but it was not until the principate that their energies were harnessed in the army and the imperial civil service.

The tribunate of Ti. Gracchus also marked the beginning of Italian agitation for the Roman citizenship, a demand eventually granted only after a brief but bitter war that broke out in 91. The enfranchisement of Italy was to have profound effects, as new candidates came forward to compete for office and new voters made the assemblies more difficult for Roman politicians to control: the local aristocrats of the Italian towns gradually began to make their way in politics, encountering resistance as long as the republic survived, but surging forward during the triumvirate and early principate.

But what was to prove the most important development of all occurred just before the end of the second century. Faced with a desperate shortage of troops, the great general C. Marius ignored the property qualification for military service and enlisted men who owned no land. Such men came to look to their general for gratuities and grants of land when their period of service came to an end and were prepared, to secure their own interests, to follow him against the state. The senate never found an answer to the problem of the rebellious commander at the head of an army. Marius himself did not use the tool he had forged, but his enemy L. Cornelius Sulla initiated the last stage in the fall of the republic by marching on Rome in 88. Ironically, as dictator in 81, Sulla tried to turn back the tide. But his settlement was rapidly undermined. Less than ten years after his death Cn. Pompeius Magnus was consul for the first time, in 70, although he had held none of the lower offices and was well below the minimum age laid down by Sulla. Pompey's unprecedented career continued with extraordinary commands against the pirates in 67 and Mithridates, king of Pontus, in 66. But a rival soon emerged: C. Julius Caesar, consul in 59. Pompey married Caesar's daughter Julia, but tension between the two men increased throughout the fifties, while Caesar was occupied with the conquest of Gaul and Pompey engaged in political juggling at Rome. Finally in 49, faced with the choice between civil war and political annihilation, Caesar invaded Italy.

The end of the civil war saw Caesar as dictator – not for six months but for life. Senate and magistrates were treated with a contempt that reduced constitutionalists like Cicero to despair. On the Ides of March 44 Caesar paid the price for attempting to ignore the rules of the political game as the Roman governing class had always played it. His assassins misguidedly hoped that with Caesar gone public life as they had known it could continue. Instead his death ushered in a further fifteen years of civil war, administrative chaos, and social and political change, before Augustus established a new order: the principate.

2. TIBERIUS' BIRTH AND INFANCY: THE TRIUMVIRATE

Tiberius Claudius Nero was born at Rome on 16 November, 42.[1] His lineage was ancient and glorious. Both his father, Ti. Claudius Nero, and his mother, Livia Drusilla, were descended from Ap. Claudius Caecus, consul in 307 and 296: Nero from one of Caecus' sons, Ti. Claudius Nero, Livia from another, P. Claudius Pulcher, consul in 249.[2] Both these branches of the patrician Claudii had played a major part in the history of the republic, and the family was renowned for headstrong arrogance and stubborn pride.[3] But the Nerones had dropped into the background – no Claudius Nero had held the highest office since Ti. Claudius Nero, consul in 202 – while the Pulchri had continued to occupy a prominent place, with consuls in 92, 79 and 54, as well as the notorious P. Clodius, Cicero's bitter enemy, tribune of the plebs in 58. By a practice common among the aristocracy, Livia's father had been adopted into another noble house, that of the Livii Drusi, and so became M. Livius Drusus Claudianus. His adoptive father was M. Livius Drusus, the famous tribune of 91, son of the opponent of C. Gracchus.

In 50 Tiberius' father had been hoping to marry Cicero's daughter Tullia,[4] but when the civil war broke out he joined the Caesarian side.

---

[1] *Fer. Cum., F. Ant., Act. Arv. (EJ* p. 54); Suet. *Tib.* 5.1, dismissing the claim that Tiberius was born at Fundi and the alternative dates 43 and 41.

[2] Tac. *Ann.* 6.51, Suet. *Tib.* 3.1 (who mistakenly gives Pulcher's *praenomen* as Appius); for Livia, cf. also Tac. *Ann.* 5.1. The date of the marriage is unknown: probably about 43 or 42. On the Claudii Pulchri of the triumviral and Augustan periods, cf. Wiseman, *HSCP* 74, 1970, 207ff.

[3] Cf. Suet. *Tib.* 2.

[4] Cic. *Att.* 6.6.1.

Quaestor in 48, he commanded the fleet in the Alexandrian campaign.[1] His services on that occasion earned him further favours from Caesar: a priesthood and the task of founding colonies in Gaul at Narbo and Arelate. But like many of Caesar's former adherents he turned against the dictator, and after the Ides of March 44 took up an extreme position in the senatorial debate of 17 March. Both Antony and Cicero spoke in favour of moderation and a general amnesty, but Nero, now an ardent republican, made the provocative suggestion that the 'Liberators' should be rewarded.[2]

During autumn 44 an ominous contest developed between the consul Antony, the senior Caesarian leader, and the nineteen-year-old Octavian, Caesar's great-nephew and posthumously adopted son, who exploited with cold daring the magic of Caesar's name.[3] The immediate prize was control of the Caesarian party and the loyalty of Caesar's veterans, whose demands for land had not yet been satisfied, but for Octavian the ultimate goal was a position of power as great as Caesar's own. Nevertheless at the end of 44 the old republic still had its champions: D. Brutus held the fortress of Mutina, M. Brutus was established in Macedonia and Cassius in Syria. Cicero, republicanism's most eloquent spokesman, dreamed of first employing the youthful Octavian as a weapon against the seemingly more dangerous Antony and then dispensing with him when he had served his purpose, just as the senatorial oligarchy had hoped a decade before to use Pompey to destroy Caesar before discarding him.

Luck, nerve and cunning protected Octavian. At first, in spring 43, he joined forces with the republicans against Antony, but in August he marched on Rome and seized the consulship. Reconciliation with Antony soon followed. In November Octavian, Antony and M. Aemilius Lepidus met near Bononia and agreed to divide power among themselves. On 27 November they were appointed by law as triumvirs to rule the state for five years. In 42 Octavian and Antony set out to deal with Brutus and Cassius. The campaign of Philippi in October of that year set the final seal on the military doom of the

---

[1] Suet. *Tib.* 4.1, *B. Alex.* 25.3.
[2] Suet. *Tib.* 4.1.
[3] On the events of this period, cf. Syme, *RR*, 97ff.

republic. The scions of many noble families were killed, and one of those who committed suicide after the battle was Tiberius' grandfather, Drusus Claudianus.[1] The only remaining centre of resistance was in Sicily, where Sex. Pompeius, the surviving son of Pompey, maintained himself at the head of a pirate fleet. The two dynasts now went their separate ways, Antony to campaign against the Parthians in the East, Octavian to deal with the settlement of veterans in the West.

Tiberius' father was praetor in 42, but at the end of the year he did not lay down his office.[2] Italy was torn by widespread discontent: the financial exactions of the triumvirs, their seizures of land to provide the veterans with allotments and the activities of Sex. Pompeius combined to produce an explosive situation. In 41, with Antony engaged in the East, trouble came to a head at home between Octavian and Antony's friends, led by his wife Fulvia and his brother Lucius, now consul. When war broke out between them Nero, like Lucius, claimed to champion the cause of the dispossessed and attempted to raise Campania.[3] Lucius' forces, penned up in Perusia, eventually surrendered to Octavian in February of 40 and were mercilessly liquidated. But Nero and Livia escaped first to Praeneste and then to Neapolis, and so by sea to Sicily, where Sex. Pompeius offered a haven to refugees.[4] At Neapolis they left the aged C. Velleius, who had served as *praefectus fabrum* (adjutant) under Pompey and Brutus as well as under Nero. Too infirm to follow, Velleius committed suicide, a deed of honour remembered with pride by his grandson, the historian Velleius Paterculus.[5]

But in Sicily Nero did not find the welcome he expected. Sextus did not grant him immediate audience and forbade him the use of the praetorian insignia that he still continued to usurp. Claudian pride could not brook such treatment, and so Nero left Sicily in a huff to throw in his lot with Antony.[6] But even in the relative safety of Greece

[1] Dio 48.44.1, Vell. 2.71.3.
[2] Suet. *Tib.* 4.2.
[3] Tac. *Ann.* 5.1, Suet. *Tib.* 4.2, Vell. 2.75.1.
[4] Suet. *Tib.* 4.2, Dio 48.15.3, Vell. 2.75.3.
[5] Vell. 2.76.1.
[6] Suet. *Tib.* 4.3, Dio 48.15.3.

9

the family almost perished – in a forest fire near Sparta, from
which Livia escaped with only her clothes scorched and her hair
singed.[1]

The infant Tiberius had accompanied his parents in their flight.[2]
Suetonius tells, with what measure of truth we do not know, how his
crying twice almost gave away their hiding-place at Neapolis. In Sicily,
despite his father's failure to come to terms with Sex. Pompeius, the
baby seems to have won the affection of Sextus' sister, who presented
him with a cape and brooches that were still on display at Baiae in
Suetonius' time.

Though Sex. Pompeius had proved inhospitable, it was the need to
solve the problem of the pirate leader that gave Nero and his family
their chance to return. In October of 40 Octavian and Antony had
renewed their alliance at Brundisium, to which Sextus had responded
by raiding the coasts and harassing the corn fleets of Italy. Octavian,
whose power and prestige were more directly affected by Sextus'
activities, was eager for a war that would simplify the situation, for
with Sextus removed he would be free to prepare for the final struggle
with Antony that was one day bound to come. Antony favoured a
reconciliation: it suited him to keep Sextus in play as a useful check to
his rival's boundless ambition, while he himself was detained by war
and pleasure in the East. The people of Italy, desperate for relief from
the horrors of war and the famine provoked by Sextus, also clamoured
for peace. In the face of such an outcry Octavian gave way, and a pact
between the three men was concluded at Misenum in spring 39. One
of its clauses was an amnesty for refugees, and under this condition
Nero, Livia and Tiberius returned to Italy.[3]

There Livia, still only nineteen, attracted the attention of Octavian.
Nero bowed to the triumvir's will and divorced Livia, pregnant as she
was.[4] On 14 January, 38 – the same date as the birthday of Antony –
Tiberius' brother, Drusus Claudius Nero, was born.[5] Only three days

---

[1] Suet. *Tib.* 6.1ff.
[2] Cf. Tac. *Ann.* 6.51.
[3] Tac. *Ann.* 5.1, Suet. *Tib.* 4.3, Vell. 2.77.3.
[4] Suet. *Aug.* 62.2, *Tib.* 4.3, Dio 48.44, Vell. 2.79.2. Tac. *Ann.* 5.1 exaggerates, as the
Fasti show; Suet. *Claud.* 1.1 is nonsense.
[5] Suet. *Claud.* 11.3.

later, on 17 January, Octavian and Livia were married.[1] Nero played no further part in public life, and Tiberius and Drusus grew up in their stepfather's house under the guidance of their proud and ambitious mother. During the years of the disintegration of the triumvirate the child Tiberius made only one public appearance. In 33 his father died and to Tiberius, aged nine, fell the task of pronouncing the public funeral oration.[2] It would be interesting to know who wrote it, and what he found to say.

3. THE AUGUSTAN PRINCIPATE

The battle of Actium in 31 gave Octavian final victory over Antony and Cleopatra. Tiberius shared in his stepfather's triumph, celebrated on 13–15 August of 29. He rode in the third day's procession on the left-hand trace-horse; the place of honour on the right was reserved for Octavian's nephew, M. Claudius Marcellus, son of C. Marcellus, consul in 50, and the princeps' sister Octavia.[3]

Now that the civil wars were over, Octavian set about making sure that no man should ever again be able to achieve such a *coup* as he had accomplished himself. During his long career as princeps – the leading man in the state – his powers were redefined on more than one occasion in order to make his unprecedented position more intelligible and more acceptable to various sections of the community. He boasted later that in 28 and 27 the republic – or constitutional government – had been restored. A grateful Rome rewarded him not only with the surname Augustus, but with a provincial command of novel scope, embracing Gaul, Spain and Syria. But, although he made frequent journeys abroad, Augustus continued to base himself at Rome and retained the consulship for year after year. This unexpected behaviour gave rise to various difficulties. In the first place it created a promotion block. The surviving members of the old aristocracy, whose support or at least acquiescence was vital to the establishment of the new order, were liable to find themselves deprived, by Augustus' constant occupation

---

[1] *F. Ver.* (*EJ* p. 46).
[2] Suet. *Tib.* 6.4.
[3] *F. Tr. Barb.* (*EJ* p. 35), *F. Ant.* (*EJ* p. 50), Suet. *Tib.* 6.4, Dio 51.21.5ff.

of one consulship, of such power and dignity as was still accessible to them, while his own supporters too might be kept from the reward that they expected as their share in their master's success. Nor was it clear what authority Augustus had to interfere, as he sometimes found it necessary to do, in the running of those provinces that were still controlled by the senate.

In 23, to obviate these problems, Augustus resigned the consulship. He now became proconsul of his own vast province, while his *imperium* was declared superior to that of the governors of senatorial provinces – a familiar and therefore acceptable expedient. At the same time he was granted the tribunician power for life. Of this he made little or no practical use: it was rather a symbol of his unceasing concern for the welfare of the common people. Nevertheless the people were not satisfied. Despite his assumption of the tribunician power, they regarded Augustus' resignation of the consulship as a first step back towards the chaos and anarchy of the nobles' bitter competition for high office. Riots were frequent, one consulship was left vacant, and demands were repeatedly made that Augustus should accept either the dictatorship or a lifelong consulship.

Augustus had learned from the errors of Julius Caesar tact, respect for the solemn façade of republican institutions and sensitivity to public opinion. So, in 19, he reformulated his powers yet again. To accede to the clamour of the mob was impossible: Caesar had disgraced the title of dictator for ever, and to resume his hold on the consulship would merely have resuscitated the problem that had prompted his resignation of it in 23. To satisfy the plebs without giving fresh offence to the upper classes Augustus devised a compromise. His *imperium* was made valid inside the city and he occupied a seat of honour between the consuls. Thus he now had the power that the people insisted he should have without the awkwardness that would have ensued if he had actually held the office of consul.

Meanwhile the senate – purged on more than one occasion – and the magistrates continued to fulfil their traditional functions in a simulacrum of the old republican order. Ultimately now, however, men owed their advancement not to the time-honoured qualifications of birth, wealth and personal glory but to the princeps' favour, though his support was often granted on the best of traditional grounds. Augustus' power was beyond any challenge. He was supreme commander of the armies of Rome, supreme guardian of the welfare of the Roman people, and his personal authority and influence were greater than any man's had ever been. For those who had ruled the republic and their descendants the dimming of their splendour and the curb on their ambition and achievement were bitter disappointments: they were not deceived by Augustus' offer of dignity without real power. But for many who would have had no hope of a career under the republic the Augustan régime held out rich rewards for loyal and honourable service. The *equites* too found new scope for their talents in military and administrative posts, while the plebs had quickly realized that Augustus was better, not only at giving games, but also at caring for the water-supply, putting out fires and making the streets safe at night. Such in outline was the new political system under which Tiberius grew to manhood, the system which, by repeated tricks of fate, he was eventually called upon to perpetuate.

II

TIBERIUS AND AUGUSTUS

1. TIBERIUS' FIRST STEPS IN PUBLIC LIFE

Tiberius' early career proceeded with the smoothness that might be expected for the stepson of Augustus. Little, however, is known of the details. Only the bare data of advancement are recorded: magistracies and military service.

At some date which is not preserved, but probably about 33, well before he came of age, Tiberius had been betrothed to Vipsania Agrippina, daughter of the great general Agrippa, whose power in the state was second only to that of Augustus himself.[1] It is possible to see in the match a scheme of Tiberius' mother Livia to strengthen the position of the Claudian house by establishing a link between it and the princeps' most prominent henchman; such an acceptance and exploitation of the realities of power would not be inconsistent with the traditions of the Claudii. But although the betrothal may have been political in conception, the eventual marriage – probably celebrated after Tiberius' return from the East in 20 – was a happy one, founded on sincere affection, and its dissolution at Augustus' behest, in order that Tiberius might marry the princeps' daughter in pursuance of Augustus' private dynastic ambitions, was to leave a lasting scar on Tiberius' personality and may have done something to determine his attitude to the principate as an institution.[2]

---

[1] Vipsania was one year old at the time of the betrothal and Atticus, who died on 31 March, 32 (Nep. *Att.* 22.3), was still alive at the time (Nep. *Att.* 19.4). If Vipsania was fourteen at the time of the marriage, this yields an approximate date of 20. Cf. also Sen. *Ep.* 21.4, *ILS* 165.

[2] Cf. Suet. *Tib.* 7.2f. on Tiberius' affection for Vipsania.

14

On 24 April, 27, Tiberius, now fourteen, assumed the *toga uirilis*,[1] the symbol of manhood, and in the next year came his first experience of military service.[2] The mountain peoples of northern Spain were still reluctant to accept the Roman yoke and Augustus thought it necessary to take command of Rome's forces there in person. Tiberius accompanied him to Spain, with the rank, despite his youth, of military tribune; so too did Augustus' nephew M. Marcellus, who was betrothed to Julia, the princeps' daughter. In 25, when the Cantabrian war was prematurely deemed to be concluded, the two young men collaborated in organizing games in the camps of the Roman army. At some point in the course of his stay in the province Tiberius was adopted as patron by the important city of Nova Carthago.[3]

When Augustus returned to Rome in 24, Marcellus and Tiberius received their share of honours in the course of the general celebrations. Marcellus, whose marriage to Julia had meanwhile been solemnized, with Agrippa presiding on behalf of the absent Augustus, was granted a seat in the senate among the ex-praetors and the right to stand for the consulship ten years before he reached the legal minimum age. Tiberius, less significantly favoured, was given the right to stand for each magistracy at five years below the legal age. Both at once attained office for 23, Marcellus as aedile, Tiberius as quaestor.[4]

In his quaestorship Tiberius, in his nineteenth year, was active in two fields. He set about dealing with the difficulties that bedevilled the corn supply at Rome and at the port of Ostia, a task which suggests that the lot or the princeps may have given him the post of *quaestor Ostiensis*, familiar from the late republic. But Tiberius then moved on to another occupation, investigating the barracks in which slaves were housed up and down Italy to ensure that no free men, victims of brigandage or kidnapping, were being wrongfully confined and no deserters evading justice.[5]

So far this is the typical introduction to public life of a young Roman

---

[1] *F. Prae.* (*EJ* p. 48).
[2] Suet. *Tib.* 9.1, Dio 53.26, Plin. *NH* 14.64.
[3] *ILS* 144.
[4] Dio 53.27f.
[5] Suet. *Tib.* 8, Vell. 2.94.1; for the importance of the corn supply and Augustus' interest in it, cf. *RG* 5.2, 18.

noble, just as it might have been under the republic, except for the accelerated advancement which was henceforth to characterize the careers of youthful members of the ruling house. Tiberius' early forensic activities too are in accordance with republican tradition, though most of the cases in which he appeared were heard not in the public courts but by his stepfather.[1] Thus he defended King Archelaus of Cappadocia before Augustus, also the city of Tralles and the Thessalians, and spoke in the senate on behalf of Laodicea, Thyatira and Chios, which had suffered damage in an earthquake and were seeking relief. In 22 he undertook his first and as far as is known his only prosecution, arraigning Fannius Caepio before the court that dealt with cases of treason for allegedly conspiring against the life of Augustus. The matter is murky, by accident or design, and the truth is never likely to be known. Tiberius' presence to demand revenge for the attempted assassination of his stepfather was of course entirely proper, and may have been intended to thrust into the foreground the theme of family loyalty and family honour in preference to less savoury political implications. Not surprisingly, Tiberius won his case.

A more important mission abroad was soon to come his way. In the East Augustus had inherited a burdensome legacy from the republic and the upheavals of the triumviral period.[2] In 53 the Parthian expedition of Crassus had ended in disaster at the battle of Carrhae, which had left Roman standards and prisoners in Parthian hands. Julius Caesar had been struck down by his assassins when he had been about to embark on a Parthian war. In the years of turmoil that had followed his death more eagles had been lost, first by Decidius Saxa in 40, then by Antony in his Median expedition of 36. Rome still waited for revenge, and there were many voices that clamoured for a Parthian war. But Augustus had no wish to stir up needless trouble. The Parthian throne was always menaced by internal dissensions, and its occupants were consequently reluctant to indulge in foreign wars of uncertain outcome which might supply occasions for revolution at home. Augustus was eager to stop short of war, provided that the

[1] Suet. *Tib.* 8, Strabo 12.8.18, Agath. *Hist.* 2.17; for Archelaus, cf. also Dio 57.17.3.
[2] On relations between Rome and Parthia, cf. Anderson, *CAH* x, 254ff.; Tarn, *Mélanges Glotz* II, 831ff.

standards and prisoners lost at Carrhae and later could be honourably recovered and a monarch friendly to Rome placed on the throne of Armenia. This valuable buffer-state had been lost to Rome by the intrigues of Antony, who had lured its king, Artavasdes, into his control and then treacherously handed him over to Cleopatra. Artavasdes had been executed by her in 30, and his son Artaxes, disgusted with the treatment his father had received at the hands of a Roman, had shown himself consistently friendly to Parthia and hostile to Rome.

To achieve his limited objectives Augustus judged that diplomacy, backed up by a discreet show of force, would be sufficient. He was by no means ill-supplied with counters to employ in the diplomatic game. At Rome he had not only Tiridates II, who had established himself briefly on the Parthian throne at about the time of Actium but had then been expelled by Phraates III and had taken refuge with Augustus after a second unsuccessful *coup* in about 26, but also Phraates, son of the Parthian king, who had been kidnapped by Tiridates and brought by him to Rome. Also in Augustus' hands were the brothers of Artaxes, the king of Armenia.

In 23 Phraates made the first move. An embassy from Parthia arrived at Rome, demanding the surrender of Tiridates and the return of the young Phraates. Augustus refused to hand over Tiridates but expressed his willingness to give back the king's son on condition that the standards and prisoners were restored to Rome. He himself travelled to Syria in 22, but for two years no progress was made. Then in 20 an opportunity to intervene arose. Armenian representatives came to complain against Artaxes and request that his brother Tigranes be installed as king. The twenty-one-year-old Tiberius was summoned to lead a force to the East, with the object of expelling Artaxes and placing Tigranes, who had now been resident at Rome for ten years, on the throne.[1] This seems to have been the limit of his responsibilities, though the over-enthusiastic Velleius credits him with a general mission to inspect and organize the oriental provinces.[2] Tiberius' task was made simple for him, since Artaxes was murdered by his native opponents before the Roman army reached Armenia. He therefore

[1] *RG* 27.2, Suet. *Tib.* 9.1, Dio 54.8f., Jos. *AJ* 15.105.
[2] Vell. 2.94.2, cf. 2.122.2.

entered the country without opposition and with his own hands placed the crown on Tigranes' head. Phraates, cowed by the presence of a Roman force, did not dispute the loss of Armenia, and the standards too were duly handed over, perhaps to Tiberius himself, on the banks of the Euphrates. This bloodless triumph was widely celebrated, both by poets and by the imperial coinage, and Augustus allowed himself to be hailed as *imperator*.[1] Tiberius too was honoured on his return with praetorian ornaments, while his younger brother Drusus was at the same time granted the privilege, conferred on Tiberius himself three years before, of standing for office at five years below the legal age.[2] It was probably about this time that Tiberius' marriage to Vipsania took place.

2. THE SUCCESSION: MARCELLUS AND THE SONS OF AGRIPPA

Meanwhile Augustus had begun to turn his thoughts to the problem of perpetuating his power. No precedent existed, and moreover the principate was not an established office, with powers prescribed and limited by constitutional law. The position that Augustus had secured for himself in the state was a purely personal one, and it was neither necessary nor certain that, if another princeps succeeded him, his powers would be the same in every detail as those of his predecessor. The foundations of the Augustan principate were on the one hand a bundle of legal powers – granted at different times and in response to differing political needs, and constantly liable to modification on grounds of practical convenience or public pressure – on the other hand his unchallenged personal authority. For his lifetime Augustus was supreme, but when he died, all that made him princeps might be extinguished. This he was determined should not happen. It was his firm intention that the principate should endure and his dearest wish that power should remain in the hands of one of his own family, by a flexible principle of hereditary succession that would allow the princeps

---

[1] Hor. *Epist.* 1.3.1ff., 1.12.26, *Carm.* 4.15, Verg. *Aen.* 7.604ff., Prop. 4.6.79f., Ov. *F.* 5.567ff., *Anth. Pal.* 9.219, 16.61 (cf. Cichorius, *Römische Studien*, 298ff., 313f.); *EJ* 26–28; cf. Sutherland, *Coinage*, 37f., 44.
[2] Dio 54.10.4.

some say in the choice of his political heir if more than one qualified candidate were available.

Augustus' desire to found a dynasty not only ran counter to republican tradition but was also to some extent discordant with the forces that had helped to build up his present position.[1] He had come to power in the troubled years that had followed the death of Caesar, ruthlessly contending with Antony for the leadership of the murdered dictator's supporters. In the war against Antony and Cleopatra and the years since Actium he had acquired, like any great Roman politician, a nucleus of loyal adherents who hoped for lasting personal power and prestige from his victory. It might prove difficult to reconcile his ambitions for his family with the claims of those who may perhaps with all due caution be termed the members of his party. Foremost among these was M. Vipsanius Agrippa, the actual victor in most of Augustus' battles. The nature of the conflict that might arise must have been vividly present to Augustus' mind when he first began to plan the creation of a dynasty, for he himself had been one of the protagonists in an earlier clash between family and party loyalties. When he had come to Rome in 44 to claim his inheritance and with it the name of Caesar, he had been coldly received by Antony. In the struggle for supremacy that followed, he had relied, at least in the early stages, on his status as Caesar's adopted son to win over Caesar's veterans and the people, thereby provoking Antony's famous gibe at the boy who owed everything to a name.[2] Good luck, good nerves and diligence in betrayal had enabled him to oust Antony. But now Agrippa stood to Augustus in a position not dissimilar to that in which Antony himself had once stood to the dictator Caesar – the most distinguished of the many adherents whom Augustus had gathered about him over the years. If Augustus nominated a successor of his own blood, he was bound to be aware of the danger that at his death there might be a repetition of that rivalry between Antony and himself which had split the party and brought about a further fourteen years of civil war. Yet his first tentative effort to secure the succession seemed fraught with peril in this quarter.

[1] Cf. Syme, *RR*, 341.
[2] Cf. Cic. *Phil.* 13.24 and in general Syme, *RR*, 112ff.

The candidate was Augustus' nephew and Agrippa's brother-in-law, M. Claudius Marcellus, who had been married to Julia in 25. On the princeps' return from Spain in 24 the young Marcellus, already a *pontifex*, was admitted to the senate with praetorian rank and granted the right to stand for the consulship ten years before he reached the legal minimum age.[1] It is perhaps not surprising that, in view of these signs of favour, when Augustus fell seriously ill in 23, many men expected Marcellus to be named as his successor.[2] These expectations were disappointed. Augustus, fearing that he had not long to live, did not designate a successor at all. Instead he consigned to the consul Cn. Calpurnius Piso a memorandum of the military and financial resources of the state and handed his signet ring to Agrippa. This was interpreted, according to Dio, as a token of preference for Agrippa. The claims of constitutional propriety and party loyalty had been respected, those of the intended dynasty set aside, at least for the moment.

It is tempting, but dangerous, to speculate about the pressures that may have influenced Augustus' decision. The sources are agreed that despite their relationship Marcellus and Agrippa were not the best of friends and that friction between them was one of the reasons why Agrippa was now sent on a mission to Syria.[3] Dio attributes resentment to Marcellus, who objected, he says, to the implication of preference for Agrippa contained in the handing over to him of the ring; so when Augustus recovered and learned of Marcellus' feelings, he dispatched Agrippa to the East in order to avoid any worsening of relations between the pair. Suetonius on the other hand makes Agrippa take offence because the youthful Marcellus was in general exalted above him and regards the mission to the Orient as no better than a voluntary exile. This interpretation is influenced no doubt by the circumstances of Tiberius' withdrawal to Rhodes. Whatever Agrippa may have thought in private about the prospect of labouring far from the public eye while Marcellus was sedulously courted and fêted at Rome, on the surface there was nothing but honour in his appointment. This pro-

[1] Dio 53.28.3f.
[2] Dio 53.30f.
[3] Suet. *Aug.* 66.3, Dio 53.32, Plin. *NH* 7.149: *pudenda Agrippae ablegatio.* This obviously goes too far, but Syme (*RR*, 342) is too hasty in dismissing the story altogether; he seems to have had second thoughts (ibid. 344).

bably brought him, as legate of the princeps, *imperium* equal with that of Augustus in the imperial provinces. Yet it is true that Augustus must have welcomed the chance to get Agrippa out of the way in this fashion. It is hard to penetrate Agrippa's mask, but Velleius indicates that men did not trust his intentions. They thought, he says, that Marcellus would succeed Augustus, but they did not expect that Agrippa would stand by and see him do so without a struggle.[1]

If, then, Augustus had died in 23, there might have ensued a contest similar to that which had taken place twenty years before. But Augustus lived, allegedly saved by the treatment of the physician Antonius Musa. Instead it was Marcellus who died, despite Musa's efforts, his death the first of the many misfortunes by which Augustus' dynastic policies were dogged.[2] For the moment the risk of a clash between dynastic heir and political lieutenant was averted, but now, if the danger arose again, it would be in an aggravated form. To pass on his power to heirs of the blood Augustus would need grandsons, born to his daughter Julia, now left a widow. It was hardly to be expected that Augustus himself would survive until a hypothetical son of Julia's next marriage attained his majority and so be able to hand over his power direct. If Agrippa did in fact have it in his head to bid for the principate at Augustus' death, he would therefore in all probability have as competitor only a defenceless boy. Augustus was confronted with a two-fold problem. Julia must be provided with a husband, in order that the princeps should have grandsons to carry on the line, and Agrippa's loyalty must somehow be secured, in case Augustus died before him, leaving as his heir a grandson too young to defend himself against a *coup*. Augustus' solution was superbly economical, one of the finest conceptions of a master politician. In 21 Agrippa was persuaded to divorce his wife Marcella, Augustus' niece, and marry Julia.[3] Dio says that the subtle Maecenas had warned Augustus that Agrippa had now been raised to such a height that the princeps had only two choices: he must make Agrippa his son-in-law or put him to death. Augustus saw in the marriage a chance to guarantee his ultimate ends. The

[1] Vell. 2.93.1.
[2] Tac. *Ann.* 1.3, Suet. *Aug.* 63.1, Vell. 2.93.2.
[3] Tac. *Ann.* 1.3, Suet. *Aug.* 63.1, Dio 54.6; cf. Syme, *RR*, 389, 416.

hoped-for grandson who would one day inherit his power would be Agrippa's son. It was not unreasonable to suppose that, whatever measures Agrippa might have adopted against a youthful heir with whom he had no personal tie, he would be unlikely to liquidate a child of his own. If Augustus died while his grandson was still a minor, Agrippa could take over the reins of power and guide the state until such time as the heir of the blood had sufficient experience to rule. The potentially conflicting claims of dynasty and party had been reconciled in advance by making Augustus' political second-in-command the father and guardian of the eventual heir. Out of this expedient devised to neutralize Agrippa there developed the concept of the guardian or regent, whose task was to rule until the time was ripe for the power to be passed on to a direct descendant of Augustus. This was the position for which, after the death of Agrippa, Tiberius was chosen by Augustus, and it is only if the repeated pattern is studied from its inception that the rôle of Tiberius in the overall design can be fully understood.

For the moment all seemed to go well. After his visit to Rome in 21 Agrippa was active in Gaul and Spain, and in 18 he was granted the tribunician power for five years.[1] Next he was sent once more to the East, and he remained there until 13.[2] Despite this constant activity as Augustus' chief administrator he found the time to beget the grandsons that the princeps so ardently desired. The eldest, Gaius, was born in 20, the second, Lucius, in 17, and Augustus made his intentions clear by adopting both boys not long after Lucius' birth.[3] Henceforth they bore the names Gaius and Lucius Caesar. Everything was now as Augustus had planned. He would be succeeded by one of his own blood, one who was at once his grandson and adopted son, and if he should die before Gaius was old enough to govern the empire without assistance, the prince's father Agrippa would be on hand to control affairs in the meantime and to ensure that the eventual transfer of power was smoothly carried out. As far as could be seen, the question of the succession had been settled.

[1] Dio 54.11f.
[2] Dio 54.28.1.
[3] Suet. *Aug.* 64.1, Dio 54.8.5, 18.1. For coins celebrating the adoption, cf. Sutherland, *Coinage*, 58. Cf. also *EJ* 76.

3. THE NORTHERN FRONTIER: RHAETIA AND VINDELICIA

In 16, despite the praetorian rank he had been granted in 20, Tiberius was praetor at the age of twenty-five.[1] The years between his tenure of this office and his retirement to Rhodes were almost entirely taken up with campaigning on Rome's northern frontier. There Augustus found much to be done.[2] His first objective was to conquer the Alpine lands, whose inhabitants sometimes launched raids into Italy and Gaul. Next he proposed the extension of Illyricum to the Danube, giving Rome control of the valleys of the Save and Drave, to link the province of Macedonia with Italy and bring it within easy reach of Gaul and the Rhine. If this plan were successful, the Rhine and Danube would serve as natural boundaries. The third theatre of war was Germany, where a series of expeditions crossed the Rhine in a speculative attempt to extend Rome's dominion to the Elbe. The motive is probably to be sought in the shorter lines of communication which an Elbe–Danube frontier would provide.

To supervise the initiation of his scheme Augustus travelled to Gaul in 16, taking Tiberius with him.[3] In the next year Tiberius and Drusus set out to subdue Rhaetia and Vindelicia. It is difficult to follow their movements in any detail. Drusus was the first to march against the Rhaeti, routing a number of them near the Tridentine Alps. For this he received praetorian ornaments, but the Rhaeti continued to harass Gaul, though they refrained from further raids on Italy.[4] Tiberius then joined Drusus, and it seems from the brief accounts of Velleius and Dio that both commanders divided their forces, putting legates in charge of subordinate detachments. The order of the names of the conquered tribes recorded on the trophy set up by Augustus at La Turbie suggests that Drusus' line of advance may have been over the Brenner into Vindelicia, then from the lower Inn valley by way of the foothills of the Bavarian Alps to upper Swabia, while Tiberius may

[1] Dio 54.19.6.
[2] On the northern frontier, cf. Syme, *CAH* x, 349ff.; Christ, *Historia* 6, 1957, 416ff.
[3] Dio 54.19.6.
[4] Suet. *Tib.* 9.1, Dio 54.22, Vell. 2.95.2, Hor. *Carm.* 4.4.17f., 4.14.7ff., *Cons. Liv.* 15, 175, 385, Strabo 4.6.9, 7.1.5, Plin. *NH* 3.136 (= *EJ* 40), *ILS* 208 (= *EJ* 363a). For subsequent control of the area, cf. *ILS* 9007 (= *EJ* 224).

have worked eastwards from Vindonissa along the Rhine valley to Lake Constance, which he crossed by boat. Then the brothers pressed forward together.

Speed of movement along the Alpine valleys and the division of forces which prevented the tribesmen from congregating to face the Romans brought quick success. The land as far as the Danube was conquered; it was not, however, occupied.[1] There were no Roman troops concentrated on the line of the river. Instead the army was based at Oberhausen, whence it could be quickly moved to meet any emergency that might arise. The reasons for this policy are probably that the land in the immediate neighbourhood of the Danube was largely uninhabited and there was no strong power on the other side of the river which might threaten the newly acquired territory with invasion. Thus troops were not needed in advanced positions either to hold down a recalcitrant population or to guard against attack from outside.

4. THE SUCCESSION: TIBERIUS' MARRIAGE TO JULIA

In 13 Tiberius, now twenty-eight, was consul.[2] One of his duties was to organize the celebrations that greeted Augustus' return from Gaul.[3] In making the seating arrangements he realistically placed the boy Gaius Caesar next to his adoptive father. For this he incurred a rebuke from the princeps, who no doubt judged such a public gesture premature.[4] In the same year Agrippa returned from the East in order to take up the command in Illyricum. His tribunician power was renewed for a further five years and he set off for the Balkans with *imperium* superior to that of the other governors with whom he might come into contact. But his constant exertions had weakened his health and the Pannonian winter proved too much for him: in February of 12 he died.[5]

His death not only deprived Augustus of his greatest general and

[1] Cf. Christ, *Historia* 6, 1957, 425f.
[2] Dio 54.25.1.
[3] *ILS* 88 (= *EJ* 36).
[4] Dio 54.27.1.
[5] Dio 54.28.

administrator; it revived the problem of the succession in a new form. Augustus now had heirs but no mature lieutenant to guard their interests should he die. The practical question was straightforward enough. Yet another husband must be found for Julia, a man who could take Agrippa's place and as stepfather to Gaius and Lucius make sure that the succession went according to plan.[1] With characteristically ruthless unconcern for the personal inclinations of his puppets, Augustus chose Tiberius. It did not matter that Tiberius was happily married to Vipsania, that Vipsania was pregnant, that she had just suffered one blow in the loss of her father.[2] With Agrippa dead, Tiberius was the empire's leading general, the only man who could step into Agrippa's shoes as the princeps' deputy. His power and influence were therefore bound to increase and to ignore him in reshaping his dynastic schemes was a risk that Augustus was not prepared to take. To marry him to Julia was the obvious answer. The destinies of the Julian and Claudian houses would be linked more closely than before, the princes would again be provided with a guardian, and any ambitions that Tiberius might have or that Livia might cherish on his behalf would be more easily restrained if Tiberius' place in Augustus' calculations was made plain to the family and the world.

So Tiberius was instructed to divorce Vipsania. He obeyed and was duly betrothed to Julia.[3] The marriage, however, was not celebrated immediately, for Tiberius was sent as a legate of Augustus to take up the command in Illyricum which Agrippa's death had left vacant.[4] It was not until 11, after two campaigns in Pannonia, that the marriage took place on Tiberius' return to Rome.[5] A potential flaw in Augustus' scheme was revealed in the following year, when Julia gave birth to a son at Aquileia. Had the child lived, Tiberius might have been inclined to favour him to the detriment of Gaius and Lucius, but the problem

[1] Cf. Syme, *RR*, 416.

[2] Suet. *Tib.* 7.2. Nothing is heard of the child, which presumably died in infancy. Their son Drusus had been born about 14; cf. Sumner, *Latomus* 26, 1967, 427ff. (His birthday was 7 October.) Sattler (in Schmitthenner, *Augustus*, 498f.) is reluctant to believe that Tiberius was unwilling to divorce Vipsania, but gives no good reason.

[3] Suet. *Aug.* 63.2, Dio 54.31.1f.

[4] *RG* 30.1, Dio 54.31.2; cf. Syme, *CAH* x, 357ff.

[5] Dio 54.35.4, Vell. 2.96.1.

was solved by his death in infancy and did not arise again, for certainly by 6 and perhaps before 7 Tiberius and Julia had ceased to live as man and wife.[1]

5. THE NORTHERN FRONTIER: ILLYRICUM AND GERMANY

In 12 both brothers had a successful year.[2] Tiberius subdued Pannonia, making good use of a friendly tribe, the Scordisci. A triumph was voted to him for his achievements, but Augustus would not allow him to celebrate it, permitting him only the triumphal ornaments. Nor was he allowed to accept the salutation as *imperator* with which his troops acclaimed him. Meanwhile in Germany Drusus had dug a canal from the Rhine to the Ijssel, won over the Frisii and invaded the territory of the Chauci. On his return to Rome he was appointed urban praetor for 11.[3]

In 11 Tiberius was confronted with a revolt of the Dalmatians, then with a revolt of the Pannonians, conquered in the previous year, who rose while he was away dealing with the Dalmatians.[4] These events are symptomatic of the defects of Roman policy in the North. Roman armies marched through Illyricum and Germany, disposing in the main of such resistance as they encountered. The regions they had traversed were duly catalogued as subdued and the armies withdrew for the winter, leaving behind them neither military control nor civil organization. Not surprisingly the tribesmen who had been thus superficially 'conquered' tended to 'rebel' as soon as the weather allowed. Drusus in this year reached the Weser, but shortage of supplies and the advent of winter, as well as unfavourable omens, deterred him from crossing the river.[5] On his way back he was ambushed, suffering serious casualties, and indeed was lucky to escape. But on his return to Rome he was honoured with triumphal ornaments and an

---

[1] Suet. *Tib.* 7.3; cf. Sattler in Schmitthenner, *Augustus*, 502f.
[2] Suet. *Claud.* 1.2, Dio 54.31.3–32, Front. *Strat.* 2.1.15. Augustus' somewhat ungenerous attitude is reflected in the absence of any celebration of the brothers' achievements on the coinage; cf. Sutherland, *Coinage*, 65ff.
[3] Dio 54.32.3.
[4] Dio 54.34.3f.
[5] Dio 54.33.

ovation, though Augustus took his imperatorial salutation. Tiberius too received ornaments and an ovation. Both men were granted proconsular *imperium*.[1]

In the next year the Dacians raided Pannonia, passing across the frozen Danube into the province. Tiberius had accompanied Augustus to Gaul, and from there he was sent to repel them and subdue the Dalmatians, who had rebelled yet again against the imposition of tribute. For the time being he succeeded in restoring order.[2] Drusus meanwhile had returned to Germany to operate against the Chatti. Augustus spent the summer in Gaul and at the end of the campaigning season all three returned to Rome together.

In 9 Drusus, now consul, marched beyond the Weser and advanced as far as the Elbe. He did not cross the river, but set up a trophy and withdrew.[3] On the return journey disaster struck. Drusus was thrown by his horse, which fell on top of him, breaking his thigh.[4] His condition worsened and his brother was summoned. Tiberius had been engaged by yet another rebellion of the Pannonians and Dalmatians, but was now at Ticinum after the campaign. On hearing of the accident he set off at once, riding day and night with a single guide, and succeeded in reaching Drusus shortly before he died.[5] The army demanded the body of its beloved commander, but Tiberius displayed a characteristic respect for tradition, imposing moderation in mourning both on himself and on others and restraining the grief of the troops within a Roman measure.[6] That he and Drusus were friends is not disputed; it is therefore reasonable to suppose that his attitude on this occasion was dictated by sincere beliefs about the manifestation of public and private grief. It may then serve as a useful guide in interpreting his later behaviour in the matter of mourning. Tiberius escorted the body on foot the whole way to Rome, amid the ardent demonstrations of colonies and country towns, which in Seneca's words gave the procession something of the air of a triumph. He pronounced a eulogy in

---

[1] Dio 54.33.5 (Drusus), 34.3 (Tiberius).
[2] Dio 54.36.
[3] Dio 55.1.1.
[4] Suet. *Claud.* 1.3, Dio 55.1.4, Vell. 2.97.3, Liv. *Per.* 142.
[5] Dio 55.2.1, Val. Max. 5.5.3, Plin. *NH* 7.84.
[6] *Cons. Liv.* 83ff., 169ff., Sen. *Dial.* 6.3.1, 11.15.5.

the Forum; another was delivered by Augustus in the Circus Flaminius. Then Tiberius celebrated a second ovation for his achievements in Pannonia and gave a feast to the people, while Livia and Julia entertained the women. The title Germanicus was posthumously conferred on Drusus and also on his descendants.[1]

Tiberius now took Drusus' place at the head of the armies of the Rhine.[2] On the Roman side the campaign of 8 was distinguished more by Augustus' treachery than by any military achievement. Tiberius crossed the Rhine and in the face of the threatened invasion all the German tribes except the Sugambri sent envoys to Augustus in Gaul to sue for peace. Augustus refused to conclude a truce unless the Sugambri too were represented. Then, when the Sugambri duly sent envoys in their turn, he had them arrested and interned in various cities. This move did not even prove expedient. In order to leave their fellow-tribesmen free to act as they pleased, without the restraint that Augustus had tried to impose, the hostages all committed suicide. So Augustus had accomplished nothing except to teach the Sugambri to hate Rome. The year was also noteworthy for the introduction to military service of Gaius Caesar, in whose name a donative was paid to the troops. The rewards for this season's work were out of all proportion to the practical results: salutations for both Augustus and Tiberius, and for Tiberius at last a triumph and a second consulship at thirty-four.[3]

On 1 January, 7, Tiberius spoke in the senate and assigned himself the task of repairing the temple of Concordia, which was to bear his name and that of his dead brother.[4] Shortly afterwards he celebrated his triumph and together with his mother Livia dedicated a precinct in her name. He himself entertained the senate at a banquet on the Capitol, while Livia feasted the women. When these solemnities were over, Tiberius again returned to Germany, where according

[1] Suet. *Claud.* 1.3ff., Dio 55.2, *Cons. Liv.* 209ff., 465f., *EJ* 80. The reason Dio gives for Augustus' choice of the Circus Flaminius would be better suited to Tiberius; there may be some confusion.
[2] Dio 55.6, Vell. 2.97.4, Eutrop. 7.9, Oros. 6.21.24.
[3] *ILS* 95 (= *EJ* 39).
[4] Dio 55.8. The temple was apparently not dedicated till 16 January, 10, cf. *F. Ver.*, *F. Prae.* (*EJ* p. 45), Ov. *F.* 1.639f. Suet. *Tib.* 20 mentions it under 12.

to Dio nothing worthy of mention took place in the course of the year.[1]

6. TIBERIUS' RETIREMENT TO RHODES

For five years the question of the succession lay dormant while Tiberius was kept busy leading the armies of Rome. Then in 6 there was popular agitation that Gaius should at once be created consul – at the age of fourteen![2] To make a mockery of the office in this way would have offended all those whom Augustus wanted to convince that even under a thinly veiled dictatorship the consulate was still a worthwhile honour. He therefore rejected the suggestion with a proper show of displeasure. But it was clear that the premature advancement of Gaius and Lucius would not be long delayed. Tiberius too was to receive a further reward for the loyalty and diligence with which he had performed his new rôle. Just as Agrippa had been elevated by the princeps to the tribunician power, so now Tiberius was granted that power for five years.[3] But he was not to be allowed to remain idle at Rome. Again like Agrippa, he was to go to the East on a conveniently important and honourable mission to deal with fresh trouble in Armenia, where the death of Tigranes II had created an extremely unsettled situation.[4] With the princes' guardian thus kept occupied, the coast would be clear for the grooming of Gaius and Lucius.

But for the first time Augustus' plans were thwarted not by fate but by another man's will. Tiberius refused to go. His mother appealed to him, Augustus complained openly in the senate that he was being abandoned and betrayed. The only response that Tiberius made to this increasing private and public pressure was to begin a hunger-strike that he kept up for four days. At last the angry princeps acquiesced in his stepson's desire to be allowed to retire to the quiet of Rhodes, a place which had first attracted him when he visited it on his way home from Armenia in 20.[5]

[1] Dio 55.9.1.
[2] Dio 55.9.2.
[3] Suet. *Tib.* 9.3, Dio 55.9.4, Vell. 2.99.1.
[4] Cf. Anderson, *CAH* x, 273ff.
[5] Suet. *Tib.* 10, Dio 55.9.5ff., Vell. 2.99.1.

Tiberius' motives have been hotly debated, in antiquity and later. Tiberius himself, if Suetonius is to be believed, offered two reasons, one at the time, one later. At the time, trying to justify a total withdrawal from public life, he pretended to yearn for a rest from his labours, claiming that he had had enough of honours, but later he is alleged to have said that his real reason for removing himself from the scene was a desire to avoid any appearance of friction. This led him to model his conduct on that of Agrippa. Suetonius also records the explanations canvassed by others. One was that Tiberius could no longer endure the increasingly flagrant misconduct of his wife and (since it would be excessively scandalous to divorce Augustus' daughter on his own initiative) preferred to retire in order to escape her presence. Another was that he resented the preferment of Gaius and Lucius and intended, by depriving the princeps of his services, to prove that he was indispensable to the state. Velleius, concerned as ever to show Tiberius in a good light, agrees that at the time Tiberius begged for repose, but gives as the real motive behind the decision that which Tiberius himself preferred, duly decked out in flattering language: Tiberius withdrew, he says, in order that his own renown might not overshadow the young men's rise.

There is little here that will stand up to examination.[1] Neither of Tiberius' own reasons is satisfactory. Had he done as Augustus intended and spent some years in control of affairs in the East, out of sight and mind of senate and people, Augustus could have proceeded unhindered with whatever plans he had in hand for Gaius and Lucius. We may be sure that Augustus wanted nothing to stand in the way of the steady advance of his grandsons. Therefore in his estimation at least the mission that he had chosen for Tiberius would not have clashed with his designs for the princes. Nor does the plea of an excess of honours sound convincing, so soon after Tiberius had accepted the tribunician power. It is likely, however, that his acceptance had been reluctant and that his choice of this pretext to explain his action bears witness to a genuine and deep distaste for such extraordinary powers

---

[1] The best discussion is by Sattler (in Schmitthenner, *Augustus*, 486ff., reprinted from *Studien aus dem Gebiet der alten Geschichte*, 1ff.); cf. also Groag, *WS* 40, 1918, 159ff.; Syme, *RR*, 417.

1 Augustus

2b Livia

2a Augustus as *pontifex maximus*

which ran counter to republican practice. The excesses of Julia will not supply a motive, not because they had been going on for some time – their effect on Tiberius' patience might well have been cumulative – but because Julia had already left him, so that Tiberius had no need to retire to Rhodes in order to avoid her.

It may be that Tiberius was calculating his prospects. Since the deaths of Agrippa and Drusus he had been without question the second man in the state. In a few years, however, Gaius would take over that position. Tiberius would then be superfluous and therefore in danger. Of his relations with his stepsons at this time and of their relations with their mother nothing is known, but it was possible that, once Gaius had come to the fore, he might easily be persuaded that Tiberius represented a threat. Tiberius' life would then be worth little. He may have hoped in withdrawing to prove, by pushing Gaius to the front too soon, that, whatever Augustus intended, the empire could not yet do without Tiberius, or, if Gaius proved competent despite his youth, at least to demonstrate a total lack of ambition, on the strength of which he might be allowed to survive.

Before Tiberius left Italy, Augustus' health had suffered a further relapse. Tiberius had reached Campania, but paused in his journey until it became clear that Augustus was not going to die.[1] Rumour of course detected dark designs in this delay, but it was simple common sense for the empire's most experienced statesman to wish to be at Rome if the princeps were in fact to succumb and only natural that Tiberius, despite their recent quarrel, should not want to appear selfishly to avoid his father-in-law's deathbed. However, Augustus recovered and Tiberius continued to Rhodes.

There he made a point of living quietly, enjoying the lectures of various philosophers in an entirely informal way and debating with them on terms of equality.[2] But he still retained his tribunician power, and Suetonius records what appears to be the only instance of its use. One day Tiberius took sides in a philosophical dispute. The discussion

[1] Suet. *Tib*. 11.1.
[2] Suet. *Tib*. 11.2f. An inscription of the Rhodian people: *EJ* 77b; victories of Tiberius at the Olympic Games and at Thespiae during this period: *SIG*³ 782 (= *EJ* 78), *SEG* XXII 385. For the tribunician power, cf. also *ILS* 147 (= *EJ* 79).

became heated, his opponent insulting. Little by little Tiberius retreated, while the argument continued, until he was within range of his own house, when he summoned an attendant to arrest the sharp-tongued scholar and convey him to prison. This incident, as Suetonius narrates it, is strikingly inconsistent with all that we know of Tiberius' general behaviour on the island and his attitude to the tribunician power. In the absence of detailed information on the nature of the philosopher's offensive remarks, it seems pointless to speculate about why Tiberius resorted to exceptional measures.

At times he found it difficult to live as quietly as he wished. All proconsuls and imperial legates on their way to serve in the eastern provinces visited Rhodes and thought it proper to pay their respects, but Tiberius lived in the country and shunned their calls as much as possible.[1] Another story told by Suetonius is significant of Tiberius' ambiguous position and of an important aspect of his character. He had happened to express a desire to visit the sick. The local authorities completely misunderstood the nature of the visit that Tiberius had in mind. They rounded up all the invalids they could find and paraded them by diseases for Tiberius' inspection. When he arrived and found what had been done he was very much taken aback and for some time could not make up his mind what to do. Eventually he went round and apologized to each man individually for the inconvenience and discomfort caused in his name.[2] Bafflement in an unexpected and embarrassing situation is characteristic of Tiberius throughout his life.[3]

Meanwhile Augustus seemed determined to prove that he could do without Tiberius. In 5 Gaius and Lucius were honoured by the equestrian order with the unprecedented title of *principes iuuentutis*, and Gaius was designated consul five years in advance, an honour repeated for Lucius in 2, when he also reached the age of fifteen.[4] There was no doubt in men's minds that Gaius would succeed Augustus,

[1] Suet. *Tib.* 12.2, Vell. 2.99.3.
[2] Suet. *Tib.* 11.2.
[3] Cf. Thiel, *Mnemos.*[3] 1935/6, 181f.
[4] *RG* 14.1f., Dio 55.9.9f., *EJ* 62, 63a–65, 67, 75.

and he was hailed as the future princeps by the poet Ovid.[1] It was in 2 that the last link was severed between Tiberius and Augustus, when Julia fell into disgrace.[2] The official reason was the immorality of her conduct. Augustus sent her a letter in Tiberius' name announcing the end of their marriage and banished her to the island of Pandateria. The affair had wide repercussions. The most distinguished of Julia's alleged paramours was Iullus Antonius, the son of Antony. He was executed, and several other men of high rank were exiled. Whether the princeps' sudden and vigorous action in defence of the sanctity of marriage concealed a suspicion of conspiracy, whether Iullus Antonius had aspired to fill the place left vacant by Tiberius beside Augustus as well as beside Augustus' daughter, we do not know.[3] Nor is Tiberius' reaction entirely clear. Suetonius says that in his heart he was glad, though he thought it his duty to plead for his erring wife in repeated letters to Augustus. He may well have had more than duty on his mind. The divorce wiped out his connection with Gaius and weakened the link between him and Augustus. It was now plain that Augustus was trusting to luck that he himself would survive until Gaius was old enough to take over, and so Tiberius was left more insecure than ever.[4]

This insecurity was increased in the following year when his tribunician power expired. It was at this point that he alleged his reluctance to stand in the way of Gaius and Lucius as an explanation of his retirement. Now that they were successfully established, he begged to be allowed to return to Rome.[5] This in itself shows the precariousness of his position. He had not been sent to Rhodes on any official mission, but had gone there of his own free will for private reasons. On the surface therefore there was no need to request permission if he wanted to return. But in view of Augustus' attitude he no doubt thought it more discreet to ask, and his judgment of the situation was disagreeably

[1] *ILS* 137 (dedication of a temple to the princes at Acerrae; cf. Taylor, *Divinity*, 224); Ov. *AA* 1.177ff., especially 194; cf. Gell. 15.7.3 (letter of Augustus to Gaius, 23 September, A.D.1). For divine honours paid to Gaius and Lucius in the East, cf. *EJ* 62, 64, 115(a); Taylor, *Divinity*, 274ff.; for their prominence on the coinage of this period, cf. Sutherland, *Coinage*, 71; *EJ* 66.

[2] Suet. *Tib.* 11.4, Dio 55.10.14, Vell. 2.100.1.

[3] Cf. Syme, *RR*, 425ff.

[4] Cf. Groag, *WS* 41, 1919, 82f.

[5] Suet. *Tib.* 11.5.

confirmed by the response to his plea. Despite the intercession of Livia, Augustus refused. All that Livia was able to gain for her son was an appointment as legate of Augustus which would serve to some extent to cloak his disgrace and leave him not entirely devoid of authority.[1]

In 1 Gaius was placed at the head of the army of the Danube,[2] only to be promoted almost at once to an even more important post. Augustus had put off dealing with the Armenian problem in the absence of Tiberius, feeling that he himself was too old and Gaius still too young to go to the East.[3] But now he thought the prince was old enough to look after himself, and so Gaius was invested with proconsular *imperium* and sent out, with M. Lollius as his mentor,[4] to negotiate with the Parthians and settle the Armenian succession. Tiberius went to pay court to his former stepson, but only the faithful Velleius suggests that he got a good reception and was honoured by Gaius as a superior (which technically of course he was not). The assertions of Suetonius are more plausible. Tiberius, he says, sensed that Gaius was hostile to him. He had been made so by the accusations of Lollius, who had reported to Gaius and apparently also to Augustus that Tiberius was tampering with Gaius' troops, issuing ambiguous instructions designed to tempt individuals to plot against Gaius.[5] When Augustus informed Tiberius of these charges, Tiberius could do no more than request that a check be kept on all his words and actions. As a result of the attitude that Lollius had inspired in Gaius, Tiberius' position grew even worse. At Nemausus, where Gaius and Lucius had inherited the popularity of their father Agrippa, his statues were overthrown, and for two years he was treated, as Suetonius says, with more and more contempt from day to day, until his very life was in danger. One day, while Gaius was at dinner, one of his entourage offered to sail to Rhodes and bring back the exile's head. The story may or may not be true, but it shows how desperate Tiberius' plight had become.

---

[1] Suet. *Tib.* 12.1.
[2] Dio 55.10.17.
[3] Dio 55.10.18.
[4] Lollius had lost a legion in Germany about 16 (cf. Suet. *Aug.* 23.1, Vell. 2.97.1), which presumably accounts for his prolonged eclipse.
[5] Suet. *Tib.* 12.2f., Dio 55.10.19, Vell. 2.101.1.

In alarm he and Livia doubled their prayers, but Augustus refused to commit himself, saying that he would make no decision in the matter which had not been previously recommended by Gaius.[1]

As long as Lollius retained his ascendancy over Gaius, Tiberius had no hope of an improvement, but suddenly Lollius fell from grace, accused by the Parthian king, and committed suicide after Gaius had renounced his friendship.[2] His place was taken by P. Sulpicius Quirinius, who was friendly to Tiberius.[3] Now, in A.D. 2, Gaius gave his consent and Tiberius was at last allowed to return, though only on the humiliating condition that he take no part in public life. Significantly, he moved from his house in the Carinae, near the Forum, to the less central residential area on the Esquiline, made popular by Maecenas.[4]

7. TIBERIUS' ADOPTION

It is hard to know what might have become of Tiberius if fate had had no more disappointments in store for Augustus. But in the same year in which Tiberius returned to Rome the younger grandson, Lucius, on his way to Spain, fell ill at Massilia and died.[5] For the moment Tiberius' position was unchanged – Gaius was still universally regarded as Augustus' destined successor. His mission to the East had been carried out with some panache.[6] He had met the Parthian king Phraataces on an island in the middle of the Euphrates and each side had entertained the other at banquets on their respective banks. The Parthian had abandoned his claim to Armenia, fearing that internal troubles might threaten his throne if he allowed himself to be involved in a war with Rome. But Armenia was plunged into civil war, as a number of its dignitaries rose against the imposition by Rome of

[1] Suet. *Tib.* 13.

[2] Suet. *Tib.* 13.2, Vell. 2.102.1, Plin. *NH* 9.118.

[3] Tac. *Ann.* 3.48.

[4] Suet. *Tib.* 13.2, Dio 55.10a.10; for Tiberius' houses, cf. Suet. *Tib.* 15.1.

[5] Dio 55.10a.9, Vell.2.102.5. For the date (20 August), cf. *F. Ant.* (*EJ* p. 51), *ILS* 139 (= *EJ* 68). Tiberius composed a lyric poem lamenting his death (Suet. *Tib.* 70.2).

[6] Vell. 2.101.2ff. (an eye-witness account; Velleius served as military tribune under the prince); cf. Anderson, *CAH* x, 273ff.

Ariobarzanes of Media as king. Gaius was constrained to military intervention, and on 9 September, A.D. 3, he was treacherously wounded by an arrow during a parley with the defenders of the fortified town of Artagira.[1] The wound left him listless and apparently incapable of taking any further interest in his career. Despite the efforts of his friends to rouse him, he begged to be excused from further participation in public life, and on 21 February, A.D. 4, when about to make his way back to Italy, he died at Limyra in Lycia.[2]

Augustus' plans were now completely shattered. He had neither a deputy nor a successor of the blood. For the past six years Gaius had combined these rôles, but now Augustus was thrown back on Germanicus, the son of Tiberius' brother Drusus. Germanicus was married to Agrippina, the daughter of Agrippa and Julia, and so his sons would preserve the direct line. But for the moment he was too young and inexperienced to rule.[3] The office of guardian to the heir and deputy to the princeps, filled first by Agrippa and then, until his retirement, by Tiberius, must be revived and the pattern repeated as before. Whatever his personal feelings, Augustus had no choice. Only one man had the ability and experience to fight Rome's wars and govern the empire until Germanicus was ready to do so. That man was Tiberius.

Augustus acted with typical decision. Tiberius was once more granted the tribunician power, despite a considerable reluctance on his part, expressed both in private and in the senate.[4] The duration of the grant is disputed: ten years according to Dio, only five according to Suetonius. Dio is perhaps more likely to be correct, since Augustus himself says in the *Res Gestae* that he accepted a colleague in the tribunician power five times in all;[5] he is unlikely to have omitted any instance that would tend to diminish the autocratic aspect of his power.

---

[1] Dio 55.10a.6ff., Vell. 2.102.3ff.; date in *F. Cupr.* (*EJ* p. 39).
[2] Date in *F. Gab.*, *F. Cupr.* (*EJ* p. 39), *F. Ver.* (*EJ* p. 47), *ILS* 140 (= *EJ* 69).
[3] He was born on 24 May, 15: *Fer. Cum.*, *Act. Arv.* (*EJ* p. 49); cf. Suet. *Cal.* 1. The year is rightly defended by Sumner, *Latomus* 26, 1967, 413ff. Yet Augustus did seriously consider adopting Germanicus at this time, cf. Tac. *Ann.* 4.57, Suet. *Cal.* 4.
[4] Suet. *Tib.* 16.1, Dio 55.13.2, Vell. 2.103.2.   [5] *RG* 6.2.

Then on 26 June, A.D. 4, he adopted Tiberius, whose name thus became Ti. Julius Caesar, and at the same time his sole surviving grandson, the brother of Gaius and Lucius Caesar, born after Agrippa's death and so known by the name of Agrippa Postumus.[1] Two features distinguished Tiberius' adoption. First, before it was carried out, Tiberius himself was compelled to adopt his nephew Germanicus, who would thus, when Augustus adopted Tiberius, become the princeps' grandson.[2] Secondly, when he announced the adoption to the senate, Augustus added: 'I do this for the sake of the commonwealth.' Most historians have seen in both these facts attempts on Augustus' part to sugar for himself the bitter pill of political necessity by humiliating the successor he disliked, first by making it plain that he was only a stop-gap, secondly by emphasizing that personal affection played no part in his decision. There are other possibilities. Tacitus believed that Augustus was trying to strengthen Tiberius' position by linking him and Germanicus in this way.[3] He does not elaborate, but it is possible to discern his meaning. Tiberius was not by blood a member of the Julian house, nor had he ever made an effort to win the love of the Roman people. If Augustus died, as was probable, while Germanicus was too young to rule, the public knowledge that he would nevertheless in due course follow Tiberius, whose own elevation was intended to be only temporary, might prevent possible discord, the consequences of which would be incalculable. Thus by planning out the succession well in advance and defining Tiberius' rôle with some precision, Augustus was in fact strengthening Tiberius and making his accession more secure, even though his main object in doing this was not to make life pleasanter for Tiberius but to leave the ultimate succession of Germanicus less open to chance. As for the words with which Augustus announced the adoption, Velleius, probably rightly, treats them as a

---

[1] Suet. *Aug.* 65.1, *Tib.* 15.2, *Cal.* 1.1, 4, Dio 55.13.2, Vell. 2.103.2ff.; for the date, cf. *F. Amit.* (*EJ* p. 49), against 27 June in Velleius – no doubt a scribal error. It is noteworthy that the *Fasti Amiternini*, inscribed in A.D. 20, do not record the adoption of Agrippa Postumus. On all matters connected with Tiberius' adoption, cf. Instinsky, *Hermes* 94, 1966, 324ff.

[2] Just. *Inst.* 1.11.11; cf. Levick, *Latomus* 25, 1966, 232.

[3] Tac. *Ann.* 1.3, accepted by Timpe, *Kontinuität*, 29.

compliment.[1] The republic stood in urgent need of a potential ruler and, as recent developments in Germany showed, of a skilled and experienced general. In Tiberius Augustus was giving the republic both, and it is plausible that the popular rejoicing recorded by Velleius was at least to some extent genuine, despite Tiberius' lack of personal popularity.

The pattern shows only slight changes from the past. The disgrace of Julia meant that it was no longer possible to unite the princeps' deputy with the family of Augustus by marriage, as had been done in the cases of Agrippa and of Tiberius before his exile. Hence the use of that other familiar device among the Roman aristocracy, adoption, to create a bond first between Tiberius and Germanicus and then between Augustus and Tiberius.[2] It was the only course now open to the princeps, but it was nevertheless, as the wily Augustus will have realized, an extremely effective one. Filial loyalty played a prominent part in the aristocratic tradition to which Tiberius was devoted. His consciousness of his position as Augustus' son is remarkable through-out the rest of his career, showing itself in a dedicated loyalty to Augustus' person, policies and precepts. Suetonius stresses the seriousness with which Tiberius regarded the legal implications of his status.[3] His position as Augustus' son was a cornerstone of his own security, even after Augustus' death, but it was also the key to Augustus' hold over him.[4] Once again the princeps had calculated wisely, and this time it was not until after his death that fate interfered with his designs.

8. THE NORTHERN FRONTIER: GERMANY AND PANNONIA

No sooner was Tiberius restored to favour than fresh military em-

[1] Thus Instinsky, *Hermes* 94, 1966, 331ff.; cf. Levick, *Latomus* 25, 1966, 229 n.1; Sumner, *HSCP* 74, 1970, 269. It is, however, noteworthy that no coins were issued to celebrate either the grant of tribunician power or the adoption; cf. Sutherland, *Coinage*, 73.

[2] On the incompatibility of the two forms of connection, cf. Instinsky, *Hermes* 94 1966, 326, 336.

[3] Suet. *Tib.* 15.2; cf. also the gibe in Tac. *Ann.* 1.26.

[4] For Tiberius' attitude to the precepts of Augustus, cf. Tac. *Ann.* 1.14, 77, 2.59, 3.24, 29, 68, 71 and above all 4.37. The kind of criticisms against which official propaganda was directed are illustrated in Tac. *Ann.* 1.7f., 2.40, 3.4. For the stress on continuity in Tiberius' coinage and the importance of the legend DIVVS AVGVSTVS PATER, cf. Sutherland, *Coinage*, 85f.

ployment for him was found, once more in Germany. With him went
the historian Velleius Paterculus, succeeding his father as *praefectus
equitum*. He paints a moving picture of the joy of those who had served
under Tiberius in the past at their reunion with their old commander –
they had clearly never expected to see him again.[1] Little is known of
the campaigns in Germany since Tiberius himself had last been active
there. But it is likely that the great expeditions of the intervening
years, like those of Tiberius himself in 4 and 5, were conceived in
preparation for an attack on Maroboduus, the king of the Marcomanni,
whose growing power, centred in Bohemia, had aroused an unfriendly
interest on the part of Rome.[2]

In 4 Tiberius prolonged his stay in Germany till December and left
his army encamped at the source of the Lippe when he returned to
Rome for what remained of the winter. His troops had penetrated
beyond the Weser, but had not yet reached the Elbe.[3] That was the
target for the combined military and naval operation which was
mounted when Tiberius returned to the front in the following spring.
All Germany, says Velleius, was visited by Roman arms, the Chauci
were subdued, the Langobardi driven from the left bank of the Elbe,
while the fleet sailed into the mouth of the river and established
contact safely with the army.[4] Velleius emphasizes the lack of casualties: the army returned unscathed to its winter quarters after fighting
only one victorious battle, and once more Tiberius hurried back to
Rome.[5] There, on 27 January, 6, he dedicated a temple to Castor and
Pollux in his own name and that of his dead brother Drusus.[6]

The result of the campaigns of 4 and 5, in the optimistic judgment of
Velleius, was that nothing in Germany remained to be conquered
except the Marcomanni under Maroboduus.[7] Despite his assurance that
he would not move against Rome unless provoked, his realm was to

[1] Vell. 2.104.3ff.; cf. Sumner, *HSCP* 74, 1970, 270.
[2] On Maroboduus and his kingdom, cf. Dobiáš, *Klio* 38, 1960, 155ff.
[3] Dio 55.28.5ff., Vell. 2.105; cf. Gelzer, *RE* 10.489.
[4] Vell. 2.106.1: *perlustrata armis tota Germania est.* Hindsight might suggest that
this is all too accurate an estimate of the Roman achievement.
[5] Vell. 2.107.3.
[6] Dio 55.27.3ff.; for the date, cf. Ov. *F.* 1.705ff., *F. Prae.* (*EJ* p. 46). Erroneously
dated to 12 by Suet. *Tib.* 20.
[7] Vell. 2.108.1.

Roman eyes a refuge for Rome's enemies and a constant threat, by virtue of its position, to Germany, Pannonia and Noricum. Ultimately Italy itself might be endangered; Rome could not or would not believe that Maroboduus' standing army was being strengthened and trained for defensive purposes alone.[1] So it was decided that in 6 the Marcomanni should be simultaneously attacked on three fronts. Tiberius, who devised the plan, was to come from the south-east, advancing from Carnuntum with the army of Illyricum. C. Sentius Saturninus, who had already done good service under Tiberius in 4, was to invade from the west, setting out from Moguntiacum. A third force was to march north from Rhaetia.[2]

But this complex operation had barely been set in motion when alarming news from Tiberius' rear brought it to an abrupt and inglorious halt. For fifteen years complacent Rome had exacted extravagant tribute from a Pannonia that had never been comprehensively subdued.[3] Now in Dalmatia to resentment of the tribute a further cause of discontent was added. The governor, M. Valerius Messalla Messallinus, about to lead his troops in support of Tiberius, demanded a contingent from the tribesmen. A small revolt broke out among the Daesitiates, instigated by a man called Bato, and this spread when the Romans failed to put it down until the whole of Dalmatia was in arms. In Pannonia the Breuci, inspired by Tiberius' absence, rebelled and marched on the Roman stronghold of Sirmium. Their leader, also named Bato, was defeated near the Drave by A. Caecina Severus, the governor of Moesia, but the Roman losses were heavy. Meanwhile Bato the Dalmatian had turned towards Macedonia. He himself was wounded in an attack on Salonae, but his men ravaged the coast as far as Apollonia.[4]

Tiberius did not hesitate to conclude a treaty with Maroboduus – who was statesman enough not to throw in his lot with the rebels – and came hurrying back to quell the revolt, sending Messalla Messallinus

[1] Vell. 2.108.3–109.2.
[2] Vell. 2.109.3.
[3] Cf. Syme, *CAH* x, 369. On the revolt, cf. ibid. 369ff.; Koestermann, *Hermes* 81, 1953, 345ff. For excessive taxation as a cause of the rebellion, cf. the remark attributed to the Dalmatian leader Bato in Dio 56.16.3.
[4] Dio 55.29.

ahead. His first objective was to reach Siscia and so bar the way to Italy. How serious the threat to Italy was is difficult to estimate. Ten days, said Augustus, might see the enemy in Rome.[1] But Augustus clearly panicked, as Velleius discreetly observes, and he may also have deliberately exaggerated the danger in order to reconcile public opinion to the unpopular measures in the fields of recruiting and taxation which were needed to cope with the rebellion.[2] Veterans were recalled to the colours, freedmen were enlisted, a tax of 2 per cent on the sale of slaves was introduced, and no public money was forthcoming for the praetorian games.[3]

While Tiberius waited at Siscia for reinforcements, Sirmium was under heavy pressure.[4] The Daesitiate and Breucan leaders had now joined forces and established themselves on a hill to the north of the city, the Mons Almus. They suffered a defeat at the hands of Rhoemetalces, king of Thrace, who had been sent against them by Caecina, but Caecina himself was unable to dislodge them from their stronghold. Soon he had to return to Moesia, which was threatened by Dacian and Sarmatian raids.

Before the end of 6 Tiberius had received some reinforcements, conducted to Siscia by Velleius Paterculus, quaestor designate for the following year, during which he was seconded to Tiberius' staff with a special appointment as a legate of Augustus.[5] Then in 7 Germanicus was sent out as quaestor at the head of another makeshift contingent. Very slowly Tiberius began to move east and south, avoiding any pitched battle with the rebels while attacking and routing scattered detachments and containing many of them in the hills between the Save and the Drave.[6] Velleius justly praises him for his prudence, but others expected more rapid and more resounding victories. That Augustus, as Dio claims, was among them is highly likely.[7] Suetonius

[1] Vell. 2.110.6; cf. Sumner, *HSCP* 74, 1970, 272.
[2] Cf. Koestermann, *Hermes* 81, 1953, 349.
[3] Dio 55.31, Vell. 2.110.7.
[4] Dio 55.30.
[5] Vell. 2.111.2f.; no doubt Tiberius had backed his candidature, cf. Sumner, *HSCP* 74, 1970, 271.
[6] Vell. 2.111.3, 112.3.
[7] Dio 55.31, accepted by Koestermann, *Hermes* 81, 1953, 358; contra Syme, *CAH* X, 371.

preserves fulsome letters from the princeps, in which he declared that the fate of the empire depended on Tiberius' safety and continuing good health,[1] and, like Velleius, singled out Tiberius' prudence for his praise.[2] These, however, probably belong a little later, when the danger was over and it was clear that Tiberius had been right to refuse to be hurried.

Late in 7 five legions were brought up from the East by Caecina and M. Plautius Silvanus. West of Sirmium the rebels waited for them and succeeded in taking them completely by surprise at the Volcaean Marshes.[3] Velleius is with good cause savagely critical of the commanders for their negligence, and total disaster was indeed only narrowly avoided. But eventually the legions won through and made their way to Siscia. Tiberius now had a huge force: ten legions, more than seventy auxiliary cohorts, ten squadrons of cavalry and over ten thousand veterans.[4] This host he led back to Sirmium, establishing his control in the valley of the Save. There he left Plautius Silvanus in charge before returning to Siscia to take up his winter quarters.[5]

In 8 Tiberius' methods brought their reward. The Pannonians, ravaged by the famine and disease that resulted from the scorched earth policy he had turned against them, capitulated at the River Bathinus.[6] Their leader Bato, despairing of his cause, betrayed Pinnes, for which he was rewarded by Rome with the chieftainship of the Breuci. But he was soon captured and executed by his namesake, who succeeded in briefly reviving the Pannonian rebellion. Silvanus, however, swiftly put down the outbreak and Bato withdrew southwards into Dalmatia.[7] The task of subduing him was left for the following year. Tiberius placed M. Aemilius Lepidus in command at Siscia – Silvanus remained at Sirmium – and set off to spend the winter in Rome.

[1] Suet. *Tib.* 21.4ff.
[2] Suet. *Tib.* 21.5: *non potuisse quemquam prudentius gerere se quam tu gesseris existimo.*
[3] Dio 55.32, Vell. 2.112.4.
[4] Vell. 2.113.1: far more than he really needed, in consequence of Augustus' initial panic and desire for quick results; cf. Sumner, *HSCP* 74, 1970, 272.
[5] Vell. 2.113.3.
[6] Dio 55.33, Vell. 2.114.4.
[7] Dio 55.34.

In 9 Tiberius moved to Dalmatia. Lepidus marched from Siscia to join him, fighting his way through country as yet untouched by the war and earning triumphal ornaments.[1] To complete the reconquest of Dalmatia Tiberius planned a three-pronged attack, with Lepidus and Silvanus moving from the north, he himself, accompanied by Germanicus, from the south. Germanicus had already done well in this year; he had captured three rebel fortresses and his courage is praised by Velleius.[2] Velleius also speaks highly of several other men who appear as consuls and governors in the years of Tiberius' ascendancy: C. Vibius Postumus, Cossus Cornelius Lentulus and his son Cn. Cornelius Lentulus Gaetulicus, L. Apronius, L. Aelius Lamia and A. Licinius Nerva Silianus.[3] Hunting down Bato proved a difficult task. Tiberius besieged him in Andretium, near Salonae, but the siege was arduous and Bato escaped before the place was captured.[4] Eventually he surrendered and was removed, like so many distinguished prisoners, to Ravenna, while the last flickerings of revolt were crushed among the Daesitiates and the Pirustae.[5]

The Pannonian revolt shows Tiberius' generalship at its best. Despite the difficulty in coming to grips with the enemy, the great advantages given to the guerrillas by the terrain, and the pressure from Rome for quick results, he kept calm and refused to abandon the methods that he knew would bring ultimate success. His patient and thorough pacification brought lasting quiet to Illyricum.[6] Velleius highlights his extreme concern for the welfare and comfort of his officers and his constant efforts to avoid casualties. To Tiberius, he says, the least risky course was always the most glorious.[7] Suitable honours were duly decreed: a triumph for Tiberius, salutations and triumphal arches in Pannonia for Tiberius and Augustus, and triumphal ornaments for Germanicus and the other commanders. Germanicus was also given praetorian rank in the senate, with the right to vote

[1] Vell. 2.115.1f.
[2] Dio 56.11–12.2, Vell. 2.116.1.
[3] Vell. 2.116.2f.
[4] Dio 56.12.3–14.
[5] Suet. *Tib.* 20, Dio 56.16, Vell. 2.115.3, Ov. *Pont.* 2.1.45f.
[6] Suet. *Tib.* 16.2.
[7] Vell. 2.114.1f., 115.4.

immediately after the consulars, and was to hold the consulship before the legal age. Even Tiberius' son Drusus, who had not taken part in the war, was given permission to attend meetings of the senate before he actually became a senator and was to vote before ex-praetors as soon as he attained the quaestorship.[1]

But Tiberius' triumph was to be delayed and rejoicing at Rome cut short almost before it had begun. Less than five days after the news of his success reached the city came tidings of disaster from Germany – the governor, P. Quinctilius Varus, dead, three legions annihilated by Arminius, the leader of the Cherusci.[2] The blame rests squarely on the shoulders of Augustus. The policy of invasion unsupported by adequate occupation or organization was his, and it was his over-confidence that had led Rome to treat Germany as pacified. The appointment of Varus, the husband of his great-niece Claudia Pulchra, underlines this fact. A former governor of the peaceful province of Syria, Varus was an administrator rather than a general, occupying himself with the hearing of lawsuits and perhaps also indulging in undue extortion.[3] His mistake, as Velleius briskly formulates it, had been to think that Germans were human beings.[4]

After Varus and his army had been ambushed in the Teutoburger-wald, Arminius sent the governor's head to Maroboduus to encourage him to join the revolt. But Maroboduus remained faithful to his treaty with Tiberius, judging that Arminius was highly unlikely to achieve any permanent success and that, even if he did, no one else would benefit by it.

Tiberius postponed his triumph, though he entered the city wearing a laurel crown and shared with Augustus the seat of honour between the consuls.[5] Then he went to take over the command on the Rhine. The army of Germany was increased to eight legions, six of them drawn

---

[1] Suet. *Tib.* 17.1, Dio 56.17. Drusus was quaestor in 11, cf. Dio 56.25.4.
[2] Dio 56.18.1, Vell. 2.117.1.
[3] Dio 56.18.3ff., Vell. 2.117. 2–118.1.
[4] Vell. 2.117.3: *concepit esse homines, qui nihil praeter uocem membraque haberent hominum.*
[5] Suet. *Tib.* 17.2. The date was perhaps 16 January, 10: cf. *F. Prae.* (*EJ* p. 45); Taylor, *AJP* 58, 1937, 185ff. This was the day of the dedication of the temple of Concordia, which Tiberius had promised in 7 to repair.

from other provinces – Rhaetia, Spain and Illyricum – for to raise entirely new forces was impossible. Tiberius' first task was to build up discipline and morale. Then he crossed the Rhine and began slowly but surely to apply the methods that had proved so successful in Illyricum.[1] It has often been believed that these expeditions were no more than punitive raids, mere gestures, but in fact Augustus still appears to have dreamed of imposing Roman rule as far as the Elbe.[2] Tiberius did not get very far with this task, because he tried to do it properly for the first time. Hence his advance was meticulously slow as he ravaged crops, burned dwellings and dispersed their inhabitants. Now more than ever Rome could not afford to lose men and Tiberius was even more careful than usual to avoid wasting lives: Velleius declares, presumably with some exaggeration, that every man returned from the field safe and sound. Tiberius' thoroughness in other matters is attested by Suetonius: all his orders were given in writing, with instructions that he was to be consulted directly on any doubtful points.[3]

For the campaign of 11 he was joined once again by Germanicus.[4] Dio records that they won no battles and reduced no tribes, for although they remained in Germany well into the autumn they did not go very far beyond the Rhine. From these disparaging remarks it may be inferred that Tiberius was proceeding with the same patience and caution he had displayed in the previous year.

In 12, the year of Germanicus' first consulship,[5] Tiberius returned to Rome and on 23 October celebrated his long-delayed Pannonian triumph.[6]

---

[1] Suet. *Tib.* 18f., Vell. 2.121.1f.; Velleius was still serving under him (cf. Vell. 2.104.3).

[2] Cf. Timpe, *Triumph*, 31f.

[3] Suet. *Tib.* 18.

[4] Dio 56.25.2 could be right in crediting him with proconsular *imperium*, but even if the grant in 14 recorded by Tac. *Ann.* 1.14 is only a renewal, it is more likely that Germanicus' proconsular *imperium* came with his appointment as supreme commander on the Rhine in 13.

[5] Dio 56.26.1.

[6] Suet. *Tib.* 20, Vell. 2.121, Ov. *Pont.* 2.1, 2.2, 3.3.85ff. The day is certain, cf. *F. Prae.* (*EJ* p. 54), the year disputed. In favour of 12, cf. Sumner, *HSCP* 74, 1970, 274 n.107.

9. TIBERIUS THE SUCCESSOR OF AUGUSTUS

In the years that followed his return to favour Tiberius' influence constantly increased. Friends and men who served under him in Germany and Pannonia secured consulships and provincial commands.[1] The Fasti show C. Sentius Saturninus in 4, C. Vibius Postumus in 5, Lucilius Longus in 7, L. Apronius and A. Vibius Habitus in 8, C. Poppaeus Sabinus, Q. Poppaeus Secundus and M. Papius Mutilus in 9, and Q. Junius Blaesus in 10. In the provinces L. Volusius Saturninus was succeeded in Syria by P. Sulpicius Quirinius, L. and Cossus Cornelius Lentulus both governed Africa, while Cn. Calpurnius Piso's tenure in Spain may also belong to this period. It is clear not only that Tiberius' friends among the old nobility – Lentuli and Pisones – were in high favour, but that new men who attached themselves to him could expect a rapid reward for good and loyal service.

That Tiberius was Augustus' choice as his immediate successor could not be doubted. Despite his simultaneous adoption, Agrippa Postumus, a young man of low intelligence and uncouth disposition, received no privileges when he assumed the *toga uirilis* in 5. Soon he was first of all confined to Surrentum and then, when his character not surprisingly worsened, placed under guard in 7 on the island of Planasia. Indeed, Augustus felt so hostile towards the youth that he had his decision to put him away for life confirmed by a decree of the senate.[2] The structure of the dynasty in Augustus' last years is repeatedly affirmed in the complaints of the exiled poet Ovid. At the head stands Augustus, with Tiberius beside him; below them are the young men, Germanicus and Drusus. Livia is regularly associated with her husband and her son; the princes' wives, Agrippina and Livia Julia, are also sometimes mentioned along with their husbands.[3] Even fuller was the arch of Ticinum, erected in 7–8, which bore statues of Augustus, Livia, Tiberius, Germanicus, Drusus, Claudius, Germani-

---

[1] Cf. Syme, *RR*, 383, 434ff., against Marsh, *Tiberius*, 44.

[2] Tac. *Ann.* 1.3, Suet. *Aug.* 65.1, 4, *Tib.* 15.2, Dio 55.22.4, 32.1ff., Vell. 2.112.7 (malicious and deliberately obscuring the interval that elapsed before Agrippa's death). On Agrippa's character, cf. Pappano, *CP* 36, 1941, 30ff.

[3] Ov. *Trist.* 2.161ff., 4.2.7ff., *Pont.* 2.2.71f., 2.8.1ff., 26ff., 3.1.163f., 4.5.23ff., 4.9.105ff. On Germanicus' position as the ultimate successor, cf. especially *Pont.* 2.5.

3a Livia

3b Agrippa

3c Gaius Caesar

3d Tiberius as a youth

4a Coin of Augustus celebrating the recovery of the standards from Parthia, with legend SIGNIS PARTHICIS RECEPTIS.

4b Coin of Augustus of A.D. 13–14: obverse Augustus; reverse Tiberius.

4c Coin of Augustus of A.D. 13–14 celebrating Tiberius' Pannonian triumph: obverse Augustus; reverse Tiberius in chariot.

cus' sons, Nero and Drusus, and the dead Gaius and Lucius, with inscriptions detailing the ties of kinship between them.[1] When Tiberius' Pannonian triumph was decreed, Augustus again made his intentions plain. Various honorific surnames were proposed – Pannonicus, Invictus, Pius – but Augustus rejected them all on Tiberius' behalf, promising that his son would be content with the name he would acquire when Augustus died: that is, that Tiberius would become Augustus in his turn.[2] The imperial coinage told the same story. Tiberius appeared on coins of 10 and 11, which celebrated his tribunician power and his imperatorial salutations.[3]

In 13 the same honours were granted to Tiberius as had once been conferred on Agrippa. At Augustus' request a consular law was passed, giving Tiberius *imperium* equal to Augustus' own throughout the empire. Coins of 13 and 14 have the head of Augustus on one side, that of Tiberius on the other.[4] Tiberius' tribunician power was also renewed, and Drusus was designated consul for 15 – his first accelerated promotion.[5] For Germanicus came an appointment as governor of the three Gauls and commander-in-chief of the armies of the Rhine.[6] Tiberius was now more secure than he had ever been, his position as Augustus' destined successor clear.

[1] *ILS* 107 (= *EJ* 61).
[2] Suet. *Tib.* 17.2.
[3] Cf. Dieckmann, *Klio* 15, 1917/8, 352ff.; Sutherland, *Coinage*, 76.
[4] Suet. *Tib.* 21.1, Vell. 2.121.3 (placing the grant earlier, before Tiberius' return to Rome to celebrate his Pannonian triumph). For the coinage, cf. *EJ* 81; Dieckmann, *Klio* 15, 1917/8, 354; Sutherland, *Coinage*, 77. Tiberius' place in Augustus' confidence is well illustrated by their joint decision in 12 to exclude Claudius from public life, cf. Suet. *Claud.* 4 (letter of Augustus to Livia). Cf. also *EJ* 81a.
[5] Dio 56.28.1; cf. Sumner, *Latomus* 26, 1967, 427ff.
[6] Suet. *Cal.* 1.1, 8.3.

III

THE ACCESSION OF TIBERIUS

I. THE DEATH OF AUGUSTUS AND THE REMOVAL OF AGRIPPA POSTUMUS

In 14, together with Augustus, Tiberius completed a census.[1] He then set out for Illyricum to begin the reorganization of the province after the great revolt. But he had scarcely arrived when a letter from Livia called him back. Augustus, who had accompanied Tiberius as far as Beneventum, had been taken ill at Nola and now lay on his deathbed. It is probable that Tiberius reached Nola while Augustus was still alive, but on 19 August the long reign of Rome's first princeps came to an end.[2]

There was only one conceivable obstacle to the unhindered assumption of power by Tiberius: the unfortunate Agrippa Postumus, still in exile on the island of Planasia. It is unlikely, despite the assertion of Tacitus, that anyone could have considered him as a serious contender for the principate.[3] But in the interests of security Agrippa had to be removed. The sources are uncertain as to where the blame should rest: on Augustus, Livia or Tiberius himself. Tacitus is chiefly concerned to exculpate Augustus and states firmly that Tiberius was lying when he claimed that Augustus had ordered Agrippa's execution.[4] Suetonius is

[1] *RG* 8.4, *F. Ost.* (*EJ* p. 40).

[2] *F. Ost.* (*EJ* p. 40), *F. Amit.*, *F. Ant.* (*EJ* p. 50). Suet. *Tib.* 21.1 and Vell. 2.123.3 are categorical that Tiberius found Augustus alive and conscious. Tac. *Ann.* 1.5 refuses to commit himself, while Dio 56.31.1 maintains that a majority of writers, and among them the best, held that Augustus was already dead when Tiberius arrived.

[3] Tac. *Ann.* 1.4; cf. Charlesworth, *AJP* 44, 1923, 149f.; Koestermann, *Historia* 10, 1961, 333 n.6.

[4] Tac. *Ann.* 1.6.

undecided between three possibilities: Augustus, Livia in Augustus' name and with Tiberius' knowledge, and Livia unknown to Tiberius.[1] Dio unhesitatingly proclaims Tiberius' guilt and dismisses as fabrications the views that Augustus had given the order before he died or that Livia had played a part.[2]

That the decision to liquidate Agrippa had been taken by Augustus cannot be doubted, however. His will did not mention Agrippa's existence, yet if Agrippa had been expected to be still alive when the will was opened he would have had in Roman law to be expressly disinherited.[3] The final version of the will had been drawn up on 3 April, 13.[4] It follows that Augustus had by then already made up his mind that Agrippa could not be allowed to survive him. He will therefore, as Tiberius insisted, have issued standing orders to the tribune at Planasia that Agrippa was to be put to death as soon as he himself was dead. These orders must not be confused – as they are in the sources – with the letter sent by C. Sallustius Crispus, the confidential adviser. The purpose of this letter must have been to inform the tribune that Augustus was dead and that the time had therefore come to carry out his instructions. Such a message could not be sent in Augustus' name, since its burden presupposed Augustus' death, but neither Sallustius nor Livia had the power to give orders to the centurion of the praetorian guard who actually carried out the execution; with Augustus dead, Tiberius alone had that right. Sallustius will have had no choice but to write in Tiberius' name, with or without Tiberius' knowledge. That he did so is confirmed by the fact that the centurion reported to Tiberius on his return that his orders had been carried out.[5] Tiberius reacted with a show of surprise and anger, denying that he had given any such orders and threatening to call the centurion to account before the senate. There is no reason to suppose that this reaction was not

---

[1] Suet. *Tib.* 22.

[2] Dio 57.3.5f. For various modern views, cf. Rogers, *Trials*, 2ff.; Hohl, *Hermes* 70, 1935, 350ff.; Pappano, *CP* 36, 1941, 30ff.; Allen, *TAPA* 78, 1947, 131ff. Tiberius' responsibility is reaffirmed, without new or convincing arguments, by Detweiler, *CJ* 65, 1970, 289ff.

[3] For the significance of this fact, cf. Hohl, *Hermes* 70, 1935, 352.

[4] Suet. *Aug.* 101.1.

[5] Tac. *Ann.* 1.6, Suet. *Tib.* 22.

genuine.[1] Augustus, knowing that Tiberius was unlikely to approve, may not have seen fit to acquaint him with his intentions, preferring to confront his successor with a *fait accompli*. The complicity of Livia need not be assumed, though no doubt she will have been pleased at the course adopted. It was presumably after his anger at these proceedings had been mollified by her arguments and those of Sallustius that Tiberius announced to a disbelieving senate what he had only just discovered himself, that Augustus had left orders for Agrippa to be executed as soon as the news of his own death reached Planasia.

The fate of her only surviving son may have hastened the death of the exiled Julia, Tiberius' former wife. Tiberius' accession brought her no relief; indeed, the princeps gave his undying hatred full rein. Augustus had confined his daughter first to the island of Pandateria and then to the town of Rhegium, but Tiberius had her kept under house arrest and deprived her of the allowance made her by Augustus on the ground that Augustus had said nothing of it in his will. Whether Julia succumbed to her despair or Tiberius had her slowly starved to death is uncertain; at all events she died before the end of 14.[2] Her confinement will not have been merely an act of revenge: security demanded that Augustus' daughter should be kept out of the hands of any potential rebels, and her allowance might have sufficed to bribe a guard.

2. THE INTERIM AND THE MEETING OF THE SENATE ON 17 SEPTEMBER

Meanwhile, in the minds of the magistrates, the senate and the people, there was no doubt that Tiberius was to be the new princeps. The consuls, Sex. Pompeius and Sex. Appuleius, were the first to take the oath of loyalty, followed by the praetorian prefect L. Seius Strabo and the prefect of the corn supply C. Turranius. Senate, armies and people followed suit.[3] Nor did Tiberius hesitate to exercise his *imperium* when it was necessary, issuing orders to the praetorian guard and sending

[1] Cf. Hohl, *Hermes* 70, 1935, 352ff.
[2] Tac. *Ann.* 1.53, Suet. *Tib.* 50.1, Dio 57.18.1a. The execution of her former lover Sempronius Gracchus is further proof of Tiberius' lasting resentment.
[3] On the oath, cf. von Premerstein, *Werden und Wesen*, 59; Syme, *Tacitus*, 410; Timpe, *Kontinuität*, 38f.

letters to the provincial armies. By virtue of his tribunician power he wrote to the senate, claiming the right to escort Augustus' body to Rome and summoning a meeting to be held on his arrival to discuss the honours due to the princeps' memory.[1]

The senate duly met, early in September. Tiberius attempted to address the house, but was overcome by his emotion and had to hand over the bulk of his speech to Drusus to read. Then Augustus' will was read. Its bitter opening words were a savage reminder that necessity had compelled Augustus to raise Tiberius to his present position of power: 'Since cruel fate has torn from me my sons Gaius and Lucius, let Tiberius Caesar be my heir. . . .'[2] The discussion of the funeral honours was doubtless preceded by a reading of the memorandum on the subject prepared by Augustus himself.[3] Tiberius was not spared further embarrassment, for in the course of the debate Messalla Messallinus proposed that the oath of loyalty to Tiberius should be renewed each year. Tiberius angrily asked if Messalla was implying that he himself had suggested this proposal to him. Messalla answered that he had spoken on his own initiative and in affairs of state would always trust his own counsel, even at the risk of giving offence.[4] Tiberius may have been well enough pleased with the reply – always suspicious of what looked like servile flattery, perhaps on this occasion he snapped too soon. But the incident, though trivial in itself, was ominous. It was to prove only the first of many where the senators, even those who had no wish to manoeuvre the princeps into awkward situations, were baffled by his inscrutable will and uncertain temper and failed to understand the part that he expected them to play.

Before the funeral Tiberius issued an edict, warning the people against any repetition of the disorders that had attended the obsequies

---

[1] Tac. *Ann.* 1.7.
[2] Suet. *Tib.* 23.
[3] Suet. *Aug.* 101.4, Dio 56.33. Dio's fourth volume is almost certainly an appendix to the third, the *breuiarium*, and Tac. *Ann.* 1.11 is surely right, against Dio, in implying that the *breuiarium* was first read at the second meeting of the senate, on 17 September. Cf. Hohl, *Klio* 30, 1937, 323ff.; Koestermann, *Historia* 10, 1961, 344; Timpe (*Kontinuität*, 45) suggests that the bare existence of the *breuiarium* had already been made public at the first meeting. For details of the honours to Augustus, cf. Suet. *Aug.* 100, Dio 56.34, 42, 46.
[4] Tac. *Ann.* 1.8.

of Julius Caesar, and on the day of the ceremony a substantial guard of honour served to ensure that Augustus' spirit might be seen to ascend to heaven without unseemly tumult upon earth. Two funeral orations were pronounced, one before the temple of Divus Julius by Tiberius, the other before the Rostra by Drusus.[1]

Then, on 17 September, the senate met again to consecrate Augustus as a god.[2] When this had been done, a motion was brought by the consuls to determine Tiberius' position.[3] The detailed content of this motion is nowhere recorded, but can perhaps be established with some precision. At the time of Augustus' death Tiberius held both proconsular *imperium* and tribunician power. It is likely that his *imperium* was also valid inside the city. If it was not, it is hard to explain the standing of the prefects who took the oath of allegiance.[4] Their power had derived directly from that of Augustus and must have been extinguished by his death. The natural explanation of their subsequent appearance is that Tiberius had the power to reappoint them and had done so. Moreover, when Tacitus mentions the edict by which Tiberius summoned the first meeting of the senate, he says that Tiberius cited in its prescript only his tribunician power.[5] The implication seems clear: Tiberius could, had he so desired, have summoned the senate to meet, inside the city, by virtue of his *imperium*. There can be no doubt whatever that during his principate Tiberius' *imperium* was valid inside the city. Dio speaks of him administering justice in the Forum.[6] Such an exercise of jurisdiction can be justified only by

---

[1] Tac. *Ann.* 1.8, Suet. *Aug.* 100.3f.

[2] This meeting is described in Tac. *Ann.* 1.10 (the last sentence) to 15.

[3] Tac. *Ann.* 1.13. For various interpretations, cf. Marsh, *Tiberius*, 48 (what meaning he attaches to the phrase 'declaring Tiberius emperor' is obscure); Charlesworth, *CAH* x, 612; Sutherland, *Coinage*, 81 (also obscure); Syme, *Tacitus*, 411 n.4; Kampff, *Phoenix* 17, 1963, 35.

[4] Tac. *Ann.* 1.7. The absence of any mention of the *praefectus urbi* is not necessarily significant: he might be subsumed under *senatus*, or, since his functions were not of vital importance, Tiberius might not have bothered to reappoint him at once. There is no record of a special grant of consular power in connection with the census of 14, nor does it seem to me that the language of the *Res Gestae* must imply one. The census too may therefore serve as evidence that Tiberius' *imperium* was already valid in Rome.

[5] Tac. *Ann.* 1.7.

[6] Dio 57.7.2, cf. Vell. 2.129.2.

imperium, and Tiberius' possession of it is confirmed by the statement of Tacitus and Dio that when he visited the praetors' courts he took a seat at the side of the tribunal so as not to make the praetor vacate his official chair.[1] This implies that Tiberius had the right to take the praetor's chair; he must therefore have held *imperium* greater than a praetor's. The only point which might suggest that he had not yet been granted this privilege at the time of the debate is the remark of Mam. Aemilius Scaurus, who in the course of the meeting found hope of Tiberius' ultimate acceptance of power in the fact that he had not used his tribunician power to veto the consuls' proposal.[2] It might be argued that if Tiberius' *imperium* were valid he could have used it to veto the motion instead of the tribunician power and that therefore Scaurus ought to have mentioned it too. But by 17 September Tiberius had already made it clear that the only power he was yet prepared to use inside the city was the *tribunicia potestas*. It was therefore reasonable for Scaurus to assume that, if Tiberius had been going to veto the motion, he would have chosen the tribunician power as his instrument, and so to mention nothing else.

There was then no formal need for a consular motion to confer on Tiberius the powers held by Augustus – he possessed them all already, and there is no reason whatever to suppose that Augustus' death had terminated their validity or even brought it into question.[3] The realization of this has led to the suggestion that Tiberius followed the example of Augustus and laid down all his powers at the beginning of the debate.[4] The point of the consular motion would then have been to beg him to take them up again. This notion is, however, demonstrably false, for Mam. Scaurus, in the speech already mentioned, rejoiced that Tiberius had not used his tribunician power to veto the motion. Therefore Tiberius was still in possession of at least one of his powers after the consuls had introduced their motion, and it is hardly likely that he retained this single attribute while laying down the others. As far as Tiberius' powers were concerned, the motion may have presumed

[1] Tac. *Ann.* 1.75, Dio 57.7.6; cf. Dio 54.30.4.
[2] Tac. *Ann.* 1.13.
[3] Cf. Timpe, *Kontinuität*, 37.
[4] Cf. Timpe, *Kontinuität*, 54.

to confirm them, though this was certainly not legally necessary and might have been construed as an impertinence, but is perhaps more likely to have confined itself to the request that he should agree to retain them and his guardianship of the state. It was not powers that Tiberius lacked but a province. When in 13 his *imperium* had been made equal to that of Augustus, the provinces of the empire had still been divided between Augustus and the senate. Augustus' provinces had been granted to him as an individual, and when he died his *prouincia* ceased to exist. Tiberius could not automatically inherit it. The most important function of the consular motion will have been to provide Tiberius with a sphere in which to exercise the powers he already held by conferring on him the province once bestowed on Augustus.

Tiberius, although he did not veto, stubbornly argued against the motion. He spoke at length on the magnitude of the task, a task so great as to exceed the capacity of any individual except the deified Augustus. His own experience under Augustus, when he had had to shoulder only a part of the burden, had taught him how hazardous and arduous it was to rule an empire. The responsibility should not, he said, be heaped on one man but should be divided up. The senate, unable to believe that he was sincere, dissolved into tearful obsecrations. Then Tiberius produced the *breuiarium*, in which Augustus had catalogued the military and financial resources of the state, and ordered that it be read to underline his point.[1] The senators continued to beseech, and Tiberius remarked, apparently quite casually, that, although he was unequal to the task as a whole, he was prepared to undertake whatever part might be assigned to him.[2] This suggestion was pounced on by C. Asinius Gallus, who demanded to know what part Tiberius wanted. Tiberius, at first reduced to silence by this sudden attack, then collected himself and replied that it would be unfitting for him to make a choice. Gallus hastily backed down, explaining that he had not expected an answer to his question, but had asked it merely to show that the imperial power was in fact one and

[1] Tac. *Ann.* 1.11; according to Dio 57.2.4 Tiberius also pleaded failing sight.
[2] Dio 57.2.4f. says that Tiberius proposed a tripartite division: Rome and Italy; the armies; 'the remaining subjects'. This is too impractical to be at all plausible.

indivisible. But Tiberius already had reason to dislike Gallus, who had married his beloved Vipsania when he had been compelled by Augustus to divorce her,[1] and he did not forget this attempt to embarrass him in public.[2] L. Arruntius also gave offence by speaking in similar vein, and as the patience of the senators began to wear thin Q. Haterius ventured to enquire just how long Tiberius intended to allow the state to remain without a head, which earned him an immediate rebuke, and Mam. Scaurus pointed out with unctuous malice that in spite of his prolonged hesitations Tiberius had after all not vetoed the motion.

At last Tiberius weakened and withdrew his objections.[3] At the same meeting of the senate on 17 September honours were conferred on other members of the imperial house. Much adulation was lavished on Livia, which Tiberius did his best to keep in check. Then, at Tiberius' request, proconsular *imperium* was granted to Germanicus and an embassy deputed to inform him of this and at the same time to condole with him on the death of Augustus. Since Drusus was consul designate and present in the senate, no similar grant was made to him.[4] It is unthinkable that arrangements such as these could have been made if Tiberius' own position had remained unsettled.[5] It may therefore be accepted that the motion of the consuls was eventually allowed to pass and that Tiberius assumed the principate on 17 September.[6] It is uncertain, however, that he did so for life.[7] Suetonius tells us that he

[1] Dio 57.2.7 even goes so far as to assert that Gallus claimed the paternity of Drusus.
[2] Tac. *Ann.* 1.12, Dio 57.2.5ff.
[3] Tac. *Ann.* 1.13, cf. Suet. *Tib.* 24.2.
[4] Tac. *Ann.* 1.14.
[5] Cf. Syme, *Tacitus*, 411; Koestermann *ad loc.*; Timpe, *Kontinuität*, 49.
[6] This is also the implication of Vell. 2.124.3, who describes the election arrangements of 14, which clearly preceded the mutinies, as *primum principalium eius operum*. The evidence of Velleius and of Suet. *Tib.* 24.2 is sufficient to refute the view that Tiberius did not accept the principate until late September or early October, after the mutinies had been dealt with, as is stated by Suet. *Tib.* 25 and Dio 57.1.1 and accepted by e.g. von Premerstein, *Werden und Wesen*, 58; Pippidi, *Tibère*, 129; Béranger, *Recherches*, 20ff. Kampff's attempt to reconcile the two views (*Phoenix* 17, 1963, 46) is unconvincing, as is that of Wellesley to date the accession debate about 3 September (*JRS* 57, 1967, 23ff.).
[7] As is suggested by Hohl, *Hermes* 68, 1933, 112 n.2; Charlesworth, *CAH* x, 612; Kampff, *Phoenix* 17, 1963, 35. For an indefinite period: Marsh, *Tiberius*, 49; Syme, *Tacitus*, 411 n.4.

accepted power only 'until such time as you judge it fair to grant me some repose in my old age'.[1] Dio records decennial celebrations during the reign, and it is likely that Tiberius' province at least was conferred in 14 for only ten years and that the grant was subsequently renewed at ten-year intervals.[2]

It was not only Tiberius' contemporaries who found it difficult to believe that his reluctance to rule was genuine. Historians concluded that he must have been dissembling and so made dissimulation the keynote of his character. It was easy to point out that from the moment of Augustus' death Tiberius had attended to all the immediate necessities of the administration and to sneer that he showed hesitancy only in the senate.[3] Many modern scholars have followed suit and have dismissed the debate of 17 September as a polite comedy in which Tiberius, after a formal show of resistance, ought benignly to have acceded to the eager prayers of the senate, a comedy, however, in which he was too tactless or too surly to play his part with a good grace, with the result that the senators in turn grew restive and improvised some awkward lines.[4] It is certainly true that in later years the initial refusal of power was an empty ceremony patiently rehearsed even by victors fresh from the civil wars that had brought them to the purple.[5] But although Augustus had once gone through some such show, in 14 there was as yet no precedent for the conferment of power on a new princeps after the death of the old, and if anything is clear about the meeting of 17 September it is that no script had been agreed on. To deny Tiberius' sincerity is perverse. He was fifty-four years old and he had had a long and tiring career, in the shadow of a man whose character and achievements he could never hope to emulate even if he wanted to. Now he was being called on to dedicate the rest of his life to the preservation of a political structure of which he had no reason to approve. There can be no doubt that he would have preferred to

[1] Suet. *Tib.* 24.2.
[2] Dio 57.24.1 (in 24: very ambiguous), 58.24.1 (in 34: here the language suggests a renewal).
[3] Tac. *Ann.* 1.7, Suet. *Tib.* 24.1; cf. Syme, *Tacitus*, 410.
[4] Cf. Marsh, *Tiberius*, 45, 50 (yet he notes the absence of constitutional precedents); Allen, *TAPA* 72, 1941, 22; Syme, *Tacitus*, 410.
[5] Cf. Béranger, *Recherches*, 137ff.

reject the principate altogether, no doubt that he meant what he said when he accepted this painful and burdensome servitude, as he called it, only as a temporary measure, in hope of retirement.[1] Yet the debate was indeed a farce, though not the orderly farce that was fashionable later, for Tiberius knew that in the end he could not refuse. Augustus' intentions were clear, and Tiberius had obeyed Augustus too often during his lifetime to be ready to betray his life's work after his death. The senators too knew that Tiberius would have to yield at the last. What they would not or could not understand was that his feelings were so strong he could not yield quickly and gracefully, but was compelled by his loathing for the task that was being forced on him to give vent to all his bitterness.[2] Perhaps indeed this was why Tiberius refused so vehemently and so long – he knew that ultimately it would make no difference, and yet he longed to make the senate at least comprehend his predicament and grew more and more irritated at its lack of understanding. The senate knew only that this awkward wrangle had for practical purposes been pointless from the first and could not see why matters need take such an unpleasant course. Hence there was all through the debate an increasing atmosphere of exasperated frustration.

[1] Suet. *Tib.* 24.2. Cf. Charlesworth, *CAH* x, 612; Sutherland, *Coinage*, 82; Allen, *TAPA* 72, 1941, 21f.
[2] Cf. Koestermann, *Historia* 10, 1961, 340ff.

IV

GERMANICUS AND DRUSUS

1. THE MUTINIES ON THE DANUBE AND THE RHINE

The death of Augustus had disturbing effects on the Roman armies in
Pannonia and on the Rhine.[1] In the summer quarters of the three
Pannonian legions (VIII Augusta, IX Hispana and XV Apollinaris)
their commander Q. Junius Blaesus, suffect consul in 10 and an uncle
of the new praetorian prefect L. Aelius Seianus, had unwisely allowed
a total relaxation of discipline as soon as he heard the news.[2] Morale
deteriorated rapidly, and a skilful troublemaker arose, Percennius, a
man with a theatrical background which now stood him in good stead.
The grievances that he and his satellites rehearsed were real: poor pay,
brutal centurions, service prolonged well beyond the appointed time,
worthless land-allotments among marshes and mountains for those
who survived till retirement. The recruitment and financing of a large
standing army had been a constant problem throughout the reign of
Augustus;[3] in particular the Pannonian revolt and the *clades Variana*
had meant that many men due for demobilization had been forced to
remain in service, while others who were hardly suitable material –
freedmen and riffraff from the city – had been signed on in desperation
to fill the gaps left by the annihilation of three legions. Now, with
Augustus dead and Tiberius not yet secure, the time seemed ripe to
protest against these abuses and demand more tolerable conditions of
service.[4]

---

[1] For the relationship between these events and Tiberius' accession, cf. above,
p. 55 n.6.
[2] The Pannonian mutiny is narrated in Tac. *Ann.* 1.16–30; cf. also Suet. *Tib.* 25.1f.,
Dio 57.4, Vell. 2.125.
[3] Cf. *RG* 16f. with Gagé's notes.
[4] Tac. *Ann.* 1.16f.

So the legions formulated their terms: increased pay of a denarius a day (still no more than half what was received by the praetorian guard) and genuine demobilization after sixteen years, with no retention of veterans under arms in the reserve. Then came the suggestion that to strengthen their position the three legions should merge themselves into one. This failed, since no agreement could be reached as to which two legions should sacrifice their identity, but the legionary standards and those of the cohorts were set up together in one place and the troops began to construct a tribunal. At this point Blaesus intervened, crying that it would be less shameful for them to murder him, their legate, than to mutiny against their commander-in-chief. Work on the tribunal went on for a time regardless, but then the men stopped of their own accord and Blaesus seized the opportunity to reason with them. Mutiny, he said, was not the way to convey their wishes to Tiberius; it would be better if they appointed envoys to represent them at Rome. This proposal won the approval of the mob, which decided that Blaesus' son should go to the city to demand demobilization after sixteen years. Once this was granted, their further conditions would follow. So young Blaesus set out and some degree of quiet was restored.[1]

Not for long, however, for the mutiny flared up again when a detachment from Nauportus, which had been employed on road and bridge building duties, perhaps in connection with the new colony at Emona, returned to camp. These men had been inspired by the news of the disturbance to run riot through Nauportus and the villages around, first abusing and then manhandling the centurions who had tried to hold them in check, and in particular their *praefectus castrorum* (camp commander), Aufidienus Rufus, a martinet who was especially hated. In an attempt to keep the majority in order Blaesus commanded a few to be flogged and put in irons, but their comrades answered their appeals for aid, the jail was broken open and the mutineers were joined by its complement of deserters and criminals. A new leader, Vibulenus, emerged, claiming that his brother had been sent on a mission to the legions in Pannonia from the army of the Rhine, but had been murdered in the night by the gladiators kept by Blaesus. The men, roused to fury, seized the gladiators and the rest of Blaesus'

[1] Tac. *Ann.* 1.17–19.

59

slaves, while others instituted a search for the corpse of Vibulenus' murdered brother. No body could be found, and interrogation of the slaves revealed that Vibulenus was an only child, otherwise Blaesus might not have escaped alive.[1]

But the discrediting of Vibulenus' tale did not curb the mutineers, who drove the tribunes and *praefectus castrorum* from the camp. One centurion, Lucilius, renowned for his love of the cane, was murdered, the rest went into hiding, except for one Julius Clemens, who was judged to be a suitable mouthpiece for the claims of his men.[2]

Such was the state of the mutiny when Tiberius took steps to put it down. Drusus was sent out with an escort composed of the leading men in the state, two praetorian cohorts, strengthened for the occasion with other picked troops, a large detachment of praetorian cavalry and some of the princeps' German bodyguard. As second-in-command and counsellor to the prince went Seianus, newly appointed, as colleague of his father Seius Strabo, to the prefectship of the guard.[3] Tacitus remarks that his influence over Tiberius was already great, and his appointment as praetorian prefect goes some way to bear this out. As a young man he had served in the retinue of Gaius Caesar in the East, and it is possible that he had then behaved in such a way as to win Tiberius' lasting favour.[4]

The chronology of Drusus' mission presents a problem. Drusus was present in the senate on 17 September.[5] He reached the camp of the mutinous legions on 26 September.[6] Such a journey is possible for a small group of men making use of the horses of the imperial post, but it is inconceivable that the praetorian cohorts could have covered the distance in this time.[7] It is perhaps possible that at this time part of the praetorian guard was stationed at Aquileia and that Drusus picked up his cohorts from there.[8] But even if this were the case, it would not

[1] Tac. *Ann.* 1.20–23; for Emona, cf. Šašel, *Historia* 19, 1970, 122ff.
[2] Tac. *Ann.* 1.23.
[3] Tac. *Ann.* 1.24, Dio 57.19.6.
[4] Tac. *Ann.* 4.1.
[5] Tac. *Ann.* 1.14; denied without good reason by Wellesley, *JRS* 57, 1967, 23ff.
[6] The date of the eclipse, cf. Tac. *Ann.* 1.28.
[7] Cf. Schmitt, *Historia* 7, 1958, 378ff.; contra Hohl, *Hermes* 68, 1933, 107.
[8] Denied, however, by Durry, *Les cohortes prétoriennes*, 45 n.2.

account for the movements of the German guard, while Tacitus certainly implies that the entire force set off from Rome. Nor is it plausible that Drusus and his advisers rode ahead, leaving the bulk of the force to follow as fast as it could. This would have exposed the advance party to far too great a risk if they had had to face the mutineers unprotected, and besides it is plain from Tacitus' narrative that Drusus would not merely have arrived but have left the camp again before the greater part of his force had reached it. The most likely explanation is that the main body left Rome as soon as possible after news of the mutiny was received, some time before the meeting of the senate on 17 September, and that Drusus and his counsellors set out post-haste on 18 September to catch them up.

When Drusus entered the camp on 26 September, he found himself little better than a prisoner as the mutineers closed and guarded the gates behind him. After the mutterings of the mob had at last died away, he read a letter from Tiberius. Its contents were guarded and not likely to please his hearers. The princeps asserted his concern for the well-being of the legions in whose company he had himself endured many campaigns. (It must have been a bitter blow to his pride that troops whom he had commanded for so long had sunk to such a level of indiscipline, even though, in Pannonia at least, the mutiny was not inspired by disloyalty to him as a commander or as an individual.) As soon as his mind was freed from its burden of grief, he would put, he promised, the demands of the legions to the senate. Meanwhile he had sent his son to grant without delay whatever concessions could be made without further authority. For the rest they must wait on the senate. In answer Clemens recited the army's demands: demobilization after sixteen years with adequate gratuities, pay of a denarius a day, and the abandonment of the practice of forcing veterans to remain with the colours. Drusus made the only reply he could: that he had no power to decide on such matters but would refer them to the judgment of his father and the senate. At this the angry mob shouted him down, asking why he had come if he had no authority to make the least concession. In the past, they said, Tiberius had sheltered behind Augustus in refusing the legions their due, and now Drusus was resorting to the same device. They had had enough of sons who were empowered to grant nothing without their fathers' permission.[1]

The mutineers dispersed, threatening violence to any of the praetorians or Drusus' friends whom they met. The especial target of their
hatred was Cn. Cornelius Lentulus, consul as long before as 14 B.C.,
an experienced commander who had seen service in the region and a
close friend of Tiberius.[2] The mob suspected him of influencing
Drusus to stand firm, caught him alone and began to pelt him with
stones. Only the arrival on the scene of Drusus' bodyguard saved
Lentulus' life. Thus the day ended on an ominous note, but the night
brought Drusus good luck – an eclipse of the moon, which struck terror
into the hearts of the mutineers and convinced them that the gods
disapproved of their actions. Drusus was quick to exploit their mood,
enlisting the assistance of Clemens and any others who had succeeded
in retaining the confidence of their men without betraying their loyalty.
The change of heart spread rapidly, as the men speedily realized the
possible advantages of being the first to repent of their excesses. The
guard on the gates was abandoned and the standards which had been
brought together at the outset of the mutiny were now restored to their
proper places. When day came Drusus addressed the troops, refusing
to be moved by threats but promising that if they put their case
modestly he would write to Tiberius in support of their claims. At the
legions' request a second embassy was sent to Tiberius, comprising
the young Blaesus once again, L. Aponius, an *eques* from Drusus'
retinue, and Justus Catonius, a centurion.[3]

Drusus and his counsellors then debated their course. Some were in
favour of humouring the troops, at least until the return of the embassy;
others, including Drusus himself, preferred sterner measures. Moderation, they thought, would merely encourage the mob. It would therefore be better to get rid of the ringleaders before the salutary effects of
the eclipse had worn off. Drusus' opinion seems to have carried the
day. Vibulenus and Percennius were arrested and executed, then other
ringleaders were cut down at random, some by centurions, some by
praetorians, others by their own comrades as proof of their renewed

[1] Tac. *Ann.* 1.25f.
[2] Cf. Koestermann on Tac. *Ann.* 1.27.
[3] Tac. *Ann.* 1.27–29.

loyalty. The spirits of the former mutineers were still further damped by the onset of heavy rain, which made it impossible for them to set foot outside their tents. The downpour was interpreted as another token of divine discontent, and the men became convinced that the only way to end this state of affairs would be to abandon the scene of their ill-starred attempt and withdraw to their winter quarters. First the eighth legion, then the fifteenth departed. The men of the ninth at first spoke in favour of waiting for Tiberius' reply to their ambassadors, but finding themselves deserted by their comrades they too left the camp. Thereupon Drusus, deciding that the danger was over, returned to Rome without waiting for the envoys.[1]

It was not only in Pannonia that Augustus' death provoked a mutiny.[2] On the Rhine there were two Roman armies, each of four legions: on the upper Rhine II Augusta, XIII Gemina, XIV Gemina and XVI Gallica, commanded by C. Silius A. Caecina Largus, consul in the previous year; on the lower Rhine I Germanica, V Alaudae, XX Valeria and XXI Rapax, under A. Caecina Severus, suffect consul in I B.C., who as governor of Moesia had played a part in the suppression of the Pannonian revolt. Their commander-in-chief was Germanicus, who was engaged at the time of Augustus' death in taking a census of the three Gauls, of which he was governor. Trouble, stemming from the twenty-first and fifth legions, broke out in Caecina's summer camp in the territory of the Ubii as soon as the news of Augustus' death arrived. Tacitus places the blame on the rabble who had been enlisted to meet the emergency created by the destruction of Varus' legions. Loving an easy life and unused to military hardships, they seized the opportunity to make the same demands as their comrades in Pannonia: demobilization for those who had served their time, higher pay for those who had not, and revenge for brutal treatment at the hands of centurions. Meanwhile the army of the upper Rhine held its hand, waiting in two minds to see what might ensue.[3]

Whereas the Pannonian mutiny seems to have been solely a protest

[1] Tac. *Ann.* 1.29f.
[2] For the Rhine mutiny, cf. Tac. *Ann.* 1.31–49, Suet. *Tib.* 25.1f., Dio 57.5f., Vell. 2.125.
[3] Tac. *Ann.* 1.31, cf. 4.18.

against intolerable conditions of service, without any political under-
tones, the mutiny on the lower Rhine had another more sinister aspect.
It was hoped, says Tacitus, that Germanicus would be unable to
endure the supremacy of another and would put himself in the hands
of the legions, who would seize power on his behalf. This motive is
given pride of place by Suetonius, Velleius and Dio, all of whom make
the legions of the Rhine unanimously urge Germanicus to claim the
principate, while Velleius and Dio strongly suggest that the army's
demands on the subject of pay and conditions were very much a matter
of secondary importance.[1] Yet in Tacitus' detailed narrative of the
outbreak this theme is kept very much in the background.[2] Only a
small minority among the mutineers attempted to push Germanicus
into rebellion, and that on the purely selfish ground that they expected
him to be more ready than Tiberius to disburse the legacies promised
in Augustus' will but not yet paid. After Germanicus' dramatic reaction, nothing more is heard of any such design. It is on balance unlikely
that it was a major factor in provoking the mutiny.

But the prominence given to this possibility by the sources is not
without significance. Tacitus, Suetonius and Dio all agree that
Tiberius feared and distrusted Germanicus;[3] it is rash to dismiss their
evidence as sheer imagination.[4] That Tiberius had no cause for alarm
is clear: whatever criticisms may be levelled at Germanicus for his
handling of the mutiny, he did at least prove his loyalty beyond doubt.
But in character the two men were far apart, Tiberius withdrawn and
for the most part careless of public opinion, Germanicus affable and
eager for popularity. Neither could understand or appreciate the
qualities of the other, and their relations were always awkward and
fumbling.[5] There is no reason to suppose deliberate malice on either
side. It was simply a misfortune for Tiberius and for Rome that he

[1] Suet. *Tib.* 25.2, *Cal.* 1.1, Dio 57.5.1, Vell. 2.125.2.
[2] Cf. Liechtenhan, *MH* 4, 1947, 52ff.
[3] Tac. *Ann.* 1.52, 2.5, Suet. *Tib.* 25.2, 52.1, Dio 57.6.2f.
[4] As does e.g. Spengel, *SB München* 1903, Heft 1, 18. The ancient testimony is
accepted in essence by e.g. Koestermann, *Historia* 6, 1957, 430 and 7, 1958, 335;
Shotter, *Historia* 17, 1968, 195.
[5] Their relationship and Tacitus' treatment of it are well discussed by Shotter,
Historia 17, 1968, 194ff. For Germanicus' love of popularity, cf. especially Suet.
Cal. 3.1, also 4.

and the successor chosen for him by Augustus were in temper utterly incompatible. The heir to the principate had of course to be entrusted with great commands and vital missions – he could not, like a Claudius, be discreetly set aside and forgotten. But Tiberius viewed with a jaundiced eye the way in which Germanicus courted the favour of the legions, abetted by his wife Agrippina, a proud and ambitious woman obsessed with her direct descent from Augustus.[1]

Caecina did nothing to check the mutineers, who set on their centurions, flogged them unconscious and threw the bodies over the rampart or into the Rhine. One, Septimius, fled to the tribunal and sought refuge at Caecina's feet, only to be given up to the fury of the mob, but Cassius Chaerea, the future assassin of Gaius, cut his way to safety through its ranks. The tribunes and *praefectus castrorum* lost all their authority; the men divided duties among themselves on their own initiative.[2]

Meanwhile Germanicus had heard of Augustus' death. He at once demonstrated his loyalty to Tiberius by administering the oath to the Sequani and the Belgae.[3] Then, learning of the mutiny, he hurried to the camp, where he was met by a chorus of complaints. Some of the men, on the pretext of kissing his hand, thrust his fingers into mouths now toothless after long years in the service, others displayed limbs bent with age. Germanicus ordered this random assembly to disperse by maniples. The troops replied that they could hear better as they were, and obeyed only reluctantly when Germanicus gave the further command that the standards of the cohorts be brought forward to produce some semblance of order. When this had been done, Germanicus began to speak. At first his words were received in silence as he reminded the troops of the veneration in which they had held Augustus and of Tiberius' victories and triumphs, especially those that he had won in Germany at their head. Italy, Gaul and the rest of the empire, he claimed, were unanimous in their loyalty.[4] But when he came to the

[1] Tac. *Ann.* 1.52, 69, 2.5; on Agrippina, cf. Tac. *Ann.* 1.40.
[2] Tac. *Ann.* 1.32.
[3] For the oath of allegiance in the provinces, cf. the example from Cyprus published by Mitford, *JRS* 50, 1960, 75ff., and best discussed by Seibert, *Historia* 19, 1970, 224ff.
[4] News of the Pannonian mutiny had therefore not yet reached the Rhine.

subject of the mutiny, the men began to flaunt their scars and urge their grievances vociferously. The veterans who had been retained in the service for thirty or forty years were particularly loud in their demands for demobilization. It was at this point that some, claiming Augustus' legacy, offered to give Germanicus their support if he wanted to seize power for himself.[1]

Germanicus leapt down from the tribunal, shouting that he would rather die than be disloyal, drawing his sword and struggling to set it to his chest while his friends clutched at his arm to hold him back. More amused than moved by this piece of play-acting, the soldiers mockingly cheered Germanicus on and one, Calusidius, drew his own sword and jeeringly offered it to the prince, saying 'Try this one – it's sharper!' At this even the rowdiest were shocked, and in the lull Germanicus was dragged to safety by his friends. Then the prince and his advisers discussed what to do. It was rumoured that the troops were preparing to send envoys to encourage the army of the upper Rhine to join their enterprise and that they intended first to sack the town of the Ubii and then to ravage Gaul. To this prospect, gloomy enough in itself, was added the fear that, if the army abandoned the bank of the Rhine, the Germans, who were watching the course of the mutiny with interest and amusement, would seize the chance to invade. It might be possible to reduce the mutinous legions by using auxiliary troops and the Gallic allies, but a civil war of this kind was hardly inviting. So Germanicus was faced with a dilemma. To stand firm was fraught with danger, to make concessions shameful. In this quandary, after much discussion, it was decided to forge a letter from Tiberius, promising demobilization after twenty years, the last four years of which were to be spent with the reserve on the understanding that such men would be called upon to fight only if Roman territory were invaded, and undertaking not merely to pay but to double Augustus' legacies.[2]

In fairness to Germanicus it must be said that this sordid expedient reflects the weakness not only of his character but also of his position. He had no authority to make concessions, and had he attempted to act as if he had, even if only to save the immediate situation, Tiberius

[1] Tac. *Ann.* 1.33–35.
[2] Tac. *Ann.* 1.35f.

might have suspected his intentions. In this respect Germanicus' position was more delicate than that of Drusus, whom Tiberius was not inclined to distrust. In the event this shallow deceit failed to serve its purpose, for the men were not fooled and demanded that the promised concessions be granted at once. Germanicus had no choice but to yield. The task of demobilization was entrusted to the tribunes and after a vain attempt to put off payment of the legacies until the legions had withdrawn to winter quarters, which was firmly squashed by the fifth and twenty-first, Germanicus was forced to find the money from the cash that he and his friends had with them for expenses. Then Caecina led the first and the twentieth legions to the capital of the Ubii, while Germanicus made his way to the army of the upper Rhine. The second, thirteenth and sixteenth legions took the oath to Tiberius without hesitation, as did the fourteenth after a brief delay that earned it the same concessions as the mutineers, even though it had not demanded them.[1]

Germanicus returned to Oppidum Ubiorum (where the first and twentieth legions were still quartered, along with the veterans freshly assigned to the reserve) in time to meet the embassy from the senate led by L. Munatius Plancus, Silius' colleague in the consulship of 13. The troops were alarmed that its purpose might be to invalidate the concessions they had just extorted. In the night they broke into the house where Germanicus had his quarters, dragged him out of bed and forced him at sword-point to hand over the standard. Then, as they wandered through the streets, they came upon the envoys, who had heard the uproar and were hurrying to join Germanicus. From insults the men progressed to violence. Plancus alone refused to run for his life, but took refuge in the camp of the first legion, seeking sanctuary by embracing its standard. This alone would not have saved him, had not the standard-bearer, Calpurnius, succeeded in turning back the mob. It was not until dawn that Germanicus entered the camp and had Plancus escorted to the comparative safety of the tribunal. The men listened unimpressed to his reproaches while the other envoys were conducted to shelter by a detachment of auxiliary cavalry.[2]

[1] Tac. *Ann.* 1.37.
[2] Tac. *Ann.* 1.39.

His officers were now loudly critical of Germanicus, though they must at least have acquiesced in the forging of the letter. He had already gone too far along the path of weakness, they said, with his concessions over pay and demobilization. Now he should take over the army of the upper Rhine and use it against the mutineers – hardly a sensible piece of advice, for the objections to civil war had already been voiced and there was no guarantee that the loyalty of Silius' troops would extend to turning their arms against their comrades. Germanicus was also attacked for allowing his pregnant wife Agrippina and their infant son Gaius, nicknamed Caligula, to remain in the camp. This seems to have given Germanicus the idea for a new piece of theatre. Despite Agrippina's protests that she, the descendant of Augustus, was ready to face any danger, he persuaded her to carry Gaius to safety. The wives of several of his friends followed this example, and so, amid much lamentation, the procession set out to seek shelter with a foreign tribe, the Treveri, from the violence of Roman legionaries. The spectacle had the effect that Germanicus intended: stricken with shame, the troops clustered round Agrippina, begging her not to go. Germanicus took full advantage of their mood in a characteristically histrionic speech. First he harped on the disgraceful paradox that the very legions Tiberius had so often led to victory were now casting the only shadow on the universal rejoicing at his accession. Then, with consummate art, he berated his friends for their folly in staying his hand when he had tried to kill himself. Calusidius, he said, had been kinder – he could at least have died without the shame of his army on his conscience, while a new leader, leaving his death unpunished, went on to avenge the slaughter of Varus and his legions. But now Rome might have to rely on the Belgae to withstand the German hordes. He ended with an appeal to the men to restore the envoys to the senate, their obedience to Tiberius, Agrippina and Gaius to himself, and to shun all contact with the troublemakers as a proof of their repentance and renewed loyalty.[1]

This fine piece of rhetoric was as successful as Germanicus could have hoped. The men clamoured for him to punish the guilty, forgive the rest and lead them against the Germans, and begged him to recall

[1] Tac. *Ann.* 1.40–43, Suet. *Cal.* 9.

Agrippina and not allow Gaius, the foster-child of the legions, to become a hostage in the hands of the Gauls. Germanicus put off the return of Agrippina on the grounds of her pregnancy and the approach of winter, but promised that Gaius would come. For the rest, he said, let them see to it themselves.[1] It is this eagerness to evade responsibility for the punishment of the ringleaders, since this might damage his popularity with the troops, that reflects more discredit on Germanicus than anything else in his handling of the situation. No doubt it was inspired by nothing more than an innocent desire for the affection of the troops, but Tiberius, devious and immune to such considerations, was bound to wonder what ulterior motive Germanicus had for valuing the legions' love so highly. The men, nothing loath, rounded up their former leaders and dragged them in chains before C. Caetronius, the commander of the first legion. Each man was displayed on a raised mound by a military tribune; the legionaries stood below with drawn swords. If a shout of guilty went up, the man was thrust headlong from the mound and butchered. Germanicus did nothing to halt this barbarous proceeding, content that any ill-feeling aroused by such savagery should fall on the heads of the perpetrators themselves, who were acting without direct orders from him.

The veterans were then packed off to Rhaetia on the pretext of defending the province against the threat of invasion by the Suebi. Germanicus went on to deal with the centurions in an equally un-precedented manner. Each centurion was summoned in turn to recite his name, rank and home, the number of his campaigns, his achieve-ments and decorations. If the tribunes and men of his legion vouched for his industry and his innocence of any charges of cruelty or corrup-tion, he retained his rank, but if their voice went against him he was cashiered.[2]

In this dubious fashion the mutiny of the first and twentieth legions was brought to an end, but that of the fifth and twenty-first (now in their winter quarters at Vetera) remained to be dealt with, for the fate of their comrades at Oppidum Ubiorum had left them undeterred. Germanicus therefore at last resolved to use force and prepared to send

[1] Tac. *Ann.* 1.44.
[2] Tac. *Ann.* 1.44.

an allied contingent down the Rhine, with the help of the fleet that had been established on the river by his father Drusus.[1]

At Rome meanwhile Tiberius had been severely criticized for refusing on various pretexts to intervene. The princes, men said, did not carry sufficient weight to suppress the mutinies by themselves; it needed the full authority of the princeps, with his long experience of command and his status as the ultimate source of both sanctions and concessions, to bring the armies to heel. Tiberius, unmoved, believed that it would be wrong for him to leave the capital and risk exposing his person. He could not be in two places at once, and whichever army he chose to visit first, the other would take offence. It was impossible to decide between them on grounds of urgency: the Rhine armies were more powerful, especially with the resources of Gaul behind them, but Pannonia was nearer to Italy, if the worst came to the worst. Better therefore to send his sons and leave distance to reinforce his own authority. Germanicus and Drusus could refer their problems to him, and if their authority was spurned it could be backed up by his own, but if he himself acted only to be ignored, there would be nobody to whom he could look for support. Nevertheless he went through an elaborate pantomime, pretending to be constantly on the point of departure, choosing companions, assembling his baggage, equipping ships, but always finding an excuse never to leave.[2]

Although he had a force ready to bring against the remaining mutineers, Germanicus was understandably reluctant to use it, preferring if he could to engineer the same kind of solution as had proved so effective at Oppidum Ubiorum. He therefore decided to give the legions at Vetera a last chance to redeem themselves and wrote a letter to Caecina, announcing that he was on his way with a powerful contingent and that, if the legions had not punished the malefactors on their own initiative before he arrived, he would apply the death penalty without regard for the guilt or innocence of individuals. Caecina secretly communicated the contents of this letter to the standard-bearers and other trustworthy elements and encouraged them to take

---

[1] Tac. *Ann.* 1.45; on the Rhine fleet, cf. Vell. 2.106.3, Florus 2.30.26.
[2] Tac. *Ann.* 1.46f., cf. Suet. *Tib.* 38; Tiberius' decision is rightly defended by Marsh, *Tiberius*, 57.

the necessary action to save the legions from disgrace and themselves from death. They accordingly assembled those they thought suitable (for the greater part of both legions had returned to their duties) and with Caecina's approval fixed a time to set upon the unsuspecting malcontents. Here there was not even the crude semblance of formal procedure that had obtained at Oppidum Ubiorum; Caecina and his tribunes kept out of the way, no doubt as eager as Germanicus himself to dodge responsibility for the massacre, which went on unchecked until the dutiful were weary of bloodshed. Only when all was over did Germanicus see fit to enter the camp, burst into tears in his horror at the disaster, as he called it, and order a decent funeral for the victims.[1]

At Vetera, as at Oppidum Ubiorum, the men, once the mutiny was over, were keen to be led against the Germans, feeling that to risk their lives against the enemy was the only way for them to expiate the slaughter of their comrades. Tacitus paints Germanicus as yielding to their request despite the lateness of the season and the lack of preparations.[2] Dio asserts that Germanicus devised the expedition to prevent the mutiny from flaring up again.[3] There is no inconsistency here.[4] Germanicus had been trying from the first to inspire such a mood; had he failed to exploit it once it had been created, the resultant frustration might well have led to a further outbreak. Despite Germanicus' rhetorical flourishes on the theme of avenging the *clades Variana*,[5] it is clear that the campaign of autumn 14 was not the first stage in a new attempt to restore Roman dominion to the Elbe, a task that had been hanging fire since Tiberius' last campaign in 12, or even a trial run for the major advance that Germanicus tried to carry out in the following year, but simply an appendage to the mutiny. Had there been no mutiny, there would have been no campaign in 14.[6]

Tactically the invasion adhered to the principles established by Tiberius in the years 10 to 12.[7] The Rhine was bridged and Germanicus

---

[1] Tac. *Ann.* 1.48f.
[2] Tac. *Ann.* 1.49.
[3] Dio 57.6.1.
[4] As is claimed by Timpe, *Triumph*, 57f.
[5] Tac. *Ann.* 1.43.
[6] Cf. Koestermann, *Historia* 6, 1957, 429; Timpe, *Triumph*, 28f.
[7] Cf. Timpe, *Triumph*, 35f.

led across it 12,000 legionaries, twenty-six allied cohorts and eight
troops of cavalry. The Germans were caught completely unprepared,
still enjoying the respite from war they had secured thanks first to the
death of Augustus and then to the mutiny. Germanicus moved quickly,
clearing a path through the forest to mark the frontier, a task begun by
Tiberius, and making camp on this line. Then, to preserve the advantage of surprise, he chose a roundabout and hitherto unused route into
enemy territory and timed his attack to coincide with a German feast.
Caecina was sent ahead with the light-armed cohorts to cut a road
through the forests for the legions, and so the force came to the
settlements of the Marsi and found them completely unguarded.
Germanicus divided his army into four and gave them orders to ravage
the land and wipe out the population over a radius of fifty miles. Men,
women and children were massacred as they wandered helplessly
about; buildings and the sacred grove of the goddess Tanfana were razed
to the ground.[1] These methods are a continuation of the policy of slow
but ruthless pacification instituted by Tiberius after the death of Varus.

The attack provoked some other tribes, the Bructeri, Usipetes and
Tubantes, who probably shared in the worship of Tanfana, to lay an
ambush for the Romans on their way back to the Rhine. Germanicus
got wind of the trap and marched in battle order, with the cavalry and
some of the auxiliaries at the head, the four legions in a square to
protect the baggage, and the remainder of the allies at the rear. The
Germans waited until the entire column had entered the woods, then
set upon the rearguard. The allied cohorts were thrown into confusion,
but Germanicus urged the men of the twentieth, which occupied the
rear of the legionary square, to wipe out the memory of their recent
disgrace. Thus encouraged, they drove the enemy back on to open
ground and there cut them down. By this time the head of the column
had emerged from the forest and was able to set about fortifying a camp.
No further incident distinguished the return to the Rhine, and the
legions, their morale restored by a campaign that had succeeded in
achieving its very limited objective, were settled in their winter
quarters.[2]

[1] Tac. *Ann.* 1.50f.
[2] Tac. *Ann.* 1.51.

When he heard of the outcome of the German mutiny Tiberius' feelings were mixed. He was naturally glad that the outbreak was at an end, but he suspected that the concessions made by the prince had been conceived with a view to winning the favour of the troops and was also worried by the wild acclaim with which Germanicus' success was greeted, not only by the people but also by the praetorian guard.[1] Nevertheless in his report to the senate he spoke at length of Germanicus' courage, though Tacitus claims that his speech was too ornate to carry conviction.[2] Even if Tacitus had the speech before him, he is hardly likely to have had evidence for its reception, but his insight or his malice here points to another factor that complicated relations between the princeps and his heir. Despite the official keeping up of appearances it was obvious that the two men regarded each other with suspicion, and so senate and people refused to believe that Tiberius ever meant anything that he said about Germanicus. His every utterance became a target for misinterpretation and inevitably the chances of friction were multiplied. Tiberius was briefer but more credible in his praise of Drusus' conduct in Pannonia. This is understandable: he trusted Drusus and Drusus, although he had had one major stroke of luck, had behaved in a manner much more likely to appeal to the traditionalist Tiberius than the histrionics of his adoptive brother. In Germany, moreover, the concessions made had been made in Tiberius' name. Perhaps Germanicus' chief reason for this was his fear of Tiberius' anger if he dared to act on his own responsibility, but Tiberius will have fastened on the fact that in the end it would be Germanicus who would win the gratitude of the men for committing the princeps to concessions against his will. He may even have convinced himself that this was what Germanicus had been aiming at from the first when he conceived the forgery. In practice Tiberius was compelled to grant the same advantages to the legions in Pannonia. But the mutineers' triumph was shortlived, for the only permanent concession they had won, the reduction of the period of service to

---

[1] Suet. *Cal.* 4: on his return to Rome the entire praetorian guard turned out to greet him, though only two cohorts had been detailed to do so. It would perhaps be naïve to wonder why Seianus did not prevent such a demonstration.
[2] Tac. *Ann.* 1.52.

sixteen years, was rescinded by Tiberius in the following year on the ground that the state could not otherwise meet its military commitments, at the same time as he announced in an edict that the one per cent purchase tax introduced by Augustus was essential to the maintenance of the military chest.[1]

2. THE GERMAN CAMPAIGNS OF 15

In Germany the campaigns of 15 were to mark the abandonment of the policy of cautious but thorough reconquest employed by Tiberius after the *clades Variana*.[2] The aim was still the restoration of the Elbe frontier, but that aim was pursued with much greater haste and vigour and correspondingly greater risk. The reason for the change is largely to be sought in the more adventurous temper of Germanicus, who was clearly given a great measure of independence, but the situation in Germany too probably encouraged him to try a major advance. Ever since the autumn of 14 internal dissensions had been rife among the Cherusci. The leaders were Arminius, the author of the *clades Variana*, and his pro-Roman father-in-law Segestes. Despite the marriage-tie their relationship had never been friendly, for Thusnelda, Arminius' wife, had already been betrothed to another man when Arminius intervened and carried her off.[3] It is likely that Arminius had taken advantage of Roman preoccupation with the mutiny to make some attempt to oust Segestes and consolidate his own position, but things had gone badly for him and Segestes had got the upper hand, even succeeding in recovering the person of Thusnelda.[4] In this alteration of the balance of power in Rome's favour Germanicus saw a chance of destroying Arminius and breaking the German resistance with a single blow. He therefore planned an ambitious campaign in the expectation of worthwhile support from Segestes.[5]

[1] Tac. *Ann.* 1.78.
[2] Cf. Timpe, *Triumph*, 41. For all matters concerned with the campaigns of this and the following year, cf. Koestermann, *Historia* 6, 1957, 429ff.; also Marsh, *Tiberius*, 69ff. (very hostile to Germanicus).
[3] Tac. *Ann.* 1.55.
[4] Tac. *Ann.* 1.57.
[5] Cf. Koestermann, *Historia* 6, 1957, 437f.; Timpe, *Triumph*, 66f.

His aim was to subdue individually and cut off from each other the three major tribes: the Chatti, the Bructeri and the Cherusci. The Chatti formed the target of the first expedition in the spring. Eight legions crossed the river, those of the upper Rhine led by Germanicus himself, with their usual commander Silius as second-in-command, and those of the lower Rhine under Caecina. Caecina also had five thousand auxiliaries and a horde of Cisrhenane Germans; the allied force under Germanicus was twice as large. Germanicus rebuilt a fort in the Taunus that Tiberius had once established, then pressed on at full speed against the Chatti, taking advantage of good conditions following a prolonged spell of dry weather. L. Apronius was deputed to follow more slowly and put in such work as was needed on roads and bridges to prevent any hindrance from rain or floods when Germanicus returned. Germanicus moved with such speed and secrecy that the Chatti were taken completely by surprise, and the Romans were once more able to indulge in a massacre of old men, women and children. The younger men escaped by swimming the Eder and for a time prevented the Romans from crossing. When they had been driven from the bank by artillery and arrows they sued for peace, but in vain. Germanicus was not prepared to leave the Chatti in their homeland, where they might repent their surrender and rebel again when the immediate threat of Roman arms had been withdrawn.[1] His refusal to grant their request achieved its objective: some joined him, while the rest, abandoning their homes, disappeared into the forests. Germanicus set the seal on their dispersal by burning their chief settlement, Mattium, and then made ready to return to the Rhine. Meanwhile Caecina, patrolling the land between the Ruhr and the Lippe, had discouraged the Cherusci from coming to the aid of the Chatti and had also defeated the Marsi in battle.[2]

The first stage of the plan had thus gone well, but the circumstances that had called it into being now no longer obtained, for the struggle for power among the Cherusci had taken a new turn.[3] Arminius had regained his ascendancy and Segestes was being besieged by his own

---

[1] Cf. Timpe, *Triumph*, 71.
[2] Tac. *Ann.* 1.55f.
[3] Cf. Timpe, *Triumph*, 73.

people. Envoys arrived from him, begging for help, among them Segestes' son Segimundus, a young man with a past to live down. At the time of the Cheruscan uprising in 9 he had been a priest at the altar of Augustus in the capital of the Ubii, but he had torn off his regalia and joined Arminius. Nevertheless Germanicus received him kindly and sent him with an escort across the Rhine. He himself went to the relief of the besieged and succeeded in rescuing Segestes. Segestes recalled his unswerving loyalty to Rome and was promised land on the Gallic bank of the Rhine. Thusnelda was taken to Ravenna, where she gave birth to a son, Thymelicus, whose fate, thanks to the loss of much of Tacitus, is unknown. Germanicus led his army back to the Rhine and, no doubt after he had made his report, was saluted as *imperator* on Tiberius' proposal.[1]

Germanicus' generous treatment of Segestes was, however, a total failure from the diplomatic point of view. Arminius, enraged at the loss of his wife and the thought that his child would be born in slavery, set out to rouse the Cherusci against Germanicus and Segestes with sneers at the noble father and the mighty commander whose vast forces had succeeded in carrying off one woman. Behind the barrage of insults, Arminius' political position is clear. Segestes might be happy to live in conquered territory while his son performed the functions of priest to a mortal man; for Arminius the Germans could never live down the disgrace that the *fasces* had been paraded between the Rhine and the Elbe. Augustus and Tiberius, he claimed, had achieved nothing and gone their ways.[2] There was therefore no reason to fear the inexperienced Germanicus and his army of mutineers. This propaganda rallied to him not only the Cherusci but also neighbouring tribes, and won him the support of his uncle Inguiomerus, who had previously been a respected friend of the Romans.[3] Thus the situation that confronted Germanicus at the outset of his summer campaign was much more complex and much less favourable than had at first been hoped for.

In the face of such unexpectedly widespread opposition Germanicus

[1] Tac. *Ann.* 1.57f., Strabo 7.1.4.
[2] The statement is not far from the truth.
[3] Tac. *Ann.* 1.59f.

was concerned to prevent the enemy from uniting. The carefully planned pincer movement against the Bructeri that occupied the major expedition of 15 must have been conceived before the rising of Arminius, but fortunately the southern Roman force served to cut off the Bructeri from the Cherusci as well as to drive them northwards into the arms of Germanicus. Caecina was sent with his four legions along the southern borders of the Bructeri to the Ems, while Albinovanus Pedo set out with the cavalry from the land of the Frisii. Germanicus himself put his four legions on board ship and sailed through the lakes that later formed the Zuyder Zee to the mouth of the Ems. After the successful rendezvous of all three contingents the attack began in earnest. The Bructeri attempted a scorched earth policy, but were dispersed by L. Stertinius, who had the good fortune to discover among his booty one of the three standards lost by Varus, that of the twenty-first legion. All the land between the Ems and the Lippe was ravaged, but the Bructeri seem to have slipped away further east without serious loss, instead of being crushed between the armies of Germanicus and Caecina.[1]

The Romans advanced to the north-eastern limit of the land of the Bructeri and found themselves not far from the site of the *clades Variana* in the Teutoburgerwald. Despite the possible effects on the morale of his men, Germanicus was determined to visit the scene and honour the dead with belated funeral rites. He moved with the utmost caution, sending Caecina ahead to reconnoitre the dense forest and build bridges and causeways over rivers and through marshes. So the army came upon Varus' camp, with its litter of bones and broken weapons, and in the neighbouring groves the altars of the Germans. Among Germanicus' troops were some survivors of the disaster, who were able to point out where the legionary commanders had fallen, where the eagles had been lost, where Varus had stabbed himself in his despair and where Arminius had harangued the victorious Germans. Appropriate ceremonies were performed for the dead, though there was no way of distinguishing Roman from German bones, and Germanicus laid the first sod on the burial mound. When reports reached him, Tiberius did not approve, allegedly for the highly

[1] Tac. *Ann.* 1.60.

technical reason that Germanicus, as an augur, should not on religious grounds have allowed himself to come into contact with the remains of the dead. He may also, as Tacitus suggests, have been afraid that the spectacle would alarm and depress the army. But if this was the case, although the supposition was hardly unreasonable, he was mistaken, for the men, though naturally grieved, were moved to greater anger against the Germans and were all the more keen to fight.[1] Whether Germanicus was gambling on this we do not know, but it would not be out of character.

With the Bructeri out of reach Germanicus set out in pursuit of Arminius, who skilfully led him deeper into the pathless forests. At last the Germans halted in a plain and Germanicus sent his cavalry forward against them. More Germans, however, appeared from the woods where they had been placed in ambush, and the Roman cavalry was in danger of being driven into a swamp had Germanicus not thrown the legions into the fray. Despite the unsatisfactory nature of this engagement the lateness of the season prohibited any further advance and the Romans withdrew once more to the Ems, where their forces were again divided into three for the journey back to the Rhine. Germanicus again used the fleet to transport his legions, the remainder of the cavalry was to make its way along the coast, and Caecina was to lead his troops back to the Rhine by way of the *pontes longi*, a causeway through the marshes built about 2 B.C. by L. Domitius Ahenobarbus, one of the most distinguished commanders in Germany during the time of Tiberius' retirement at Rhodes.[2] The mission was not an enviable one – Caecina was ordered to march with all possible speed, which hints that Germanicus was aware of the danger that the Germans might outstrip him and lay an ambush. It is true that Germanicus had no choice – he certainly did not have enough ships for Caecina's men – but it is difficult not to see here the unfortunate result of his decision to go ahead with the summer campaign as planned, despite the strengthening of the German opposition. For rapidly though Caecina may have marched, the Germans, less weightily armed and without the major hindrance of a slow-moving baggage train, easily overtook the

[1] Tac. *Ann.* 1.60–62, Suet. *Cal.* 3.2.
[2] Tac. *Ann.* 1.63.

Roman column, so that Arminius was able to occupy the woods on either side of the causeway. Nor was this Caecina's only problem. The causeway itself was in a state of considerable dilapidation and needed repairs before it could be crossed in safety. In this awkward predicament Caecina made camp and divided his forces, sending some to work on the causeway while others repelled the attacks of the enemy. But the conditions told heavily in favour of the Germans. By nightfall the legions were beginning to get the worst of the battle and during the evening the Germans succeeded in undoing much of what little the Romans had achieved in the way of repairs. In the night the ghost of Varus appeared to Caecina in a dream, beckoning him to destruction in the marshes. On the next day the Romans began to struggle on across a narrow strip of level ground with the first legion in the van, the fifth on the right flank, the twenty-first on the left and the twentieth bringing up the rear. But the fifth and twenty-first failed to keep position and were soon floundering in the mud. Arminius wisely waited till the chaos was virtually complete before loosing his men for what he hoped would be a repeat of his victory over Varus. But the greed of the Germans for booty saved the Romans from annihilation, and when evening came the legions managed to struggle back on to firm ground. There they spent a miserable night in a makeshift camp, for a large part of their tools, tents and first-aid kit had been lost in the swamp and such food as they had was fouled with blood and slime. There seemed no reason to doubt that the next day would see their destruction. The desperately low morale of the Romans is shown by an incident during the night. A horse that broke loose and ran through the camp created a panic among the troops. Thinking that the Germans had breached the defences, they made a mad rush for the gates. Caecina tried to check them, but orders, pleas and main force all proved of no avail until he threw himself across the opening. The troops hesitated to trample their commander and at last listened to the tribunes and centurions who were trying to explain that their fears were groundless. When calm was restored, Caecina gave the order for a mass sortie that would bring the army to the Rhine. Whether he could have succeeded if the Germans had adhered to the admirable tactics that Arminius had employed so far must remain doubtful, but fortunately for the Romans

G   79

a dispute arose between Arminius, who wanted to let the Romans leave their camp and then finish the massacre begun on the previous day, and Inguiomerus, who, flushed by success, was eager to storm the camp and so save the booty from getting needlessly muddy. The foolish counsel of the older man prevailed and when day came an attack was made. At first it seemed as if it might succeed, but the legions held firm and began to fight back with a savage joy that at last they had the Germans on decent level ground. The attackers' confidence rapidly deserted them and the day ended in a resounding Roman victory. Arminius himself escaped unscathed, but Inguiomerus was seriously wounded.[1]

Meanwhile rumours had reached the Rhine that Caecina's army had been surrounded and that the Germans were heading at full speed towards the river, which had of course been stripped of its garrison. The message provoked a panic, and there were those who wanted to destroy the bridge at Vetera. Only the determination of Agrippina prevented this disgrace and so left the way clear for the battered survivors of Caecina's legions to return to base, where Agrippina was waiting at the bridge to welcome them and congratulate them on their courage before setting to work to distribute clothing and bandages to all who needed them. She had performed a real service in a moment of crisis, but Tiberius already viewed with wary distaste her unwomanly interest in the legions and saw only a further proof of impatient ambition. Always prompt to divine or invent the ulterior motive, he could not believe that Agrippina courted the favour of the legions for any honest purpose. Not only was his respect for tradition offended, his authority was impaired when Agrippina showed that she had more power over the troops than their officers or their commanders. This attitude, says Tacitus, was fostered by Seianus, who knew Tiberius' character and so stoked the fires of suspicion and resentment that would one day burst into flame.[2]

Germanicus' army too had not been immune from disaster. To lighten the burden on his ships in the shallow coastal waters the prince had decided to send two legions by land along the shore: the second and fourteenth under P. Vitellius. At first all went well, but then an

[1] Tac. *Ann.* 1.64–68.
[2] Tac. *Ann.* 1.69.

equinoctial gale sprang up and floods engulfed men, beasts and baggage, till Vitellius at last succeeded in leading the way on to higher ground. Fortunately the waters receded on the following day and the army was able to reach the mouth of the Rhine, where the men embarked once more for the journey upriver to their base.[1] Germanicus again seems open to criticism, for although the storm was a major misfortune such gales were not uncommon at this season, and the contingency which made it necessary for two of the legions to travel by land would not have arisen if Germanicus had had enough ships.

Nevertheless the events of this campaign did nothing to damage his popularity. Gaul, Spain and Italy vied with one another to make good with weapons, horses and money the losses sustained by the army, and Germanicus delved deeply into his own pocket to help his troops to re-equip themselves. His affability and obvious concern for their welfare seem to have done much to wipe from the memory of the legions the largely unnecessary hardships they had suffered under his command. For official purposes the campaign was declared a success. Triumphal ornaments went to Caecina, Apronius and Silius (about whose part in the expedition we know nothing),[2] and the steady crescendo of honours for Germanicus now reached its climax. A triumph was voted him,[3] and a triumphal arch, the dedication of which took place at the end of the following year,[4] must also have been decreed at this time.[5] Despite the comment of Tacitus,[6] the message behind these tributes was plain: for Tiberius the war was at an end. The site selected for the arch of Germanicus was only 150 yards from the arch erected by Augustus to celebrate the return of the standards from Parthia. The establishment of this architectural parallel reveals the direction of Tiberius' thoughts. Emphasis was to be subtly directed away from the regaining of lost territory to the recovery of the standard found by Stertinius, and this partial and accidental success was to mark

---

[1] Tac. *Ann.* 1.70.
[2] Tac. *Ann.* 1.72.
[3] Tac. *Ann.* 1.55; for the date, cf. Timpe, *Triumph*, 43ff.
[4] Tac. *Ann.* 2.41.
[5] Cf. Timpe, *Triumph*, 50.
[6] Tac. *Ann.* 1.55: *decernitur Germanico triumphus manente bello.*

the termination, at least for the time being, of a war in which, the public will have been meant to understand, the same spirit of loyal co-operation had reigned between Germanicus and Tiberius as had once united Tiberius and Augustus.[1] With scrupulous politeness and lavish flattery, Germanicus had been recalled.

3. THE GERMAN CAMPAIGN OF 16

But Germanicus pretended not to understand and stayed where he was. His progress from uneasy subordination to something approaching studied disobedience can only have deepened Tiberius' distrust, and the princeps had the added frustration of being helpless. Openly to order Germanicus home might lead to an equally open refusal. Such a public clash would be a political disaster, even if it could be eventually overcome without recourse to the uncertainties of civil war. Tiberius had no choice but to essay further persuasion.

Almost immediately fortune seemed to favour him. In 16 fresh trouble broke out in Armenia, and we may well believe that, as Tacitus says, Tiberius was delighted to have an honourable pretext for severing Germanicus' link with the armies of the Rhine by sending him to settle the affairs of the East.[2] But Germanicus was determined to press on with his attempt to reconquer Germany. Despite the disappearance of the factors that in 15 might have justified an adventurous strategy, the prince had no intention of returning to the thorough, cautious methods that Tiberius had adopted after the *clades Variana* and that he himself had briefly imitated in autumn 14. He saw the failures of the previous year as entirely the result of tactical and logistical problems, and here he can undoubtedly be given credit for learning from his mistakes of the previous year when he came to plan the campaign of 16. He had realized the advantages that accrued to the Germans from the wooded and marshy terrain and the brevity of the summer and he understood that the chief hindrances to the Romans were the long marches they were called on to undertake and the danger caused by a cumbersome baggage train. He therefore decided to make the fullest

[1] Cf. Timpe, *Triumph*, 52ff.
[2] Tac. *Ann.* 2.5.

possible use of sea-transport, which would be at once quicker and less exhausting and would prevent casualties *en route*.[1] This reasoning was sound enough; an adequate transport fleet in the previous year would have prevented the disasters to both Caecina's and Vitellius' forces. The winter was therefore devoted to building ships to special designs for safety and seaworthiness in the waters in which they would have to operate.

While the ships were assembling at the mouth of the Rhine, Germanicus sent Silius with a small force to make a raid on the Chatti. That such a deterrent should have been considered necessary, so soon after the attack of spring 15, reveals once again the impermanence of the results of the policy of conquest without occupation. He himself took six legions to the relief of the Roman fort on the Lippe, which was being besieged. The enemy dispersed at the news of his approach, though not before they had destroyed the burial mound of the victims of the *clades Variana* and an altar once erected by Drusus in the neighbourhood. Germanicus restored the altar but, probably because of Tiberius' response to its erection, did not rebuild the tumulus. He then made a thorough job of renewing all the Roman defence works between the fort of Aliso and the Rhine. Meanwhile heavy rain had prevented Silius from achieving much, though he did capture two additions to Rome's collection of royal German females: the wife and daughter of Arpus, leader of the Chatti.[2]

By this time the fleet had massed and Germanicus, with a prayer for success to his father Drusus, set sail by the usual route for the mouth of the Ems. For reasons that are by no means clear he left the fleet in the western arm of the river and wasted some days in bridging the stream instead of landing the army on the right bank in readiness for the march to the Weser.[3] While Germanicus was measuring out the camp on the Weser, news came that the Angrivarii had risen in his rear, and so Stertinius was sent to punish their defection. The Romans occupied the west bank of the Weser; on the east bank the Cherusci under Arminius were drawn up, though the Germans can hardly have intended

---

[1] Tac. *Ann.* 2.5f.
[2] Tac. *Ann.* 2.7.
[3] Tac. *Ann.* 2.8; cf. Meister, *Hermes* 83, 1955, 92ff.

to try to hold the river. Arminius requested leave from Germanicus to talk to his brother Flavus, who had spent long years in the service of Rome and had lost an eye in one of the German campaigns of Tiberius. Permission was granted, and Tacitus reports a shouting-match between the brothers as they extolled respectively the might and clemency of Rome and the claims of Germany's gods and her ancient freedom.[1] The debate quickly became acrimonious, and Stertinius was forced to restrain the furious Flavus, who despite the not inconsiderable obstacle of the Weser was calling for his arms and horse, while on the far bank Arminius could be descried, hurling insults in the Latin he remembered from his years in the Roman army.

On the next day the Cherusci formed up in battle order, but Germanicus was unwilling to risk taking the legions across before bridges had been built and garrisoned. He ordered the cavalry to ford the river and entice the Germans from the bank. The Cherusci simulated flight in their usual style and lured the Batavian contingent into a clearing in the woods, in which the customary ambush had been laid. The Batavi eventually broke out, with the assistance of the Roman cavalry, but not before their leader Chariovalda and many others had been killed.[2]

When Germanicus had crossed the Weser he learned from deserters that Arminius had already picked his spot for the battle to come and that the other allies of the Cherusci had assembled in a grove sacred to Hercules and were planning a night attack on the Roman camp. Scouts confirmed the presence of a large enemy force not far away. At this critical juncture Germanicus, eager to secure some reliable information about the mood of the troops, resorted to a characteristically theatrical device and wandered in disguise among the legionaries, listening to their talk. The results of this investigation were reassuring: the men were devoted to their commander and eager for the fray, and their hatred of the enemy was only increased when a Latin-speaking German rode up to the rampart, offering in Arminius' name lands, women and high wages to deserters. The night attack too came to nothing, for although the Germans rode up to the camp they withdrew

[1] Tac. *Ann.* 2.9f.; the physical possibility of this altercation has been doubted.
[2] Tac. *Ann.* 2.11.

without initiating hostilities as soon as they realized that the Romans were awake and on guard.[1]

Next morning Germanicus addressed his men and endeavoured to show that even the forests and swamps could be turned to their advantage. Arminius scathingly dismissed the Romans as the fastest runners in Varus' army, who had mutinied two years before rather than fight and now travelled everywhere by sea to avoid the risk of battle. The battle, which defies reconstruction, was fought on the plain of Idistaviso, probably located between the north bank of the Weser, east of Minden, and the Wesergebirge.[2] The Cherusci suffered heavy casualties, though Arminius and Inguiomerus both escaped.[3] Tacitus presents the victory as a massacre, but the readiness of the Cherusci to fight again so shortly afterwards suggests that some exaggeration has taken place. The troops hailed Tiberius as *imperator* – not Germanicus. No doubt Germanicus was belatedly trying to be tactful, but it seems that Tiberius refused to accept the salutation.[4] This is hardly surprising, for had he accepted it it would have appeared that he had withdrawn his disapproval of the expedition, as Germanicus will have intended.

At first the Germans, in panic and depression, had even considered retiring east of the Elbe, but soon their anger got the upper hand and they made a sudden attack on the Romans. An ambush was laid in the neighbourhood of the wall built by the Angrivarii to divide their territory from that of the Cherusci.[5] But scouts or deserters brought Germanicus news of the plan, and so he was again prepared. His first major objective, the capture of the wall, was achieved after an initial setback and he pressed forward into the woods. For once the Germans had allowed themselves to be caught with marshy ground behind them and so were unable to vanish in the face of his advance. A bitter struggle ensued, in which neither side could afford to yield, for the Roman line of retreat was barred by the river. But a pitched battle in a confined space told against the Germans, who were unable to wield their long

[1] Tac. *Ann.* 2.12f.
[2] Cf. Koestermann, *Historia* 6, 1957, 452ff.
[3] Tac. *Ann.* 2.14–18.
[4] Cf. Koestermann on Tac. *Ann.* 2.18.
[5] Tac. *Ann.* 2.19.

spears to the best advantage or to exploit their superior mobility. If Tacitus is to be believed, the day ended in a further massacre, for Germanicus had made it clear that he wanted no captives, claiming, with a large measure of truth, that only the annihilation of the German forces could put an end to the war.[1] In the monument to Mars, Jupiter and Augustus that he set up to celebrate the victory Germanicus again displayed great tact towards the offended princeps. His own name was not mentioned at all; the inscription recorded only that the peoples dwelling between the Rhine and the Elbe had been conquered by the army of Tiberius Caesar.[2] But here again the courteous wording might imply a claim to the official authorization that the campaign lacked.

This year Germanicus was determined not to be caught by the weather, and so he advanced no further. A section of the force was sent back to its winter quarters by land, but the greater part was embarked on the fleet and sent down the Ems for the voyage home. Then, despite all Germanicus' preparations, disaster struck. The fleet was caught in a storm and many ships were lost. Germanicus' own ship was driven ashore in the territory of the Chauci. At first in his despair he thought that the entire fleet was lost, but when the storm abated a few ships began to limp in. More men were recovered up and down the coast: some who had fallen into enemy hands were ransomed and returned by the Angrivarii, some were sent back from as far away as Britain.[3] For this calamity Germanicus can take no blame, and his reaction to it was entirely sensible. To prevent the disaster from destroying the morale of his army and raising that of the Germans, he immediately sent out Silius against the Chatti, while he himself marched against the Marsi, who still had in their possession, as he had recently learned, another of the eagles lost by Varus. The mounting of these expeditions confirms that Germanicus must have returned from the Weser well before the end of summer and perhaps suggests that the losses caused by the storm were by no means as great as had at first been feared.[4] Their material results were insignificant, but their

[1] Tac. *Ann.* 2.20f.
[2] Tac. *Ann.* 2.22.
[3] Tac. *Ann.* 2.23f.
[4] Tac. *Ann.* 2.25.

psychological effects were as great as could be desired. Not only was the eagle recovered, but, more important, the Germans were reduced to despair by this proof of Roman tenacity and resilience. Germanicus had some cause to feel cheerful when he led the men into winter quarters.[1]

He was convinced that if he were granted one more year he could bring the war to a successful conclusion, but repeated letters from Tiberius, who was no doubt growing increasingly impatient, summoned him home to his triumph. Quite apart from the question of Germanicus' over-independence, Tiberius can hardly have approved of his approach to the war. The strategy of far-ranging expeditions without military or political consolidation had proved itself a failure in the time of Augustus. A return to it now was unlikely to produce any lasting gain. Since Germanicus would not be ruled, it was better to abandon the policy of intervention, at least for the time being. The princeps too made an effort to be tactful. He gave Germanicus credit for his victories, but he underlined that the campaigns had also brought heavy losses, although this was through no fault of Germanicus' own. In his own long experience of Germany, he said, he had always accomplished more by diplomacy than by force: the surrender of the Sugambri, the undermining of the power of Maroboduus. The campaigns had been necessary to avenge Rome's honour. Now that this had been achieved, the Cherusci and the other rebels could be left to their internal quarrels.[2] It has often been assumed that Tiberius was renouncing for ever the attempt to recover the lands between the Rhine and the Elbe. But this is to force his words. His interpretation of the object of the war – the recovery, not of territory, but merely of honour – was of course devised to justify the cessation of hostilities and Germanicus' recall, but it cannot be said to have committed him to the view that Rome should never interfere in Germany again. His advice that the Germans should be left to cut each others' throats need only apply to the immediate problem of how to deal with Arminius' rebellion.[3] In less decorous terms Tiberius might have said that, since Germanicus had proved incapable of dealing with Arminius and no

[1] Tac. *Ann.* 2.26.
[2] Tac. *Ann.* 2.26.
[3] Cf. Timpe, *Triumph*, 63.

other general was on hand who was likely to do better, the only possible course was to withdraw and give Arminius rope to hang himself. This decision did not automatically exclude renewed intervention once Arminius was out of the way.

Germanicus still begged for one more year to finish what he had begun. But Tiberius skilfully played on his pride and his affection for Drusus. To the offer of a second consulship he added the request that, if further fighting in Germany proved necessary, Germanicus should leave his brother the chance to acquire some military glory.[1] This time Germanicus resisted no longer and returned to Rome. No doubt he too wanted to avoid the open breach that might result from a refusal to obey; certainly his compliance proves yet again his innocence of all disloyal ambition. He did not celebrate his triumph, over the Cherusci, Chatti, Angrivarii and all the other peoples as far as the Elbe, until 26 May, 17, when Tiberius distributed three hundred sesterces per man to the plebs in the prince's name.[2]

Suetonius claims that Tiberius dismissed Germanicus' glorious deeds as futile and his splendid victories as ruinous to the state.[3] This judgment is in essence no more than a less politic version of the opinion ascribed to Tiberius by Tacitus, and harsh as it is, it rests on a solid basis of fact. Germanicus did not conquer Germany, any more than Drusus or Tiberius had before him, nor is there any reason to suppose that his methods would have brought success in one more summer or indeed over a longer period. Conquest, as Tiberius had learned, involved more than annual victories over an enemy who returned to the fray refreshed after the close season. To hold down Germany would have called for an outlay in men and money greater than Rome could afford. From this viewpoint Germanicus' expeditions, like all the others that had ravaged Germany under Augustus, were indeed futile, and there is no doubt that they had brought heavy losses both of men and money. Therefore, it has been said, the expeditions should never have been undertaken in the first place: Tiberius should either have

[1] Tac. *Ann.* 2.26; for the friendship of Germanicus and Drusus, cf. Tac. *Ann.* 2.43, *EJ* 130a.
[2] Tac. *Ann.* 2.41, Vell. 2.129.2, Strabo 7.1.4; cf. Timpe, *Triumph*, 47f.
[3] Suet. *Tib.* 52.2.

pursued the war to its conclusion, using the revenues of the new province Cappadocia to finance it, or never have allowed it to be started at all.[1] This criticism is doubly misconceived. In the first place there was little hope that continuation of the war would produce a conclusion in the immediately foreseeable future. More important, Tiberius did not start the war or even allow it to be started; it was a legacy from Augustus.[2] Augustus, not Tiberius, had appointed Germanicus to the Rhine, and Augustus had surely intended the prince to press on with the task of once more extending Roman rule to the Elbe. Tiberius was faced with a conflict between his loyalty to Augustus' wishes, which forbade him openly to reject this policy, and his desire to recall Germanicus, motivated partly by unjustified suspicion of Germanicus' political designs and partly by a just conviction that Germanicus would never win durable success. For Tiberius to accomplish the latter aim, the war had to be interrupted, for to recall Germanicus, even to a triumph, and replace him immediately would be little better than a public accusation of incompetence. Yet the war could not be interrupted with honour unless it had already been won. Hence objectives that had been partially achieved were thrust into the foreground: the avenging of Varus and the recovery of the standards.

4. THE TRIAL OF LIBO AND THE RISING OF CLEMENS

Tiberius was troubled in the course of 16 not only by his awkward relations with Germanicus but also by threats of conspiracy and revolution in Rome and Italy. In September came the trial of M. Scribonius Libo Drusus, who was charged with plotting against the princeps.[3] Suetonius lists the designs of Libo among the factors that made Tiberius hesitate to accept the principate. This is false, but the detailed account of Tacitus confirms that his suspicions against Libo had been formed as long ago as 14.

The agent of Libo's destruction was one of his closest friends, the

[1] Cf. Koestermann, *Historia* 6, 1957, 468; contra Marsh, *Tiberius*, 74ff.
[2] Cf. Timpe, *Triumph*, 16, 21, 31f.
[3] Tac. *Ann.* 2.27–32, Suet. *Tib.* 25, Dio 57.15.4f., Vell. 2.129.2, 130.3.

senator Firmius Catus. Firmius saw that Libo was a gullible man – Seneca calls him as stupid as he was noble[1] – and set out to inspire in him hopes of the principate, harping on the nobility of his descent and persuading him to consult astrologers. Tacitus offers no opinion as to Firmius' motives; presumably he was moved entirely by the prospect of the rewards that might be his as the result of his revelations. His scheme, as Tacitus remarks, was the earliest symptom of a canker that grew to alarming proportions later, and in this respect Libo's high birth is significant, for descendants of the old nobility were peculiarly vulnerable to charges of conspiracy against the new order – especially when related, like Libo, to the imperial house.

When Firmius thought he had collected enough evidence, he sought access to Tiberius through the intermediary of Vescularius Flaccus, an equestrian friend of the princeps.[2] If Suetonius were correct, his approach would have to belong before Tiberius' accession, since this was the first knowledge Tiberius acquired of the alleged plot against him. But in Tacitus' account Tiberius was already princeps when Firmius made contact with Vescularius.[3] The date will therefore have been autumn or winter 14. Tiberius chose to bide his time, allowing Libo to hold in 15 the praetorship for which he must already have been designated before Firmius laid his information, and inviting him to dinner, though Suetonius claims that he took certain precautions, providing Libo with a lead knife when they officiated together at a sacrifice and leaning heavily on his arm whenever they walked and talked together.

Throughout spring and summer 16 Tiberius still did nothing. Then the issue was forced without his knowledge or instruction.[4] One of the fortune-tellers whom Libo had consulted and asked to raise the spirits of the dead reported the transaction to L. Fulcinius Trio, who was already becoming notorious as a prosecutor. Trio wasted no time in

---

[1] Sen. *Ep.* 70.10. His mother was the granddaughter of Pompey; more important, Scribonia, wife of Augustus and mother of Julia, had been his great-aunt.

[2] On Vescularius' longstanding link with Tiberius, cf. Tac. *Ann.* 6.10.

[3] Tac. *Ann.* 2.28: *aditum ad principem postulat.*

[4] Note the injustice of Dio's claim that Tiberius waited till Libo was too ill to defend himself. The consulship of L. Libo is a more plausible ground for the initial delay in 16.

bringing a charge before the consuls and the senate was summoned to investigate the matter.

Libo put on mourning and appealed to all his relations to speak in his defence. All were afraid and refused on various pretexts. On the day the senate met Libo, ill as well as afraid, was brought to the senate-house in a litter and entered supported by his brother Lucius, who had been consul earlier in the year. Tiberius received him with total impassivity and read the charges with the utmost care neither to minimize nor to exaggerate them. Two other accusers had joined themselves to Trio and Firmius, Fonteius Agrippa and C. Vibius Serenus, and a squabble ensued as to who should have the honour of speaking last. Most of the evidence produced was utterly absurd – the kind of question Libo had asked the astrologers was whether he would ever be rich enough to cover the Appian Way with money all the way to Brundisium. But Vibius produced one booklet in Libo's hand in which the names of members of the imperial family and prominent senators were followed by mysterious and sinister symbols. Libo denied that the writing was his, and it was decided that his slaves should be tortured to discover the truth. Since ancestral custom forbade slaves to testify against their master, a device was employed that was already known under the republic: the slaves were bought by the state.[1] Libo requested an adjournment, which was granted, and on reaching home he sent a last appeal to the princeps by the hand of his kinsman and Tiberius' old friend, Sulpicius Quirinius.

Tiberius' only reply was that he should address his prayers to the senate. Meanwhile soldiers guarded Libo's house, but in the evening, after vainly trying to persuade his slaves to kill him, Libo summoned up the courage to stab himself. Next day the prosecution continued in the senate with as much energy as if Libo had still been alive, but Tiberius declared under oath that, though Libo was guilty, he would have begged for his life to be spared, had he not resorted to this over-hasty suicide.

The prosecutors received their rewards: Libo's property was divided among them and praetorships were granted to those who were senators. M. Aurelius Cotta Messallinus then proposed that Libo's

[1] Cf. Koestermann on Tac. *Ann.* 2.30.

image should not be carried in the funeral processions of his descendants and Cn. Lentulus that no Scribonius should in future take the *cognomen* Drusus. It is not unlikely that Libo's body was also exposed on the Scalae Gemoniae. This custom was probably instituted under Tiberius and was well established by 20; this seems the most plausible occasion for its introduction.[1] L. Pomponius Flaccus proposed a thanksgiving to the gods, while L. Plancus, Asinius Gallus, Papius Mutilus and L. Apronius brought motions that offerings should be made to Jupiter, Mars and Concordia and that 13 September, the day of Libo's suicide, should be a public holiday.[2] A further resolution decreed the expulsion of fortune-tellers and astrologers from Italy.

Tiberius cannot be criticized for his conduct in this case. He clearly believed that Libo was guilty – he himself took astrology very seriously indeed – and his frustrated desire to intervene on the side of mercy must have been inspired by the fact that Libo presented no real danger. That Libo was the head of a serious conspiracy or proposed single-handed to wipe out the imperial house is utterly absurd. There is no suggestion in any of the sources that Libo had accomplices and his fall brought nobody else into danger. The Fasti Amiternini speak of the nefarious plans conceived by Libo concerning the safety of Tiberius, his sons, other leading men and the state.[3] Comparison of this with the language of Tacitus makes it clear that the official view of Libo's designs was entirely based on an interpretation of the names and symbols in Libo's cabbalistic notebook. In practical terms it was believed that Libo intended to liquidate all possible rivals by black magic and so attain the principate himself.

Nevertheless the trial was disquieting. The unseemly eagerness of the professional accusers to scramble for a share in the profits of prosecution, the fear of Libo's friends to perform a service demanded by Roman tradition, and the baneful effect of Tiberius' desire to be impartial: all these hinted at the shape of things to come and gave the lie to Tiberius' cherished illusion that he was just another senator.

[1] Cf. Münzer, *Hermes* 47, 1912, 174f.
[2] For a dedication to Concordia probably in this connection, cf. *ILS* 153.
[3] *F. Amit.* (*EJ* p. 52); faithfully followed by Vell. 2.129.2 and taken seriously by Marsh, *Tiberius*, 59, 110 (with naïve reasons); contra Syme, *Tacitus*, 400.

The second, more material, disturbance of 16 was a belated consequence of the removal of Agrippa Postumus. As soon as he heard of
Augustus' death, Clemens, one of Agrippa's slaves, had decided to sail
to Planasia and engineer Agrippa's escape to the German armies, where
he obviously expected to gain the support of Germanicus and Agrippina. But he was forced to travel on a slow-moving merchant ship and
so, thanks to Augustus' forethought and Sallustius' promptitude,
arrived too late to put this plan into operation. For the moment he had
to be content with stealing his murdered master's ashes. Then for a
year he lay in hiding at Cosa, on the coast of Etruria opposite Planasia,
growing his hair and beard in preparation for the attempt to exploit
his natural resemblance to Agrippa. When he was ready he began to
spread rumours that Agrippa was still alive, skilfully supported by
fleeting appearances first in one town then in another. Popular imagination did the rest, and the news was believed at Rome. When Clemens
felt strong enough to risk a visit to Ostia, a large crowd assembled to
welcome him, and by this time he already had secret bands of adherents in the city itself.

Tiberius was in a quandary. To take Clemens seriously and send
troops to intervene might be seen as an admission of the weakness of his
own position and so inspire contempt if not a more serious rebellion,
but to ignore him might also prove dangerous. In the end he turned
again to Sallustius Crispus. The subtle minister sent two of his
retainers to insinuate themselves into Clemens' confidence. When
Clemens was captured and brought secretly to Rome, he refused to
reveal the names of his confederates and is said to have told Tiberius
that he had the same right to call himself Agrippa as Tiberius had to
call himself Caesar. Tiberius thought it best to hush up the whole
affair. Clemens was quietly executed, and although many distinguished
persons were said to be implicated, no enquiry was held.[1]

5. DRUSUS IN ILLYRICUM

Drusus was not sent to Germany when Germanicus returned to Rome,
but there is no inconsistency here: the war was for the moment at an

[1] Tac. *Ann.* 2.39f., Suet. *Tib.* 25, Dio 57.16.3f.; cf. Mogenet, *AC* 23, 1954, 321ff.

end, so there was no immediate need of Drusus' presence, as the wording of Tiberius' appeal to Germanicus had made clear.[1] Instead the princeps sent his son to Illyricum to get a taste of military life. It seems that Drusus was living an easy and luxurious life among the pleasures of the capital, and Tiberius thought that it would be better for the prince, as well as for his own security, if he were given command of an army.[2] The military pretext was a request from Maroboduus for aid against Arminius and the Cherusci. Now that Roman forces had been withdrawn, Tiberius' prediction was already proving true. Arminius had secured a momentary advantage through the defection of two Suebian tribes, the Semnones and the Langobardi, from Maroboduus' empire, but this was cancelled out when Inguiomerus, refusing to take orders any longer from his nephew, went over to Maroboduus. An indecisive battle had been fought, after which Maroboduus had withdrawn to the heart of his realm in the forests of Bohemia. It was at this point that he made his request for Roman aid. Tiberius naturally had no desire for renewed embroilment in the troubles of Germany and refused help on the obvious ground that Maroboduus had no right to expect Roman assistance against the Cherusci when the Romans had received no aid from him in their campaigns against the same enemy. But whereas Maroboduus had remained strictly neutral, Drusus was now sent out to further Roman interests at Maroboduus' expense. During the summer of 18 he carried out this policy to good effect and brought even greater pressure to bear on Maroboduus' crumbling power. The instrument was Catualda, a distinguished young man among the Gotones who had once had to run away from Maroboduus and now believed that the time was ripe for revenge. He led a powerful force into the territory of the Marcomanni and stormed the royal stronghold. Maroboduus escaped, but the only course left open to him was to seek refuge with Rome. Crossing the Danube into Noricum, he wrote to Tiberius, who offered him honourable asylum at Ravenna, where he lived for twenty-two years. Not long afterwards Catualda too was forced to apply for sanctuary after a defeat by the Hermunduri; he was accommodated at Forum Julii in Narbonese Gaul. The

[1] Tac. *Ann.* 2.26.
[2] Tac. *Ann.* 2.44.

Silver cups from Boscoreale:
5a Augustus as ruler of the world
5b A triumph of Tiberius

6a The Gemma Augustea: in the centre Roma and Augustus as Jupiter. On the left Tiberius is descending from the chariot; the youth is probably Gaius Caesar (at the triumph of 7 B.C.), perhaps Germanicus (at that of A.D. 12). The figures on the right may be the World, Ocean and Earth. In the exergue soldiers erecting a trophy and prisoners.

6b The Grand Camée de France: Tiberius as Jupiter and Livia occupy the centre, flanked by Agrippina with the young Gaius Caligula, Germanicus, Antonia, Tiberius' son Drusus and Livia Julia. The seated figure may be a Parthian prince. Above are Tiberius' brother Drusus, Augustus and Germanicus astride a winged horse. In the exergue prisoners, a river god and armour.

dependants of both Maroboduus and Catualda were settled beyond the Danube, between the Morava and either the Gusen or the Vah, and Vannius, from the tribe of the Quadi in Moravia, was appointed as their king.[1]

Tiberius was delighted by Maroboduus' final collapse and delivered an unusually exultant speech in the senate. In it he rated the fallen leader of the Marcomanni as an enemy as dangerous to Rome as Pyrrhus or Antiochus the Great had been, because of his qualities of leadership, the ferocity of the people he had ruled, and the proximity of the centre of his power to Italy.[2] There may be less exaggeration in this than has sometimes been claimed – the potential threat of Maroboduus' power may have been underestimated because he was too wise ever to attack the Romans. The degree to which he had succeeded in expanding to the north shortly before his confrontation with Arminius suggests that he might well have been a force to be reckoned with.

Arminius did not long survive the removal of his rival. Once the threat of the Romans and Maroboduus was removed, his desire for supreme power turned his people against him. A leader of the Chatti, Adgandestrius, wrote to the senate offering to poison Arminius if poison could be sent from Rome, an offer scornfully rejected as unworthy of the Roman people, but after a fluctuating civil war Arminius eventually fell victim in about 21 to a plot hatched by his own kinsmen. He was thirty-seven. As Tacitus remarks in his obituary notice, he had rendered the freedom of Germany secure and, although his success in battle had been uneven, he had never been defeated in a war.[3]

Drusus' diplomatic achievements were rewarded with the voting of an ovation by the senate, probably in spring 19, and a triumphal arch was built, with images of Germanicus and Drusus, beside the temple of Mars Ultor.[4]

---

[1] Tac. *Ann.* 2.45f., 62f., Vell. 2.129.4; *ea aestas* in Tac. *Ann.* 2.62 is 18, as is *priore aestate* in 3.11 (i.e. prior to the voting of the ovation in 19).
[2] Tac. *Ann.* 2.63.
[3] Tac. *Ann.* 2.88.
[4] Tac. *Ann.* 2.64; cf. Koestermann *ad loc.*

6. GERMANICUS IN THE EAST

The disturbance that was to take Germanicus on his fatal mission to the East broke out in 15, when the Parthians expelled their king, Vonones. Vonones was the eldest son of Phraates IV and had been handed over to Augustus as a hostage along with his three brothers.[1] When Augustus had placed him on the throne of Parthia, he had at first been warmly welcomed, but gradually his popularity waned in the face of nationalist feeling, which regarded it as a disgrace that Parthia should accept as king the choice of her enemy, a man whose life in exile had imbued him with the enemy's ways. Vonones himself made matters worse by scorning the vigorous pursuits of his ancestors and Parthian habits in general. Even his virtues were counted against him, for friendliness and approachability were foreign to the royal traditions of Parthia. So in 15 Artabanus III was summoned by the enemies of Vonones. This prince, who had grown up among the Dahae, a Scythian tribe, was an Arsacid on his mother's side. After an initial defeat he retired to Media, but then succeeded in driving out Vonones, who took refuge in Armenia.[2]

At the time of Vonones' arrival there in 16, that perennial trouble-spot lacked a ruler. Artavasdes III, the successor of Ariobarzanes, had been murdered towards the end of the reign of Augustus. The subsequent reigns of Tigranes IV and of Erato, the sister and former queen of Tigranes III, had been brief. So the exiled Vonones was able to seize the vacant throne.[3] But Tiberius refused to recognize him as king, while Artabanus too showed no signs of accepting the situation. The governor of Syria, Q. Caecilius Metellus Creticus Silanus, afraid that he might find himself involved in a Parthian war in defence of Vonones' claim, summoned him to Syria and kept him under guard, albeit with the honour due to his rank.[4]

For the moment Tiberius did nothing, but other problems besides that of Armenia soon arose in the East. The empire had just acquired a new province, Cappadocia, which had been ruled for fifty years by its

---

[1] *RG* 32.2, 33, Tac. *Ann.* 2.1f.; cf. Anderson, *CAH* x, 264.
[2] Tac. *Ann.* 2.2f.; cf. Marsh, *Tiberius*, 79ff.; Anderson, *CAH* x, 278.
[3] Tac. *Ann.* 2.3f., Jos. *AJ* 18.46–52.
[4] Tac. *Ann.* 2.4, Jos. *AJ* 18.51.

king, Archelaus.[1] Tiberius had once defended Archelaus,[2] but during his voluntary exile at Rhodes Archelaus had failed to treat him with any respect. The king had been misled by intimate friends of Augustus, who had pointed to the flourishing estate of Gaius Caesar and hinted that too friendly an attitude towards the disgraced Tiberius might be dangerous. Tiberius remembered, and the workings of fate had now put Archelaus at his mercy. Livia wrote, summoning him to Rome. The letter did not attempt to gloss over Tiberius' hostility, but promised that the king could hope for clemency if he came to Rome to plead his cause in person. Archelaus hastened to obey, but was coldly received and soon found himself accused before the senate, on what charge is uncertain. Anxiety and old age did their work, and Archelaus died before any verdict was reached, either a natural death or by his own hand. Tiberius declared his intention of turning the kingdom into a province and announced that the new revenues would make it possible to reduce the tax on the sale of goods throughout the empire from 1 per cent to $\frac{1}{2}$ per cent. At the same time the deaths of Antiochus III of Commagene and Philopator II of Cilicia had led to trouble in their kingdoms, where the nobles were eager for Roman rule but the mass of the people was loyal to the dynasties. The provinces of Syria and Judaea too were clamouring for a reduction in their tribute.[3]

Plainly the time had come for a member of the princeps' family to visit Asia Minor and make some attempt to restore order. Tiberius raised the question in the senate and argued that the problems of the Orient could be solved only by the wisdom of Germanicus. He himself, he claimed, was too old for the task, his other son Drusus too young.[4] Tiberius' reasons for this choice were no doubt complex. His duty to emphasize Germanicus' position as heir by entrusting him with honourable and important missions, his eagerness to exploit a pretext that would separate Germanicus from the armies of the Rhine without any loss of face on the prince's part, the fact that, although only a couple of years older than Drusus, in character Germanicus was quite

---

[1] Tac. *Ann.* 2.42, Suet. *Tib.* 37.4, Dio 57.17.3ff., Strabo 12.1.4.
[2] Suet. *Tib.* 8, Dio 57.17.3; cf. above, p. 16.
[3] Tac. *Ann.* 2.42.
[4] Tac. *Ann.* 2.43, Suet. *Cal.* 1.2; on all matters concerning Germanicus' mission, cf. Koestermann, *Historia* 7, 1958, 331ff.

genuinely more suitable for this task: all these considerations will in some measure have influenced the princeps. So, by decree of the senate, Germanicus was granted *imperium* in the provinces on the other side of the Adriatic, greater than that of all governors with whom he might come into contact, whether they held their appointments from the senate or directly from the princeps. But despite this façade of confidence, Tiberius' caution inspired him to take further measures which will have made what had gone before seem hollow both to the people and to Germanicus himself. First he recalled the legate of Syria, Creticus Silanus. This was eminently reasonable: Silanus had been in the province since 11. But his daughter was betrothed to Germanicus' eldest son Nero, and this connection was the only explanation men could find for his supercession at precisely this time. In his stead he appointed, with the approval of the senate,[1] Cn. Calpurnius Piso, consul with Tiberius himself in 7 B.C., a man notorious for his savage tongue and independence of spirit. Piso's own ancient nobility was reinforced by the standing of his wife Plancina, sister of Plancus the consul of 13; if Tacitus is to be believed, he was reluctant to concede first place to Tiberius and looked down on the princeps' sons as his inferiors. Piso was convinced that he had been appointed to keep Germanicus in check, and he will surely have had, as some of Tacitus' sources claimed, secret instructions from Tiberius, though in what degree these may have differed from the orders that every legate of the princeps must have received before proceeding to his province it would be rash to conjecture in the face of hostile sources.[2] No doubt Tiberius was afraid that Germanicus would, if left to his own devices, quickly win a place in the hearts of the troops in Syria similar to that he had secured in the affections of the legions of the Rhine. His chief concern will have been to introduce as their immediate commander a close friend of his own, who would provide an alternative focus of loyalty. To Germanicus Piso's appointment will have been clear proof that Tiberius still did not trust him.[3] To some extent it followed the

[1] Tac. *Ann.* 3.12: striking, since Tiberius was under no obligation to consult the senate when appointing a legate to an imperial province.
[2] Cf. Marsh, *Tiberius*, 100; Koestermann, *Historia* 7, 1958, 338.
[3] Cf. Koestermann, *Historia* 7, 1958, 338.

pattern whereby a tried and trusted man was sent to watch over a young and inexperienced prince. But Germanicus was neither so young nor by any means so inexperienced as Gaius Caesar had been when he made his ill-starred visit to the East, and any implication that he needed a mentor could only be interpreted by him as a further sign of lack of confidence or worse on Tiberius' part. So in trying to reconcile his desire to honour Augustus' intentions for Germanicus and his concern to take precautions for his own security Tiberius had created a situation in which trouble was virtually bound to arise from Germanicus' resentment and Piso's lack of tact.

The year 18 brought Germanicus a further honour: his promised second consulship, with the princeps as his colleague – another public demonstration of his position as heir to Tiberius' power. The prince had already begun his journey eastward by paying a visit to Drusus in Dalmatia, for despite the efforts and intrigues of would-be partisans at Rome the two remained the best of friends.[1] Then, accompanied by Agrippina and Gaius,[2] he made his way down the coast of Illyricum and assumed the consulship at Nicopolis, the city founded by Augustus to commemorate his victory at Actium over Antony and Cleopatra. If he did so on his own initiative, it was a wildly tactless gesture, but it is more likely that Tiberius had given his sanction to an act that heralded the approaching fiftieth anniversary of Actium as it marked out Germanicus as the future ruler of the empire Actium had secured.[3] Germanicus naturally spent some time inspecting the spoils dedicated by Augustus and the camp of his grandfather Antony while his fleet was being repaired after suffering some damage from bad weather. His next port of call was Athens, where he showed himself characteristically affable and went about escorted by only a single lictor, a compliment which won the hearts of the Athenians. From Athens he sailed to Lesbos by way of Euboea. There Agrippina gave birth to her last child, Julia Livilla, and was promptly deified by the appreciative

[1] Tac. *Ann.* 2.43. There is no reason to believe in a 'party of Germanicus' and a 'party of Drusus', as posited by Marsh, *Tiberius*, 85; cf. Allen, *TAPA* 72, 1941, 4.

[2] Suet. *Cal.* 10.1, cf. Tac. *Ann.* 3.1 (i.e. Gaius and Julia Livilla).

[3] Tac. *Ann.* 2.53; a provocative act according to Koestermann, *Historia* 7, 1958, 339.

inhabitants.[1] She and the child remained at Lesbos while Germanicus combined tourism with administration on a journey to the Propontis by way of Perinthus and Byzantium. On his return he was eager to land on Samothrace, but was prevented by unfavourable winds. Then, after the obligatory visit to Troy, he moved southwards to Colophon, where he consulted the oracle of the Clarian Apollo. Later rumour told that the Milesian priest had warned him in riddling verses of his early death.[2]

Meanwhile Piso too had set out for his post. At Athens he had caused alarm and consternation by his violent behaviour and in speeches had indirectly criticized Germanicus for his excessively friendly attitude to a people who were no longer the Athenians of old but a motley rabble, supporters of Mithridates against Sulla and Antony against Augustus. Piso had a private motive for his acerbity as well as the desire to be opposite to Germanicus, for he had tried by his influence to secure the acquittal of a dependant of his, Theophilus, who was accused of forgery before the Areopagus, and had failed. From Athens he sailed at full speed through the Cyclades and caught up with Germanicus at Rhodes. When he was close to the island a storm arose and he found himself in danger of shipwreck, but Germanicus sent triremes to his aid. This did not make Piso any better disposed towards the prince and after staying on Rhodes for only one day he pressed on to Syria. There he behaved in a manner which confirms that Tiberius' principal motive in arranging his appointment had been to secure the loyalty of the Syrian legions and keep them from any close attachment to Germanicus. Bribes, says Tacitus, were distributed, promises made, disciplinarians dismissed and replaced by Piso's creatures. The troops found themselves free to idle away their time, in camp or in the pleasures of the cities, and Piso soon acquired the sobriquet of Father of the Legions. Even honest soldiers were prepared to acquiesce in what went on, because it was assumed that what Piso was doing was done with Tiberius' approval. Plancina too played her part, aping her rival Agrippina by her presence at parades and cavalry

---

[1] Tac. *Ann.* 2.54, Suet. *Cal.* 3.2, *ILS* 8788 (= *EJ* 95), *IG* XII 2.208, 213b, 258; for Germanicus on Lesbos, cf. *EJ* 94.
[2] Tac. *Ann.* 2.54.

exercises.[1] This is prosecutor's language: new blood, promotions and bonuses were natural concomitants of a change in command, there was little else for the troops to do except parade and exercise, while the first duty of a legate was to guarantee his army's loyalty to the princeps, especially after the disquieting events of 14. But the most striking aspect of the episode is the trust that Piso must have had in Tiberius. For although he was acting in Tiberius' interests and even on Tiberius' instructions, on the surface his favours to the troops were designed to bind them only to himself – it was he, not Tiberius, whom the men called Father of the Legions – and the distortions that colour the account of Tacitus show how easy it would have been, if Tiberius chose to disclaim responsibility, for any prosecutor to 'prove' that Piso had been planning a *coup d'état*.

Germanicus was not unaware of what was going on in Syria, but for the moment he did nothing, for the affairs of Armenia had first claim on his attention. The problem of the throne was simplified by the affection of both nobles and people for Zeno, son of Polemo of Pontus, who from childhood had shown himself enamoured of Armenian ways. Thus the choice of Zeno as king imposed itself, and Germanicus himself placed the diadem on Zeno's head in the capital, Artaxata, amid general rejoicing. Zeno took the name Artaxias and ruled peacefully for fifteen years.[2] Germanicus – or Tiberius, if Germanicus, as is likely, was acting under orders – can be given credit for concurring in the wishes of the Armenian people. Cappadocia and Commagene were now dealt with. Q. Veranius was sent to the former to superintend its organization as a province; to render the prospect of Roman rule more attractive, some of the taxes that had been levied by the kings were reduced. Despite its position on the frontier, it did not receive a legionary garrison and was entrusted to an equestrian governor.[3] Commagene was entrusted to Q. Servaeus; it was subsequently attached to Syria.[4]

[1] Tac. *Ann.* 2.55.
[2] Tac. *Ann.* 2.56; cf. Koestermann, *Historia* 7, 1958, 342 n.27, 343 n.31. For Zeno, cf. *EJ* 173. Coins illustrating the coronation (*EJ* 182) were probably struck by Gaius in memory of his father, not by Germanicus himself at the time.
[3] Dio 57.17.7.
[4] Tac. *Ann.* 2.56.

Germanicus had quickly and efficiently performed all the tasks with which he had been entrusted: the grievances of Asia, the Armenian succession, the establishment of Roman rule in Cappadocia and Commagene had all been satisfactorily settled. But despite these successes Germanicus was unhappy, for he knew that a showdown with Piso was at hand. He had sent instructions to Piso – as his superior *imperium* unquestionably entitled him to do[1] – that either he or his son should lead a detachment of troops to Armenia, probably rather as a guard of honour than because of any expectation of trouble. This order Piso had simply ignored. The two commanders met at Cyrrhus, north-east of Antioch, the winter quarters of the tenth legion. Piso was determined not to show fear, while Germanicus was eager not to appear to browbeat a man who, though technically his inferior, was his superior in age and experience. But his friends did their best to embitter the prince, harping on such charges as were true, inventing false ones and bringing all kinds of accusations against Piso himself, Plancina and their sons. When Germanicus and Piso met, in the presence of a few close associates, they parted open enemies. From that moment, when Germanicus was dealing with judicial business, Piso rarely put in an appearance in court, and when he did take his place among Germanicus' advisers it was only to make his disagreement manifest. The irredeemable incompatibility of their characters showed itself again at a banquet given by the king of the Nabataeans.[2] Heavy gold crowns were presented as gifts to Germanicus and Agrippina, crowns of lesser weight to Piso and the other guests, whereupon Piso snarled that the banquet was being given for a Roman princeps' son, not the son of the king of Parthia, threw away the crown offered to him and gave vent to a further attack on luxurious living which, like his behaviour at Athens, bears witness to an extreme devotion to Roman tradition, unmollified by tact. Germanicus bore this outburst in silence – Pisow as after all Tiberius' friend, and the prince must have known that on such matters Tiberius' views were not unlike Piso's own.

[1] If precedents were needed, he had those of Tiberius himself and Gaius Caesar on their visits to Armenia; cf. Koestermann, *Historia* 7, 1958, 345.
[2] Tac. *Ann.* 2.57.

So far Germanicus had had no dealings with Artabanus of Parthia. But now envoys arrived from the king to remind him of the treaty concluded between Augustus and Phraates IV and to seek its renewal. To demonstrate his respect for Germanicus Artabanus was ready to meet him at the Euphrates. In the meantime he asked that Vonones should no longer be maintained in Syria and that the nobles of Parthia should not be incited to rebel. The king's request hints that Germanicus may at least have begun to investigate the possibility of causing trouble in Parthia. The prince made appropriate diplomatic noises in reply, but courteously declined the invitation to a meeting, presumably for fear that it might offend Tiberius. Vonones was removed to Pompeiopolis, a city on the coast of Cilicia, not only to oblige Artabanus but to spite Piso, who had become devoted to Vonones' cause, allegedly thanks to the exile's cultivation of himself and his lavish presents to Plancina.[1]

But despite his caution where Parthia was concerned, in 19 Germanicus made a far greater error by going on a voyage to Egypt. His real motive, according to Tacitus, was tourism,[2] but a recently discovered papyrus, containing a fragment of a speech to the Alexandrians, confirms that the visit was also an official one and makes it clear that in Germanicus' estimation Egypt was simply one of the transmarine provinces, the affairs of which he had been sent by Tiberius to settle.[3] He was received with wild enthusiasm in Alexandria, where his grandfather Antony was still remembered with affection, and, as at Athens, his abandonment of all formality and adoption of Greek dress did much to enhance his popularity. Indeed the demonstrations in his favour were so great and took such forms that Germanicus was forced to check them. An edict survives in which he rebuked the people of

[1] Tac. *Ann.* 2.58; Germanicus' tact in avoiding a meeting with Artabanus is stressed by Koestermann, *Historia* 7, 1958, 346 n.37.

[2] Tac. *Ann.* 2.59: *Aegyptum proficiscitur cognoscendae antiquitatis sed cura prouinciae praetendebatur*. Even before the discovery of the papyrus the last words were sufficient to refute Gelzer's view (*RE* 10.454) that Germanicus did not want to be regarded as an official personality and was therefore aware that his command did not entitle him to visit Egypt.

[3] *P. Oxy.* 2435.9ff. (*Oxyrhynchus Papyri* XXV, 102ff.); Germanicus is defended by Koestermann, *Historia* 7, 1958, 350 n.46.

Alexandria for hailing him and Agrippina with titles suited only to
Tiberius and Livia.[1] The implication seems to be that in premature
excitement the Alexandrians had acclaimed Germanicus not only as a
god and their saviour, but also as Augustus.[2] If this was so, Germanicus
did well to be alarmed, for at best Tiberius was bound to be resentful,
while at worst, if Germanicus appeared to make no protest, the
princeps' suspicious mind might inflate this harmless show into
evidence of open usurpation.

After dealing with a famine by ordering the granaries in which the
previous year's grain crop had been stored to be thrown open,[3]
Germanicus went on a cruise up the Nile as far as Syene, unaware that
an angry letter from the princeps was on its way. Tiberius began with a
mild rebuke for Germanicus' undignified affability and Greek clothes,
but went on to complain bitterly because the prince had entered Egypt
unauthorized, in defiance of the rule laid down by Augustus that no
senator should set foot in the country without the express permission of
the princeps.[4] To Tiberius it must indeed have seemed that Germanicus was not only spurning the precepts of Augustus, for which he
himself had such ingrained reverence, but also conducting himself as
if he were already princeps and not merely the heir. Nothing in fact was
further from Germanicus' thoughts, as his edict shows. To him Egypt
was just another province on his list, and if he thought of the question
of authority to enter it at all, he would have assumed that it was covered
by the blanket commission that had put him in charge of the eastern
provinces. The prefect of Egypt may have thought the same, for he
made no attempt to refuse Germanicus entry, though even if he had his
private doubts, he might well have thought it excessively rash to oppose
the prince's will. In Tiberius' judgment, on the other hand, Egypt was
equally clearly not a province in the normal sense at all, but retained its
special status as a private estate of the princeps and so did not fall
within the terms of Germanicus' appointment. This misunderstanding
about the status of Egypt – for at bottom it was no more – reveals yet

[1] *EJ* 320(b); cf. Cichorius, *Römische Studien*, 376.
[2] Cf. Cichorius, *Römische Studien*, 380; in general the views of Wilcken, *Hermes* 63,
1928, 48ff., are followed here, but on this point Cichorius is probably right.
[3] Cf. Wilcken, *Hermes* 63, 1928, 61ff., refuting Cichorius, *Römische Studien*, 382ff.
[4] Tac. *Ann.* 2.59.

again the total lack of warmth and trust between Tiberius and Germanicus. Had they been on better terms, Tiberius would not have reacted so violently to a matter of so little real importance, while Germanicus might have been prepared to ascertain in advance that the princeps would have no objection.

On his return from Egypt Germanicus found that all his measures to enforce discipline in the army and put in order the affairs of the Syrian cities had been rescinded or reversed in his absence by Piso.[1] Such opposition is comprehensible – it was after all Piso's army and Piso's province – yet pointlessly provocative, since when Germanicus returned to Syria he could once more overrule Piso, whose chief purpose was probably just to restore his self-esteem. Germanicus complained bitterly and Piso replied in kind. Then came the first news of Germanicus' illness, but a temporary recovery was celebrated by sacrifices, which at Antioch were broken up by Piso's lictors. From Antioch Piso moved to Seleucia, at the mouth of the Orontes, to await developments, for the prince had suffered a relapse. In his illness Germanicus formed the conviction that Piso had had him poisoned, and human bones, ashes and spells against the prince were found beneath the walls and floor of the house in which he was lying, giving colour to the accusation of witchcraft. Germanicus, sure that his death was at hand, was determined that Piso should not profit by it. He sent a formal letter renouncing Piso's friendship, and according to most of the authors whom Tacitus consulted, ordered Piso to leave Syria.[2] It is unlikely that his *imperium* gave him the right to do this, since in a sense he would be ordering Piso to commit treason by abandoning his command. At best it was tactless towards Tiberius to give an order that was tantamount to the reversal of one of his decisions. But Germanicus by now had been driven too far to give tact any further thought. At all events Piso saw fit to obey, though he sailed slowly, ready to return to the province if Germanicus' illness proved fatal. Despite a brief resurgence

[1] Tac. *Ann.* 2.69. Koestermann supposes (*Historia* 7, 1958, 352) that Piso must have had orders from Tiberius to do so, but there is no cogent reason for such an assumption.

[2] Tac. *Ann.* 2.69f. According to 2.69 Piso decided to leave Syria before receiving Germanicus' letter, but later he wrote to Tiberius that he had been driven out (Tac. *Ann.* 2.78).

of hope, the prince's friends soon found themselves summoned to his deathbed. The dying Germanicus was firm in his accusations against Piso and Plancina, equally firm that, should they claim to have been acting under instructions, they would be lying. He called on his friends to bring the murderers to justice and they swore that they would die rather than leave their commander unavenged. In his thirst for vengeance Germanicus had cried 'Show the people my wife, the grandchild of Augustus!' but in his last words to Agrippina he begged her for the sake of their children to tame her proud spirit and learn to accept the blows of destiny, for fear that her undisguised claim to power might provoke those more powerful than herself.[1] The clash between these two pieces of advice is a last poignant reminder of the unenviable position in which Germanicus had lived since Augustus' death, as he tried to follow the middle way of legitimate aspiration between Agrippina's impatience and Tiberius' distrust.

The funeral was conducted without ceremony at Antioch. Then the friends of Germanicus, since Piso had left the province, set about choosing one of their number to govern Syria. The honour was disputed for some time between C. Vibius Marsus, suffect consul in 17, and Cn. Sentius Saturninus, suffect as long ago as 4, before Marsus finally gave way to the senior man. Sentius then arrested a notorious poisoner, Martina, who had become an intimate friend of Plancina, on a charge of complicity in the death of Germanicus and sent her to Rome, while Vitellius, Veranius and Germanicus' other friends set about preparing their case, as if Piso and Plancina had already been committed for trial. Agrippina sailed for home with her husband's ashes.[2] Meanwhile news of Germanicus' death had been brought to Piso, who was now on the island of Cos, and was allegedly greeted with celebratory sacrifices by both Piso and Plancina.[3] Some centurions too

---

[1] Tac. *Ann.* 2.71f.; Germanicus died on 10 October, 19, cf. *F. Ant.* (*EJ* p. 53).
[2] Tac. *Ann.* 2.73-75; for Sentius in Syria, cf. *EJ* 284, showing that Tiberius confirmed his appointment.
[3] If the charge is true, the most likely explanation is that they regarded Germanicus as a declared enemy of Tiberius: thus Marsh, *Tiberius*, 95; Koestermann, *Historia* 7, 1958, 357, cf. 354. But the truth, duly exploited by Piso's accusers, may be only that the news of Germanicus' death happened to coincide with the customary sacrifice to mark the end of mourning for Plancina's sister.

came from Syria to the island, assured him of the continuing loyalty of the legions and encouraged him to return to the province, of which, they said, he had been illegally deprived. Technically they were correct, for the council of officers which had chosen Sentius had no right to appoint governors and Piso had not been dismissed from his command by Tiberius, the only man with authority to recall him. But in the circumstances it would undoubtedly have been wiser to abstain from any arrogantly self-righteous course, and indeed Piso's son Marcus advised him to make all speed to Rome. Nothing but empty slanders had so far been urged against him; his quarrel with Germanicus might earn him hatred but was no crime, and his enemies would rest content with depriving him of his province. If on the other hand he returned to Syria, Sentius would resist and there would be civil war. The adhesion of centurions and troops could not be relied on, for in the long run their deepseated loyalty to the Caesars would prevail. But instead of listening to this wise advice Piso was swayed by the words of his friend Domitius Celer – and no doubt by his own temperament. Celer insisted that Piso, not Sentius, was still the only legally appointed governor of Syria, and that if Sentius did resort to armed resistance Piso would be entirely justified in crushing it. Besides, he said, it would be better to wait until popular feeling had had time to die down. Tiberius and Livia were delighted that Germanicus was dead, but they could not provoke public outrage by showing their joy. There would be no advantage in arriving at Rome while Agrippina's lamentations were still loud in the ears of a sympathetic populace.[1]

Strengthened in his natural bent by these arguments, Piso wrote a letter to Tiberius, again accusing Germanicus of arrogance and luxurious habits. He himself, he said, had been expelled from the province so that the field would be clear for Germanicus to prepare to seize power, but now he was setting out to recover control of the army in the same spirit of loyalty in which he had commanded it before. Sending Domitius Celer ahead, he organized a force of deserters, as Tacitus rather emotively describes them, and sailed to the mainland, where he intercepted and took under his command a squadron of recruits on its way to Syria. He also wrote to the princes of Cilicia

[1] Tac. *Ann.* 2.75–77.

107

demanding troops from them. In all this he was loyally supported by his son Marcus, despite the young man's disapproval of his father's scheme. As he was sailing down the coast of Lycia and Pamphylia he encountered the squadron on which Vibius Marsus was escorting Agrippina home. Insults were exchanged, and Marsus, in the premature manner characteristic of Germanicus' friends, ordered Piso to come to Rome and defend himself in court. Piso cheerfully replied that he would present himself on the day appointed by the president of the appropriate tribunal.[1]

Domitius had put in at Laodicea, intending to make for the winter quarters of the sixth legion, which he judged the most likely to support Piso's cause, but he found himself forestalled by its commander Pacuvius. Sentius meanwhile prepared for war and wrote to Piso, warning him not to try to tamper with the army or invade the province. Piso, however, occupied Celenderis with his motley force of 'deserters', recruits, slaves and Cilician auxiliaries. In his harangue he insisted that he was the governor of Syria, the province to which Tiberius had appointed him and which he was now defending against the usurper Sentius. Despite his assurances that the legions would not fight against the man whom they had called their father, battle was joined and swiftly reached its inevitable outcome. Piso stood on his legal position to the last, demanding that on surrender of his arms he be allowed to occupy Celenderis until Tiberius had decided who in his opinion was governor of Syria. But Sentius not surprisingly refused this request and Piso was granted nothing but a safe-conduct to Rome.[2]

In the city the people had been kept on tenterhooks, for the long voyage from Syria to Rome had meant that the news of the progress of Germanicus' illness was always out of date. The first announcement of the prince's fever had unloosed a wave of hatred against Tiberius and Livia. Rumour-mongers eagerly leapt to the obvious conclusions: now it was clear why Germanicus had been packed off to the back of beyond, why Piso had replaced Silanus in Syria – this was what Livia and Plancina had been plotting in private. The tales grew wilder: it was even claimed that Germanicus had been murdered because, if he

[1] Tac. *Ann.* 2.78f.
[2] Tac. *Ann.* 2.79–81.

had come to power, he would have restored the old republican constitution – just as his father Drusus had been poisoned, for the same reason, by Livia and Augustus. While Tiberius the republican savoured the bitter irony of these accusations, news came that Germanicus was dead. Even before the official edicts and decrees had instituted mourning, squares were deserted and houses closed, and public life came to a standstill. Then some traders arrived in the city, who had left Syria before Germanicus' death, and at once the story spread that the prince was still alive.[1] In the night the rejoicing reached such a pitch that the princeps was woken by the din of the cheering crowds as they chanted 'Rome is saved! Germanicus is saved!'[2] Tiberius ignored the demonstration, waiting in contemptuous silence for time to convince the revellers of the truth. When the people realized that Germanicus was really dead, this brief interlude of delusive hope only rendered their grief and their sympathy for Agrippina more intense, their hostility to Tiberius more bitter, and their lust for revenge against Piso more savage.[3]

In this atmosphere, tense and heavy with hatred, Tiberius waited to face Agrippina and Piso. All the honours that ingenuity or affection could devise were heaped on Germanicus by the senate. Only once did Tiberius intervene to keep matters within traditional bounds.[4] By a stroke of irony it was at this time that Germanicus' sister, Livia Julia, the wife of the princeps' son Drusus, gave birth to twins. The event, and Tiberius' unconcealed delight, seemed to the people merely to emphasize the blows that had fallen on the house of Germanicus, which that of Drusus now seemed fated to overshadow.[5]

A sympathetic crowd was waiting when Agrippina's flotilla landed at Brundisium. To escort her and the ashes of Germanicus to Rome Tiberius had sent two praetorian cohorts, while the municipal magistrates of Calabria, Apulia and Campania had orders to perform the appropriate ceremonies, but no member of the princeps' family was present. As the cortège slowly made its way towards Rome, Drusus

[1] Tac. *Ann.* 2.82, cf. Suet. *Claud.* 1.4.
[2] Suet. *Cal.* 6.1f.
[3] Tac. *Ann.* 2.82.
[4] Tac. *Ann.* 2.83.
[5] Tac. *Ann.* 2.84, *CIG* 2630, *EJ* 91.

and Claudius, together with Germanicus' other children, met it at Tarracina. But Tiberius and Livia made no public appearance, whether because they thought it beneath their dignity or, as Tacitus malignly prefers to believe, because they would have been unable to mask their joy. Grief, ill-health or the wishes of the princeps kept the dead prince's mother Antonia too within doors.[1] The people were not inclined to forgive this lack of propriety, and the crowds that gathered on the Campus Martius to see the ashes of Germanicus placed in the mausoleum of Augustus openly lamented that the state had fallen in ruins and that now there was no hope left. All this Tiberius might have shrugged off with characteristic unconcern, but the enthusiasm of the public got the better of its wisdom and there were passionate demonstrations of affection for Agrippina, who was hailed as the ornament of the fatherland and the only true descendant of Augustus, while prayers were offered that her children at least might be preserved from further misfortune.[2] Ironically, but inevitably, these adjurations sowed the seeds of their own frustration, for they destroyed any chance that Tiberius' dislike and distrust of Agrippina might abate with the disappearance of Germanicus. The denial of a state funeral for the prince was bitterly resented. Tiberius might have adopted an extreme attitude to the public expression of grief when his brother Drusus had died, but he had travelled hundreds of miles on foot in escorting the body back to Rome. Now, men muttered, he was not prepared to go even to the gates of the city for Germanicus. Tiberius' only response was an edict affirming his grief and imposing moderation, with precedents drawn from the practice of Julius as well as that of Augustus. Principes, he said, were mortal; only the state lived for ever.[3]

It is difficult to estimate Tiberius' reaction to the news of Germanicus' death. That his feeling was one of unadulterated pleasure, as hostile sources urge, may be rejected out of hand. He had neither liked nor trusted the prince, despite Germanicus' proofs of loyalty, and his dislike of Agrippina was even stronger. He had, however,

[1] Tac. *Ann.* 3.1–3; the more hostile explanation of the behaviour of Tiberius and Livia is accepted by Koestermann, *Historia* 7, 1958, 361.
[2] Tac. *Ann.* 3.4.
[3] Tac. *Ann.* 3.5f.

7 Tiberius

8 Gilt bronze plaque from a sword-sheath: Tiberius, with shield inscribed
FELICITAS TIBERII, receiving a Victory presented by Germanicus on his
return from the German war. The other figures are Mars and Victory.

accepted the principate only reluctantly, because the will of Augustus had left him no choice, stating clearly that he regarded his acceptance as no more than a temporary measure.[1] Germanicus had been the successor designated by Augustus and, whatever he may have felt about the passing over of Drusus, Tiberius had always accepted Germanicus as such. There is nothing to suggest that he ever dreamed of reversing Augustus' decision on this vital point, and although his lack of affection for Germanicus seems to have made him delay the final step – Germanicus had never been granted the tribunician power – it is likely that he would soon have retired in Germanicus' favour, despite any pressure that Livia might bring to bear. The situation created by Germanicus' death was not an agreeable one. While Germanicus was alive, Agrippina was more of a nuisance than a danger, and Tiberius had only to retire and so satisfy her yearning to be empress for her to cease to be a thorn in his flesh. But now more time would have to elapse before Drusus, the obvious successor – at least until one of Germanicus' sons was old enough to replace him – was ready to take over from his father, and all that time an unattached Agrippina would be constantly pressing for the rapid advancement of her sons in her impatience to rule as the princeps' mother, now that her dream of ruling as the princeps' wife had been shattered. It is inconceivable that Tiberius welcomed this prospect, for himself or eventually for his son. On a personal level he can have felt no sorrow that Germanicus was dead. His refusal to parade a semblance of the grief he did not feel may seem a pointless provocation of public displeasure, even in one who scorned the judgment of the mob as much as he did. But Tiberius must have realized that for him nothing could come of Germanicus' death but hatred. It was firmly fixed in the minds of senate and people that Germanicus had been murdered, and murdered at Tiberius' instigation. That conviction could not be overthrown, no matter what face Tiberius displayed to the public and no matter what happened at the impending trial of Piso. Since hypocrisy would have brought no political gain, it is perhaps after all not so surprising that Tiberius, immersed in thoughts of a troubled future, did not bother to don a mask.

[1] Tac. *Ann.* 1.11, 13, Suet. *Tib.* 24.2.

7. THE TRIAL OF PISO

Piso was making no haste about returning to Rome, but suspicions as to what lay in store at the trial were roused when the poisoner Martina succeeded in exercising her art upon herself at Brundisium. Inevitably foul play was seen in the demise of this promising witness. Piso had sent his son Marcus on ahead with letters to mollify the princeps, while he himself went to call on Drusus, who had set out once more for the army in Illyricum. Tiberius, with scrupulous impartiality, received the young Marcus courteously and made him the customary grant to defray his expenses in the public service. Drusus, who may have had instructions from his father, avoided any private converse with Piso, who naïvely expected him to be pleased at the removal of a rival; in public he confined himself to expressing the hope that the charges bruited against Piso would prove to be false and that Germanicus' death would bring no one else's ruin in its train. Piso landed at Ancona and proceeded to Rome. On his way he encountered the ninth legion, in transit from Pannonia to Africa, and travelled with it down the Via Flaminia, giving rise to rumours that he intended to march on the city. So Piso changed his mode of transport, sailing from Narnia down the Nar and the Tiber. But he allowed himself to be greeted on landing by a host of retainers, who escorted him to his house, which overlooked the Forum and was gaily decorated to celebrate its master's return.[1] This pomp fanned the fury of the mob – though, had Piso entered the city in furtive quiet, this would no doubt at once have been seized on as proof of his guilty conscience.

The agents of vengeance wasted no time. Next day Fulcinius Trio, the principal accuser of Libo in 16, laid charges against Piso before the consuls in the senate.[2] Trio made his name as a prosecutor, and his career is symptomatic of the change in forensic life that came with the principate, for under the republic it was frowned on for a man with any claim to social standing to make a habit of appearing on the prosecuting side. His eagerness to take the lead in bringing Piso to book underlines all that we know about the attitude of senate and people. Men like

[1] Tac. *Ann.* 3.7-9.
[2] Tac. *Ann.* 3.10; cf. Rogers, *Trials*, 42ff.

Trio wanted cases that would be easy to win but notorious enough to bring fame: the prosecution of Piso must have seemed ideal. But Vitellius, Veranius and the rest of Germanicus' friends at once intervened, claiming that the whole affair was none of Trio's business – it was they who had a sacred duty to answer Germanicus' dying call for revenge. The dispute was settled to Trio's disadvantage – he was given leave only to deal with Piso's earlier career, while the meat of the case was entrusted to the others. The consuls then asked Tiberius to take the case.[1] Their reluctance to shoulder the responsibility themselves is hardly surprising. Vitellius and company could not object, though no doubt they wanted the senate to be charged with the enquiry – they may well have believed that Tiberius would save Piso if he dared. But Germanicus had been Tiberius' adopted son and destined successor, and to complain if the princeps chose to take the case would be tactless in the extreme, since the implication of such a complaint would be that Tiberius could not be trusted with the investigation because of his suspected complicity in Piso's 'crime'. Piso himself had less complex reasons for welcoming the suggestion. He knew that he had no hope of a fair hearing in the senate, even if the populace could be restrained from lynching him, whereas Tiberius was unlikely to be moved by irresponsible rumours or the public outcry for his blood, and would also, Piso hoped, be subject to the favourable influence of Livia. But Tiberius refused to accept the burden.[2] He knew that if Piso were acquitted *in camera* this would be seen as conclusive proof that he had had Germanicus murdered. For public opinion he may have cared nothing, but it would have been politically irresponsible to risk the riots that might have ensued. Nor did he see any reason to bear alone the task of condemning his old friend, should he prove to be guilty, while the senate enjoyed the luxury of revenge without responsibility. So true to his policy of attempting to force the senate to perform its functions instead of thrusting them all upon the princeps,[3] after a

---

[1] Thus Kierdorf, *Hermes* 97, 1969, 248ff. The run of the passage suggests that this is correct, though Kierdorf's argument (p. 249) that Germanicus' friends would not have had Tiberius take the case if the choice had lain with them is not cogent.

[2] Tac. *Ann.* 3.10.

[3] Cf. Tac. *Ann.* 3.35.

brief preliminary hearing of both sides he sent the case back to the senate without prejudice – though for Piso of course this in itself was an immense blow, proving as it did that Tiberius proposed to make no special effort to save him.

Meanwhile Drusus, returning from Illyricum, had entered the city, postponing his ovation. Piso approached various distinguished men in the hope that they would act as his advocates, but Arruntius, P. Vinicius, Asinius Gallus, M. Claudius Marcellus Aeserninus and Sex. Pompeius all refused, concocting diverse excuses. Only his brother L. Calpurnius Piso, M. Aemilius Lepidus and Livineius Regulus consented to appear on his behalf. So the trial began, in a fever of popular excitement, with all eyes fixed on Tiberius to see what he would do.[1]

The princeps' opening speech was a model of reason in the midst of hysteria. He recalled that Piso had long been his friend and had also served as a legate of Augustus and that his appointment as Germanicus' counsellor in the East had been approved by the senate – a typical touch. He then attempted to insist on a distinction between the charge of murder and the smokescreen of irrelevancies with which it had been blanketed. If Piso had exceeded the duties of his office, behaved insultingly towards the prince and rejoiced at his death, that, he said, was no concern of the senate but his own private affair, to be privately avenged by a renunciation of friendship. The only crime in point was that of murder, and the only question that the senate had to settle was whether Germanicus had been murdered. The princeps also clearly defined the possible grounds for a charge of treason: the senate must decide whether Piso had been guilty of sedition in his treatment of the armies and whether he had tried to regain control of Syria by force, or whether these charges had been falsely put about or exaggerated by the prosecutors, whose excessive zeal now met with a well-deserved rebuke, in particular their attempt to prejudice the poisoning question by displaying Germanicus' naked corpse in public at Antioch. Finally Tiberius emphasized that the senate should not allow itself to be influenced by his personal connection with the case. The only special concession that had been made to Germanicus was the hearing of the

[1] Tac. *Ann.* 3.11.

case in the senate instead of in the standing courts. Therefore the senate should ignore his sorrow – and any false tales that might be brought forward against him.[1]

It was decided that two days should be assigned for the prosecution to put its case and that then, after an interval of six days, three days should be given to the defence. Trio began with trivialities from Piso's past career, in particular his conduct as governor of Spain, then Vitellius, Veranius and Servaeus took the field. They claimed that Piso had set out to win the affections of the worst elements in the legions out of hatred for Germanicus and a desire for revolution, that he had always shown himself savagely hostile to Germanicus' companions, and had finally brought about Germanicus' death by poison and black magic. Then, after he and Plancina had celebrated their triumph with impious sacrifices, he had taken up arms against the state and had had to be defeated in battle before he could be brought to trial.[2] The defence found itself in a quandary, since Piso's abuses as general and as governor and his enmity for Germanicus were too blatant to be denied. So they devoted all their efforts to refuting the charge of murder, in support of which the prosecution had produced a tale so grotesque that even Tacitus dismisses it as absurd.[3] But the voice of reason had no chance of being heard, for the senate could not be budged from its blind conviction that Germanicus had not died a natural death. Tiberius on the other hand could not forget that Piso had begun a civil war, however brief. That Piso had some legal grounds for doing so is true, but the situation he had created by taking such a step without authority from the princeps was more than Tiberius could overlook. Even if the senate had been inclined to waver, the mob outside was making it abundantly clear that the only alternative to conviction was a lynching. It seems that a demand was made for the production of the correspondence between princeps and legate, but

---

[1] Tac. *Ann.* 3.12.

[2] Tac. *Ann.* 3.13; for Vitellius' speech, cf. also Plin. *NH* 11.187.

[3] Tac. *Ann.* 3.14. Nevertheless the story of the murder is regarded as certain by Dio 57.18.9. Suetonius is more cautious, though violently hostile to Piso, in *Tib.* 52.3, *Cal.* 1.2 and 2, but apparently sure of Piso's guilt in *Cal.* 3.3 and *Vit.* 2.3. Josephus (*AJ* 18.54) has no doubts. The problems facing the historian are well summarized by Tac. *Ann.* 3.19.

Tiberius and Piso were united in their refusal. Piso's statues were torn from their pedestals and dragged to the Gemoniae and would have been smashed had not Tiberius sent troops to intervene. At the end of the day Piso was escorted home in a litter by a tribune of the praetorian guard. There he found that Plancina had abandoned him. At first, while there seemed to be some hope, she had remained loyal, but when it became clear that Tiberius was going to let matters take their course, she began to dissociate her cause from her husband's and threw herself on Livia's mercy. Nevertheless, encouraged by his sons, Piso appeared next day in the senate, but the open hostility of the senators and in particular the lack of any sign of sympathy from the princeps convinced him that further resistance was futile. He reached home after the session without incident, but in the morning he was found with his throat cut, his sword by his side.[1]

Tiberius' reaction to the news was striking, foreshadowing the haunting fear of persecution which dominated him more and more in his last years. He complained in the senate that Piso had chosen suicide in order to shift the burden of hatred on to him,[2] and quizzed Piso's son Marcus at length as to how Piso had spent his last hours. The young man answered as best he could and read Piso's last message, which was hardly calculated to ease Tiberius' mind. In it Piso begged Tiberius, for the sake of their friendship and his unbroken loyalty, to spare his sons, of whom Gnaeus had been in Rome throughout, while Marcus had advised against the invasion of Syria. About Plancina he said nothing. Tiberius absolved Marcus from any charge of treason on the grounds that once Piso had refused to take his advice the young man had had no alternative but to follow his father's lead. Two days were then devoted to the trial of Plancina, for whom, in acute embarrassment, Tiberius interceded, openly avowing that he did so at Livia's request. In vain he urged Piso's sons to defend their mother; loyal to their father, they refused, and Tiberius was left to bear alone the odium of snatching the murderess from the grasp of justice, for so public opinion saw his action. Inevitably this confirmed the impression that Tiberius and Livia had contrived Germanicus' death, and people

[1] Tac. *Ann.* 3.15.
[2] Tac. *Ann.* 3.16: *suam inuidiam tali morte quaesitam.*

feared that Agrippina and her children too might soon succumb to poison.[1]

When the proceedings were over, the consul Cotta Messallinus proposed that Piso's name should be erased from the Fasti, that half his estate should be confiscated, the other half granted to his innocent son Gnaeus on condition that he changed his *praenomen*, but that Marcus should be expelled from the senate and exiled for ten years. Not content with opposing Tiberius on this last matter, Cotta added the suggestion that it should be recorded that Plancina had been spared specifically on account of Livia's intercession. Without responding directly to the insult, Tiberius set about mitigating the motion. He refused to allow Piso's name to be removed from the Fasti, a disgrace that even Antony and Iullus Antonius had been spared.[2] He also insisted that M. Piso should suffer no penalty and should receive his fair share of his father's estate. There followed proposals for a golden statue in the temple of Mars Ultor and an altar to Vengeance, but both were rejected by the princeps as suitable only to victories over foreign enemies, not to the perpetuation of domestic griefs. A final proposal, no doubt at least in part ironical, decreed the expression of thanks to Tiberius, Livia, Antonia, Agrippina and Drusus for their part in avenging Germanicus. Claudius was at first forgotten but added later.[3] A few days later the victors received their rewards. Priesthoods were granted by the senate to Vitellius, Veranius and Servaeus on the motion of the princeps, who also promised his support to Trio in his future career, while warning him against excessive violence in speaking.[4] Not long afterwards, on 28 May, Drusus celebrated his ovation.[5]

Exasperation with himself for choosing the wrong man and guilt at his enforced abandonment of the friend who had so obviously relied on his support certainly sharpened Tiberius' feeling that Piso had betrayed his trust. But Piso's death had a profound and lasting effect

---

[1] Tac. *Ann.* 3.16f.
[2] It was however erased from some inscriptions, cf. *ILS* 95 (= *EJ* 39); Rogers, *Trials*, 50 (citing other instances).
[3] Tac. *Ann.* 3.17f.
[4] Tac. *Ann.* 3.19.
[5] For the date, cf. *F. Ost.* (*EJ* p. 41), *F. Amit.* (*EJ* p. 49). An ovation, not a triumph: cf. Tac. *Ann.* 2.64, 3.11, 19; in *F. Ost. ouans*, rather than *Caesar*, could be restored.

on him at a much less superficial level than this. Piso's conception of his mission had been crude almost to the point of caricature. Politically he had not only failed in what was required of him; more important, the manner of his failure had shown that he could not comprehend or would not make allowance for the complex ambiguities of Tiberius' relationship with Germanicus. On a personal level his blunt, insensitive behaviour had revealed a total lack of understanding or sympathy for the unceasing inner conflict that tormented Tiberius, the constant friction between his loyalty to the dictates of Augustus and his own political beliefs and private feelings. It was this, more than mere political ineptitude, that roused Tiberius' obsessively self-centred resentment. Yet Piso's fate meant even more to Tiberius than the failure of an old and trusted friend to understand the frustrations and pressures that the principate brought with it. Piso had remained a true republican, preserving his independence and refusing any compromise, while Tiberius' acceptance of power had condemned him to conjure with political half-truths and hypocrisies. Nevertheless he had struggled against overwhelming odds to keep alive some semblance of republican freedom of action and of speech. But while he had tried to pretend that the republic was not just a dream, Piso had behaved as if it really existed and had paid the inevitable penalty. For Tiberius it must have been as if Piso had died for taking him at his word. His despair at this bitter confirmation of his failure must have doubled his longing to be rid of the cares of state. Not many days after Drusus' ovation he was once more cruelly reminded of all he had already suffered at Augustus' behest as well as of what still lay in store, when he heard the news that Vipsania was dead.[1]

8. THE SUCCESSION: DRUSUS AND THE SONS OF GERMANICUS

In spite of the public lamentations it provoked and the suspicions it aroused against Tiberius, Germanicus' death created no dynastic crisis. The prince left three sons, Nero, aged fifteen, Drusus, twelve, and Gaius Caligula, now nearly eight. Augustus had clearly intended

[1] Tac. *Ann.* 3.19.

that Germanicus should succeed his adoptive father, and from this it would follow that he had also wished Germanicus' descendants to rule in the direct line.[1] There appeared to be no obstacle; Nero was as yet of course too young, but if Tiberius died before he reached maturity there was an obvious candidate for the post of guardian to Nero and his brothers: Tiberius' own son Drusus. Drusus, it is true, had twin sons of his own, born in 19,[2] whose interests he would have to set aside, but for this there was cogent precedent in Tiberius' refusal to allow the claims of Drusus to interfere with the destined advancement of Germanicus. For Drusus indeed the task might be easier, since his affection for Germanicus and his sons is attested,[3] whereas Tiberius had had to conquer deep distrust and lack of sympathy.

Tiberius soon made his intentions plain. Nero assumed the *toga uirilis* on 7 June, 20, and Tiberius commended him to the favour of the senate, requesting that he be excused the lowest magistracy, the vigintivirate, and allowed to stand for the quaestorship at five years below the legal age.[4] These concessions, once made to Tiberius and his brother at the request of Augustus, were naturally granted. Nero was also honoured with a priesthood and a donative was given to the people to celebrate the occasion.[5] To publicize and cement the relationship between Tiberius' son and the children of Germanicus, Nero, who had once been engaged to the daughter of Creticus Silanus,[6] was now betrothed to Drusus' daughter Julia Livilla. This news was well received, but the popular delight was marred by the apparently simultaneous announcement that the dignity of the praetorian prefect Seianus was to be increased by an alliance with the ruling house: his daughter was betrothed to Drusus, son of Claudius and Urgulanilla.[7] Such a match was widely regarded as a disgrace, but it was broken

---

[1] Cf. Dio 57.18.11.

[2] Tac. *Ann.* 2.84; celebrated on coins, cf. *EJ* 91. One was Ti. Gemellus; the other, who died in 23, was called Germanicus, cf. *CIG* 2630, *ILS* 170, *EJ* 115(b). According to Dio 57.14.6 Drusus had had another son who had died in 15.

[3] Tac. *Ann.* 2.43, *EJ* 130a (Germanicus and Drusus); Tac. *Ann.* 4.4 (Drusus and Germanicus' sons).

[4] Tac. *Ann.* 3.29; for the date, cf. *F. Ost.* (*EJ* p. 41).

[5] Tacitus says a pontificate, but this is inconsistent with *ILS* 182 (= *EJ* 96).

[6] Tac. *Ann.* 2.43.

[7] Tac. *Ann.* 3.29, Dio 58.11.5.

when only a few days later Junilla's fiancé met his death in grotesque fashion.[1]

That Drusus had taken Germanicus' place in Tiberius' plans for the succession was confirmed in 21, when for the first three months of the year the prince was consul for the second time, with Tiberius as his colleague.[2] But another more ominous development marked the beginning of the year. On grounds of ill-health Tiberius left Rome and withdrew to Campania. It may be, as Tacitus suggests, that he wanted to leave Drusus in control of affairs in order to test his son's capacity to rule, but it is clear that his distaste for public affairs and his longing for the peace of retirement were growing ever greater. Indeed, he prolonged his absence well beyond Drusus' consulship; only when Livia fell seriously ill in 22 was he reluctantly constrained to return in haste to the city.[3]

A trifling dispute gave Drusus his first chance to shine in the senate.[4] An ex-praetor, Cn. Domitius Corbulo, father of the great general, complained that a young man of noble birth, L. Cornelius Sulla, had failed to offer him his seat at a gladiatorial show. The incident provoked a major debate between defenders of tradition and the rights of age and Sulla's distinguished relatives, who included Mam. Scaurus and Arruntius. However, Drusus effected a reconciliation.

Not long afterwards trouble was stirred up by Caecina Severus, who proposed that the wives of provincial governors should no longer be allowed to accompany their husbands abroad.[5] In his speech the former commander on the Rhine named no names, but he criticized women's eagerness for power and their influence over the troops, remarking that a woman had recently been seen presiding at manoeuvres and parades. No doubt the shaft was primarily aimed at Plancina, but Caecina's words might equally apply to Agrippina, of whose behaviour he had of

---

[1] Suet. *Claud.* 27.1. He threw a pear into the air, caught it in his mouth and choked.
[2] Tac. *Ann.* 3.31. Tiberius resigned after three months (Suet. *Tib.* 26.2); two suffects were in office on 30 May (cf. Degrassi, *Fasti consolari*, 8). It is therefore virtually certain that Drusus gave up his office at the same time as his father. For stress on Drusus' place in the dynastic line, cf. *ILS* 168, 176 (= *EJ* 92), which show the similarity between his position and that of Germanicus; *EJ* 90, 91, 148, 177, 269.
[3] Tac. *Ann.* 3.64.
[4] Tac. *Ann.* 3.31. [5] Tac. *Ann.* 3.33f.

course had first-hand experience.[1] His views won little support from the senators, and Messalla Messallinus spoke convincingly against the motion. Drusus argued briefly in support of Messallinus, pleading indulgence for the imperial house, who often had to visit distant regions of the empire. He cited the telling precedent of Augustus, who had often taken Livia with him on his journeys abroad, and admitted that he himself would not look forward with enthusiasm to further tours of duty in the provinces if they brought with them an enforced separation from his wife. So Caecina's proposal was defeated.

Drusus won further favour when he intervened to check the abuse of the right of sanctuary inherent in the princeps' image.[2] A complaint was brought in the senate by C. Cestius Gallus, who was being publicly abused under this safeguard by Annia Rufilla. The senators plainly felt that a lead in such a delicate matter could only be given by a member of the princeps' family and so begged Drusus to take action. Drusus eventually acceded to the request, and Annia was arrested and imprisoned.

Drusus also got the credit for the condemnation of two *equites*, Considius Aequus and Caelius Cursor, who had brought false charges of *maiestas* against a praetor, Magius Caecilianus.[3] It is unlikely, however, that the prince was responsible; at all events the senate's verdict had Tiberius' authority, presumably conveyed by letter. In his private life Drusus showed himself much addicted to luxury, but this did nothing to diminish his popularity, for the public regarded such behaviour as natural in a young man and a welcome change from Tiberius' forbidding and parsimonious ways.

Thus as consul Drusus was a success, but towards the end of the year he fell ill.[4] No details are known, but the untimely elegy of Clutorius Priscus, which brought about the poet's execution,[5] indicates that his life was believed to be in danger. Drusus' illness did not cause Tiberius to return to Rome, but this may serve as evidence rather for the princeps' aversion to the city than for any lack of affection between father and son.

[1] Cf. Tac. *Ann.* 2.55 (Plancina), 1.69 (Agrippina).
[2] Tac. *Ann.* 3.36.
[3] Tac. *Ann.* 3.37.
[4] Tac. *Ann.* 3.49.
[5] Tac. *Ann.* 3.49–51, Dio 57.20.3f.; cf. below, p. 158.

Before his return to Rome in 22 Tiberius took a decisive step towards designating Drusus as his successor. In a letter to the senate he asked for his son to be granted the tribunician power.[1] Only two men had received this honour from Augustus – first Agrippa and then Tiberius himself – and despite his loyalty to the dictates of his predecessor Tiberius had never brought himself to bestow the tribunician power on Germanicus. But now Drusus was to share the symbol of supreme power.[2] The letter spoke in realistic terms of his character and achievements. He had a wife and three children and had now reached the age at which Tiberius himself had first received the tribunician power from Augustus. Eight years of military and public service, during which he had earned an ovation and two consulships, had fitted him to share the labours of the principate. The senate responded with abject adulation, as its members vied with one another to plumb new depths of flattery.[3] Their efforts culminated in the proposal of Q. Haterius that the decrees of the senate passed on that day should be inscribed in the senate house in letters of gold. This and other excesses were rejected by Tiberius as contrary to ancestral custom.[4] Drusus, who had joined his father in Campania, perhaps by way of convalescence after his illness, wrote in similar vein, but the modesty of his letter did nothing to quell the resentment aroused by his failure to appear at Rome in person. Tiberius, it was felt, might plausibly put forward old age and exhaustion as excuses for his absence, but Drusus' arrogance was beyond justification.

Although Drusus' illness had not brought Tiberius to Rome, later in 22 he hurried to the city when news reached him that his mother was gravely ill. Supplications and games were decreed by the senate to assist her recovery, while the *equites* promised an offering to Fortuna Equestris.[5] Despite her age Livia survived to live another seven years.[6]

---

[1] Tac. *Ann.* 3.56; if the statement here about his age is accurate, Drusus was thirty-five.

[2] Tac. *Ann.* 3.56: *summi fastigii uocabulum*, a description of the significance of the tribunician power as exact as it is concise.

[3] Tac. *Ann.* 3.57.

[4] Tac. *Ann.* 3.59.

[5] Tac. *Ann.* 3.64, 71.

[6] She died at the age of eighty-six (Dio 58.2.1) in 29.

V

TIBERIUS AS PRINCEPS, A.D. 14–26

1. SENATE AND MAGISTRATES

In his summary of the 'good years' of Tiberius' reign Tacitus speaks with guarded praise of the dignity and power accorded by the princeps to the senate and the magistrates.[1] Not only public business but the most important private matters too were debated in the senate; leading men were free to express their opinions, while adulation was checked by Tiberius himself. Men rose to high office on the best of traditional grounds: noble birth, military glory and distinction in the arts of peace. With an enthusiasm innocent of Tacitus' reservations Velleius exclaims that under Tiberius magistrates, senate and courts increased in dignity and power.[2] Suetonius and Dio too record that Tiberius consulted the senate on every issue, no matter how trivial or how vital it might seem, and made no complaint if his motions were defeated or if he found himself in the minority in a division.[3] Even when abuse was directed against himself and his family, he asserted the principle that in a free state men must be free to think and speak as they pleased.[4] His overall view of his position is preserved by Suetonius in Tiberius' own words to the senate: 'I say now, as I have often said before, that the duty of a good and beneficent princeps, to whom you have granted such great and unfettered power, is to be the servant of the senate, and often of the citizen body as a whole, and of individuals too. I do not

---

[1] Tac. *Ann.* 4.6; but cf. below, p. 257.
[2] Vell. 2.126.2.
[3] Suet. *Tib.* 30, 31.1, Dio 57.7.2ff.
[4] Suet. *Tib.* 28: *in ciuitate libera linguam mentemque liberas esse debere.*

regret my words: you have been, and still are, good, fair and generous masters.'[1]

Indeed, Tiberius strengthened the power of the senate by one of his very first acts as princeps in 14, when, no doubt in accordance with instructions left by Augustus, the right to elect the magistrates was transferred from people to senate.[2] Popular election had been an empty show since A.D. 5, when a group of senatorial and equestrian centuries had received the task of preparing for the assembly a list of candidates that included only the same number of names as there were places.[3] Henceforth it was the senate that produced such a list and passed it on for formal approval first by the destination centuries and then by the people.[4] The masses had become too accustomed to the loss of their liberty to make any complaint, and the senators were delighted to be relieved of the degrading duties of canvassing and bribery.[5] They asked that the number of praetors should be increased, but Tiberius restricted the number of places to twelve, as had been usual under Augustus, and bound himself by an oath not to exceed it when an attempt was made to press him.[6] He gave his personal commendation to only four of the candidates for these twelve places, among them Velleius Paterculus and his brother.[7] Although this had no legal force, men so commended could be sure of election without the need to canvass in the senate.[8]

[1] Suet. *Tib.* 29; in general, cf. Charlesworth, *CAH* x, 613f.
[2] Tac. *Ann.* 1.15. For the problems presented by the elections under Tiberius, cf. Tibiletti, *Principe*, 141ff.; Lacey, *Historia* 12, 1963, 167ff.; Shotter, *CQ* 60, 1966, 321ff.; Levick, *Historia* 16, 1967, 207ff.; Astin, *Latomus* 28, 1969, 863ff.
[3] The so-called *Tabula Hebana* (text *EJ* 94a) has excited more discussion than it deserves; most rewarding: Tibiletti, *Principe*, 17ff.; Brunt, *JRS* 51, 1961, 71ff.
[4] There is no reason to suppose that the destination centuries were abolished in 14. For their existence in 19 and 23, cf. *EJ* 94a.5ff. (additional centuries as part of Germanicus' funeral honours); 94b (a similar honour for Drusus).
[5] Tac. *Ann.* 1.15.
[6] Tac. *Ann.* 1.14. It is probable that Tiberius meant his refusal to apply only to the present year. To reinforce so ephemeral a decision with an oath may seem strange, but Tiberius more than once resorted to this device in quite trivial matters when he was upset or eager to forestall discussion (cf. Tac. *Ann.* 1.74, 2.31, 4.31). If the oath was meant to hold good for the future, it was not always observed: cf. Dio 58.20.5.
[7] Vell. 2.124.3f.
[8] Tac. *Ann.* 1.15.

Tiberius' conduct with regard to the consular elections is difficult to understand; Tacitus found himself confronted with conflicting data not only in historical sources but also in Tiberius' speeches, and so his account is extremely tentative.[1] It appears that Tiberius sometimes followed the curious practice of making a normal speech of commendation, but with the name of the subject omitted, while on other occasions he commended no one at all, simply instructing the candidates not to disturb the proceedings by canvassing and promising that he himself would do what was necessary. Most commonly he announced that the only candidates were those whose names he had declared to the consuls, though others were welcome to stand if they had confidence in their influence or deserts. Despite this appearance of liberty, it is unlikely that any man would dare to put himself forward against those of whom the princeps had implied his approval in this way, or that, if he did, he would stand any chance of success. But there is nothing in Tacitus to suggest that Tiberius was in the habit of announcing that only two men wished to stand; he was probably ready to allow the senate a choice between candidates, all of whom were acceptable to him.

In 16 the subject of praetorian elections brought Tiberius into conflict with Asinius Gallus.[2] Gallus proposed that at a single sitting magistrates should be elected for a period of five years in advance, that men appointed to the command of a legion before they had held the praetorship should be automatically regarded as praetor's designate, and that Tiberius should each year present a list of twelve candidates for the praetorship – that is, a list of as many candidates as there were places. At first sight this proposal might seem to imply a major increase in Tiberius' power, since he would have complete control of the praetorship at least for a long period in advance. Certainly Tiberius in his reply chose to treat it in this light. It would put great strain on his moderation, he said, to control the destinies of so many men. Even under the system of annual elections, where consolation might rapidly follow defeat, it was hard enough to avoid giving offence, and the hatred of men whose hopes had been dashed for five years would be

[1] Tac. *Ann.* 1.81.
[2] Tac. *Ann.* 2.36.

far worse to bear. Besides, it was impossible to know in advance what changes might affect a man's character, his fortune and his family over such a space of time. Men grew arrogant enough when they were designated for magistracies only one year in advance; during five years of designate status they might well become intolerable. This speech made a good impression, although, as Tacitus is quick to remark, Tiberius was not making any sacrifice of power.

Tiberius was telling almost the whole truth. Yet Tacitus was right to see in Gallus' proposal a tampering with the very foundations of the principate, for it would have robbed Tiberius' patronage in this sphere of all its flexibility and so of much of its value. If a man knew well in advance that his place was secure, he might grow not merely arrogant but dangerously independent, and it would be odious, if not impossible, to remove his name once the list had been compiled. Others might become discontented and potentially disloyal if the just reward for their services or talents was inordinately delayed by such a system. For Tiberius it was much more desirable to exercise whatever measure of control he thought prudent as circumstances might dictate from year to year.

Though the conduct of the consular elections is obscure, the names of the men who hold office under Tiberius reveal certain clear and, in the main, predictable patterns.[1] Throughout the reign the honour of the post of *consul ordinarius* is reserved, with very few exceptions, for members of the old republican noble families and the sons of men who had reached the consulate under Augustus. Noteworthy among the noble *ordinarii* are several Cornelii Lentuli – Cossus in 25, his brother Cn. Gaetulicus in 26, and probably Ser. Cornelius Cethegus in 24 – two Junii Silani in 19 and 28, L. Calpurnius Piso in 27 – he had changed his *praenomen* from Gnaeus to Lucius in accordance with the decree passed after his father's trial in 20[2] – L. Cassius Longinus in 30 and Cn. Domitius Ahenobarbus in 32, to both of whom Tiberius gave

---

[1] The Fasti are analysed by Tibiletti (*Principe*, 245ff.), but his misleading use of the term *nobilis* robs his statistics of most of their interest; cf. also Bird, *Latomus* 28, 1969, 73ff.
[2] His brother Marcus, despite Tiberius' leniency towards him, did not attain the consulship.

daughters of Germanicus as wives, and Ser. Sulpicius Galba, the future emperor and a former favourite of Livia, in 33 – his elder brother Gaius had been consul in 22. Other men of more recent consular descent include Sisenna Statilius Taurus in 16, whose father, one of Augustus' most trusted lieutenants, had been consul twice, two sons of Asinius Gallus and Tiberius' former wife Vipsania – C. Asinius Pollio in 23 and M. Asinius Agrippa in 25 – M. Vinicius in 30, who also married a daughter of Germanicus and to whom Velleius dedicated his history, and in 32 L. Arruntius Camillus Scribonianus, son of M. Furius Camillus, consul in 8, and adopted by that prominent senator L. Arruntius, consul in 6. Throughout, an even balance is maintained between the survivors of the old nobility and the scions of the newer families that had risen under Augustus. But before the fall of Seianus in 31 only three men not of consular descent appear as *ordinarii*: in 17 L. Pomponius Flaccus, a bosom companion of the princeps, in whom Tiberius had great trust, in 29 the mysterious L. Rubellius Geminus, and in 31 Seianus himself.[1] This paucity gives way in the last years to a sudden increase: L. Vitellius in 34, the energetic C. Cestius Gallus in 35, Sex. Papinius Allenius in 36 and Cn. Acerronius Proculus in 37. Of these Vitellius is the most interesting. Father of the emperor, he was consul for a second and third time under Claudius, with whom he held the censorship. Of his brothers, Aulus was suffect consul in 32 but died in his consulship, Publius, the friend of Germanicus, was involved in the fall of Seianus, and Quintus had been removed from the senate in 17. His sister was married to A. Plautius, suffect consul in 29, brother-in-law of P. Petronius, suffect consul in 19, and possibly brother of Q. Plautius, consul in 36. The Vitellii at this time are an excellent example of a family growing in influence and distinction despite some major reverses. Nothing is known of Acerronius, but later an Acerronia, perhaps his daughter, is recorded as a friend of the younger Agrippina. His colleague, C. Petronius Pontius Nigrinus, was perhaps the adopted son of C. Petronius, suffect consul in 25.

The Fasti suggest that under Tiberius the practice of appointing

---

[1] These statistics underline just how striking a step Seianus' elevation to the consulship was.

suffect consuls was not abused in a way that might cheapen the office.[1] No more than two suffects are recorded for any year, except under 18 and 31, when Tiberius himself was consul and resigned after only a brief tenure. The republican noble families are again represented: two Junii Silani in 15 and 28, the unsavoury Mam. Scaurus in 21, in 24 P. Cornelius Lentulus Scipio, reaping a rapid reward for his services against Tacfarinas, with perhaps another P. Lentulus in 27, C. Cassius Longinus in 30, succeeding his brother Lucius, and Faustus Cornelius Sulla in 31, two years before his brother Lucius was *ordinarius*. Whether P. Gabinius Secundus in 35 and M. Porcius Cato in 36 were descended from republican bearers of their names is uncertain. Members of the new consular families are rarer: M. Cocceius Nerva, grandfather of the emperor, by 24, in 26 Q. Junius Blaesus, son of Seianus' uncle, and L. Antistius Vetus, brother of Gaius, *ordinarius* in 23, in 27 C. Sallustius Passienus Crispus, son of L. Passienus Rufus, consul in 4 B.C., and adopted son of Sallustius Crispus, in 29 A. Plautius and L. Nonius Asprenas. All through the reign the suffect consulship was used to give new men their chance, with a great upsurge in the years after Seianus' fall. Most are mere names, but some stand out: in 18 Livineius Regulus, who dared to defend Cn. Piso, and C. Rubellius Blandus, in 31 the notorious L. Fulcinius Trio and his distinguished opponent P. Memmius Regulus, in 33 L. Salvius Otho, father of the emperor, in 34 Q. Marcius Barea Soranus, father of the Stoic philosopher executed under Nero, and above all in 35 D. Valerius Asiaticus from Vienna in Gaul, consul for a second time in 46 before falling victim to the intrigues of Messallina. At this time he was a friend of L. Vitellius and like him cultivated Antonia.

What brought the unknowns their success we cannot tell. Perhaps before 31 it was the favour of Seianus, but it is worth emphasizing that no consul is recorded, whether *ordinarius* or suffect, who to the best of our knowledge owed his elevation entirely to his friendship with Seianus. Friends and relatives of the prefect appear, but with claims of their own. L. Seius Tubero, suffect in 18, was Seianus' adoptive brother, but he was also a close friend of the princeps in his own right

---

[1] On the other hand Dio 58.20.1ff. accuses Tiberius of wildly capricious behaviour where the consulship was concerned, but there is nothing to support his assertions.

and had served under Germanicus, with whom he shared office after Tiberius' resignation of it. The career of the elder Blaesus too had been such that his son might expect advancement regardless of the family connection with Seianus. Fulcinius Trio had received the promise of support from Tiberius himself before Seianus had attained any great degree of power. The trial of Titius Sabinus in 28 is instructive in this context. Four men joined in the prosecution because they wanted the consulship, to which, says Tacitus, there was no access except through Seianus.[1] Yet as far as is known only one, M. Porcius Cato, ever reached his goal – and he was suffect in 36, by which time his services to Seianus had presumably, happily for him, been forgotten.

Tacitus' chronicle of senatorial business affords abundant confirmation of Tiberius' desire that the senate should perform its functions without constantly waiting upon his own opinion. In 15 a serious outbreak of rioting at a theatre inspired a motion in the senate that actors should be subject to flogging, from which a decision of Augustus had rendered them immune. The tribune D. Haterius Agrippa vetoed and was violently attacked by Asinius Gallus. Tiberius sat silent, allowing the debate to take its course, and Haterius' veto stood, though other regulations were introduced to preserve the peace at theatrical performances.[2] The senate was similarly allowed complete freedom when measures to prevent the flooding of the Tiber were debated in the same year.[3] In 16 a vigorous discussion took place on proposed sumptuary laws.[4] The principal advocates of stricter control, Q. Haterius and Octavius Fronto, were eloquently and subtly opposed by Asinius Gallus, who carried the day. Tiberius took no part in the controversy except to add a brief word in support of Gallus.

But however much Tiberius tried to be impartial and to force responsibility upon the senate, the senate's inclination to servility still found expression. In 16 Tiberius announced that he was about to leave the city, and so it was asked – and the question itself is significant of the

---

[1] Tac. *Ann.* 4.68, cf. Juv. 10.91ff.
[2] Tac. *Ann.* 1.77.
[3] Tac. *Ann.* 1.79.
[4] Tac. *Ann.* 2.33.

senate's temper – whether all business should be postponed until his return.[1] Cn. Piso proposed that the senate should meet as usual, saying that it would be a credit to the state if the senate and the equestrian order proved capable of performing their duties even in the absence of the princeps. Asinius Gallus spoke for postponement on the ground that any matters discussed in Tiberius' absence would thereby be made to appear trivial. No doubt Tiberius was entirely in agreement with Piso, but ironically, in the interests of free debate, he felt it incumbent on him not to intervene. So he sat in silence through a vehement discussion and allowed the eventual vote for postponement to pass unchallenged. A similar incident occurred in 17.[2] A praetor, Vipstanus Gallus, had died and a dispute arose over the appointment of his successor. Germanicus and Drusus, who were both in Rome, joined in supporting Haterius Agrippa, who was related to both Germanicus and Agrippina, but many voices were raised in defence of the law, which laid down that candidates with three children should be given preference. In trying to bend the law in the interests of their friend the princes were doing no more than any noble might have done in the days of the republic, and Tiberius again took no part in the debate, delighted to see the senate make a serious effort to decide between the authority of his sons and the letter of the law. But once more servility won the day and Haterius was appointed, though only after a long debate and by a small majority.

Tiberius' position was in fact such that a show of neutrality on his part was simply not enough to secure a genuine freedom of decision. The lesson of the trials of Libo and others, where the princeps' scrupulous impartiality was damaging to the defendant, is underlined by an incident in 20.[3] In that year D. Junius Silanus was allowed to return to Rome, largely in response to the pleas of his brother Marcus, suffect consul in 15. Silanus had gone into voluntary exile after Augustus had formally renounced his friendship because of his adultery with the princeps' granddaughter, Julia. Now, when M. Silanus made a speech of thanks, Tiberius replied that he too was glad that Decimus had

[1] Tac. *Ann.* 2.35.
[2] Tac. *Ann.* 2.51.
[3] Tac. *Ann.* 3.24.

returned after so long a stay abroad, as he had every right to do, since no law or decree of the senate had ordered him to leave.[1] But for himself, he added, Augustus' renunciation of Silanus' friendship still held good. Thereafter D. Silanus lived in Rome, but attained no office.[2] When such a declaration of private enmity by the princeps could without question end a man's career in this fashion, it was clearly vain for Tiberius to keep up the pretence that the princeps was just another senator like all the rest.

The senate equally let pass no chance to shirk responsibility. Not long after Tiberius had left Rome for Campania at the beginning of 21, the province of Africa was troubled, not for the first time, by the nomad leader Tacfarinas. The princeps wrote to the senate, which still appointed the governors of Africa and Asia, instructing it to select for Africa a man physically strong and experienced in war.[3] Sex. Pompeius made this the occasion for a savage attack on M'. Lepidus, whom he dismissed as unfit even to govern the peaceful province of Asia. The senate at large took a more favourable view of Lepidus' character, and so he was duly appointed to Asia. But despite his attempt to force the senate to exercise its rights, a decree was passed asking Tiberius to choose a governor for Africa. At the next meeting of the senate his reply was read.[4] Albeit indirectly, he criticized the senators for trying to throw the burden of all decisions on the princeps and refused to allow them to evade all responsibility, ordering them to choose between two men, M. Lepidus and Q. Blaesus. Lepidus professed a great reluctance for the post, urging his health, the age of his children and the need to find a husband for his daughter. He did not mention what was uppermost in men's minds, that Blaesus was Seianus' uncle. For form's sake Blaesus too protested his reluctance, but with less conviction, and so attained the post. Yet it should not be too easily assumed that Tiberius had given the senate no real freedom of choice. He was no doubt happy at the advancement of a relative of his favourite, but both Blaesus and Lepidus were competent men, and Tiberius

[1] But it would have been as impossible for Silanus to return without permission as it had been for Tiberius himself on Rhodes.

[2] Tac. *Ann.* 3.24: *fuit posthac in urbe neque honores adeptus est.*

[3] Tac. *Ann.* 3.32; for M'. Lepidus in Asia, cf. Tac. *Ann.* 4.56.

[4] Tac. *Ann.* 3.35.

might not have been unduly annoyed if the senate had had the courage to appoint Lepidus.

In 22 the question of the sumptuary laws arose again.[1] The senate, perhaps mindful of Tiberius' earlier promise that he would take action should it ever prove necessary,[2] at once referred the matter to him without making any recommendation. Tiberius complimented the aediles who had raised the matter on their devotion to duty, but pointed out firmly that such things were not really his concern. He was not an aedile, a praetor or a consul; the princeps had to deal with more exalted affairs. It was his task, he reminded the senate in his closing words, to hold the empire together and ensure that the provinces supplied the many needs of Italy, despite the daily dangers of wind and weather; if he failed in this, the state would fall to ruin. If any magistrate was energetic and severe enough to deal with the problem, he would thank him for relieving him of a part of his burden, but if all that the instigators of the debate wanted to do was to stir up trouble and then leave it for him to settle, he would point out to them that he too had no love of quarrels, of which he had to bear sufficient for the sake of the state not to want to be involved in new ones that benefited nobody. The senate promptly shelved responsibility again by referring the matter back to the aediles. It was to act in the same way a little later in the year, when embassies from various provincial cities came to Rome to defend the right of their temples to grant asylum.[3] The claimants were numerous, their arguments involved, and the senate, quickly tiring of its task, entrusted all disputed cases to the consuls.

Small wonder that every time he left the senate Tiberius is said to have muttered in Greek 'O men fit for slavery!'[4]

Nor was it easy for Tiberius to maintain the appearance of republican freedom in his dealings with individual senators. He might ask the pardon of Q. Haterius, as one senator to another, for disagreeing with him rather vehemently in the senate,[5] but this same Haterius had

---

[1] Tac. *Ann.* 3.52–55; cf. below, p. 141.
[2] Tac. *Ann.* 2.33.
[3] Tac. *Ann.* 3.63; such a matter could admittedly best be dealt with by a small committee.
[4] Tac. *Ann.* 3.65.
[5] Suet. *Tib.* 29.

fallen on his knees before Tiberius to beg forgiveness for his impudent remarks in the accession debate, and had almost been killed by the princeps' bodyguard when Tiberius, jumping back to prevent this unseemly exhibition, had tripped and fallen.[1] Tiberius treated the consuls with such honour that he always rose to receive them in public and made way for them in the street, but envoys from Africa referred, as was proper, to the consuls, complained that they had been sent to the princeps and were being prevented from fulfilling their mission.[2] Not only provincials but provincial governors too had to be rebuked, for failing to send their reports to the senate and for referring the award of decorations to Tiberius.[3]

Even the princeps' own family did not make his task easy. In 16 L. Calpurnius Piso the augur, brother of Gnaeus, delivered a violent attack on the corruption of the courts and the savagery of the delators and announced his intention of abandoning public life and retiring to some distant rural retreat. Tiberius, deeply upset, begged him to stay and roused his relations to exert all their influence. Piso stayed, but a little later clashed with Livia by bringing an action against Urgulania, a woman who thought that her friendship with the princeps' mother placed her above the law. Urgulania ignored the summons and went instead to Tiberius. Piso followed and insisted on taking her to court. At this Livia, who plainly shared Urgulania's opinion,[4] complained that her dignity was being spurned. Tiberius, certain that Piso was in the right, made only one concession to his mother, promising to appear in person before the court in support of Urgulania. But on his way he stopped repeatedly to talk with friends, deliberately taking as long as he could. This tactic proved effective; by the time he arrived at the court, Livia had ordered the sum at stake to be paid. Both Tiberius and Piso gained credit by their actions, but Urgulania did not learn her lesson. She was later cited as a witness in a case that was being tried before the senate. She refused to appear, and so a

---

[1] Tac. *Ann.* 1.13, Suet. *Tib.* 27.

[2] Suet. *Tib.* 31.2, cf. Dio 57.11.3 for Tiberius and the consuls.

[3] Suet. *Tib.* 32.1. The specific incident from which Suetonius is probably generalizing involved L. Apronius, governor of Africa in 20 during the war with Tacfarinas (Tac. *Ann.* 3.21); Gell. 5.6.14 presumably refers to the same occasion.

[4] Cf. in general Dio 57.12.

praetor was sent to her home to take her deposition, even though in the past, as Tacitus remarks, even Vestal Virgins had testified in public.[1]

Tacitus praises Tiberius for his liberality in cases where there was just cause and concedes that he still manifested this virtue even when he had put aside all others.[2] Senators were more than once the beneficiaries. In 15 a senator, Aurelius Pius, complained that his house had been damaged by the building of a road and an aqueduct and asked for compensation from the senate. The praetors in charge of the treasury resisted, for Aurelius had no legal claim and financial reserves had fallen dangerously low during the last years of Augustus. Tiberius appreciated their argument, but recognized the justice of Aurelius' claim, and so paid for the damage himself. When a former praetor, Propertius Celer, begged leave to resign from the senate because of his poverty, Tiberius made him a gift of 1,000,000 sesterces – the minimum senatorial census established by Augustus – once he had ascertained that Propertius' financial straits were a heritage from his father and not the result of his own profligacy. When other similar requests were made, he instructed the senate to investigate the circumstances. This strictness was looked upon with disfavour, and there were some who preferred to endure their poverty in silence rather than to submit to public humiliation.[3] It is clear that Tiberius had no intention of keeping wastrels at his own or the state's expense; he went so far as to expel from the senate some who could produce no adequate explanation of their lack of funds. The sum vouchsafed to Propertius Celer reveals his outlook; he had made it possible for Propertius to maintain himself as a senator provided that he exerted himself in the future and did not let matters slide in the hope of further charity.

That this was the principle on which Tiberius worked receives detailed confirmation in a much more famous case which came before

[1] Tac. *Ann.* 2.34.
[2] Tac. *Ann.* 1.75.
[3] Tac. *Ann.* 1.75, Suet. *Tib.* 47, Dio 57.10.3f., Sen. *Ben.* 2.8.1; a list of those expelled or allowed to retire from the senate by Tiberius because their poverty was of their own making is given in Tac. *Ann.* 2.48 (for Q. Vitellius, cf. Suet. *Vit.* 2.2). Tiberius' principles, though overlaid with flattery, are still discernible in the wording of Vell. 2.129.3.

the senate in 16.[1] The protagonist was M. Hortensius Hortalus, grandson of Q. Hortensius, the famous orator of the Ciceronian age. He had already received a grant of the senatorial census from Augustus, to enable him to marry and raise a family and so prevent the extinction of so distinguished a line. Now, when the senate was in session in the Palatine library, where a likeness of the great Hortensius was displayed among those of other famous orators of the past, Hortalus lined up his four children at the door and appealed for more money. It was not of his own will, he said, that he had had a family, but only at the request of Augustus reinforced by his piety towards his ancestors. Had he not obeyed, he would have had enough for his own modest needs and would have been a burden to no one. The implication of his speech was plain: Augustus had landed him in difficulties and so Augustus' successor owed him a living. The senate was sympathetic, and its attitude stirred Tiberius to make his position clear. If every pauper in Rome came begging money for his children, the state, he said, would soon be bankrupt. Hortensius' action was not an appeal but a shameless demand that was entirely out of place, since the meeting had been convened to discuss other matters, an attempt to exploit the delicacy of the senate and to force the princeps to draw from the treasury in order not to appear mean. When Augustus had made his gift he had not been under pressure of this sort, and he had not intended that the donation should be repeated whenever Hortalus wished. He himself was not prepared to tolerate a state of affairs in which men did nothing to help themselves and lived in carefree idleness as a burden to the state. His sternness and the violence of his language shocked the senate – as they clearly did Tacitus too – and after a short pause Tiberius announced that he had made his answer to Hortalus but that, if the senate thought it proper, he would grant his sons 200,000 sesterces each, an offer which Hortalus received in silence.

It is perhaps not surprising that many preferred to be poor rather than run the risk of such devastating criticism. Seneca confirms what Hortalus' reaction suggests, that Tiberius' way of giving won him no friends. He tells the story of Marius Nepos, who fell into debt and

---

[1] Tac. *Ann.* 2.37f., Suet. *Tib.* 47; cf. Gelzer, *KS* I, 151f. (= *Nobility*, 159); Geiger, *CR* 84, 1970, 132ff.

appealed to the princeps. Tiberius ordered him to supply a list of his creditors, then wrote him a letter to announce that they had been paid, in which he admonished Nepos in an insulting fashion. By so doing he freed the man from his creditors, but did not bind him to himself.[1]

But despite his concern for the treasury Tiberius was not prepared to replenish it by dubious means. In 17 the property of Aemilia Musa, a rich woman who had died intestate, was claimed by the treasury; presumably no heirs on intestacy could be found. Instead Tiberius directed that it should go to M. Lepidus, whose wealth did not match his noble birth and strength of character, on the fictitious ground that Aemilia was a member of his family. He was scrupulous too in private financial matters. When named as part heir by a rich *eques*, Pantuleius, he ensured that the estate went to M. Servilius, who, he found, had been named as heir in an earlier will. In general he refused to accept legacies except from his friends, rejecting those that came from persons unknown to him or who wanted to defraud their natural heirs.[2] Another instance of his generosity occurred in 19, when Occia died after fifty-seven years as a Vestal. Fonteius Agrippa and Domitius Pollio both offered their daughters to replace her; Pollio's daughter was preferred because Agrippa had divorced his daughter's mother. Tiberius therefore granted Agrippa's daughter a dowry of 1,000,000 sesterces by way of consolation.[3]

2. THE EQUESTRIAN ORDER AND THE PEOPLE

Tiberius made no significant innovations in the part played by the *equites* in the running of the state. Careers in the army and as procurators in charge of provincial finance or the estates of the princeps and his family, and for the few the great equestrian prefectures – the corn supply, the *uigiles*, the guard and Egypt: these were as they had been under Augustus. But the term *equites* had always been ambiguous, for many criteria might be used as the occasion demanded: possession of

[1] Sen. *Ben.* 2.7.2. Nepos cannot have learned his lesson, since the incident presumably precedes his removal from the senate.
[2] Tac. *Ann.* 2.48.
[3] Tac. *Ann.* 2.86.

the equestrian census of 400,000 sesterces, membership of the equestrian decuries from which jurors were drawn, or possession of the privilege of sitting in the first fourteen rows at the theatre. This imprecision led to disputes as to what qualified a man to wear the gold ring, the distinguishing mark of the order. The problem came to a head in 22, when the consul C. Sulpicius Galba introduced measures directed against the keepers of food-shops. Some tried to protect themselves by claiming equestrian status. As a result the situation was clarified once and for all and the following rules were laid down. To be entitled to wear the gold ring a man must be of free birth himself and likewise his father and grandfather before him, he must possess the equestrian census and be eligible for a seat in the fourteen rows.[1] The emphasis placed on free birth in an attempt to protect the dignity of the order from being cheapened by the influx of a multitude of wealthy freedmen is characteristic of Tiberius' respect for tradition.

In his dealing with the people Tiberius was at a great disadvantage compared with Augustus. He cared nothing for their affection, provided that he retained their respect.[2] Their favourite amusements were of no interest to him and he could not or would not pretend the contrary. Unlike his son,[3] he did not enjoy gladiatorial shows, and Suetonius records that he limited the number of bouts that might be put on.[4] The theatre had caused trouble immediately after the death of Augustus, when at the newly founded *ludi Augustales* one of the actors struck for higher pay. Riots broke out in support of his demand and the tribunes were forced to summon the senate and request authority to spend more than their allowance.[5] Tiberius did not feel that his position was sufficiently secure to suppress an entertainment that habit had led the people to regard as a right. Indeed, during the early years of the reign he forced himself to appear at theatrical shows, largely in the hope that his presence might act as a restraining influence.[6] Even when

---

[1] Plin. *NH* 33.32; cf. Henderson, *JRS* 53, 1963, 67ff.
[2] Already under Augustus he had coined his famous election slogan (Suet. *Tib.* 59.2): *oderint dum probent* (let them hate me, so long as they respect me).
[3] Tac. *Ann.* 1.76, cf. Dio 57.13.1.
[4] Suet. *Tib.* 34.1.
[5] Tac. *Ann.* 1.54, Dio 56.47.2.
[6] Tac. *Ann.* 1.54, Dio 57.11.5.

serious riots occurred in 15, in which not only spectators lost their lives but also soldiers, including a centurion, and a tribune of the praetorian guard was wounded while attempting to restore order, Tiberius allowed Haterius Agrippa to veto the motion put to the senate by the praetors, that actors should be rendered liable to flogging, because Augustus had declared them immune. Pay restrictions were, however, introduced and various decrees passed to keep spectators in check. No senator was to enter an actor's house, no *eques* was to accompany an actor in public, private theatrical performances were banned and misconduct by spectators was made punishable by exile.[1] The princeps' attitude did not change over the years, and finally in 23, when grief at Drusus' death had made him even less concerned about public opinion than before, he raised the subject again in the senate.[2] This time actors were banished from Italy, not to be recalled, despite popular clamour, until the reign of Gaius. When the people of Pollentia would not let a centurion's funeral procession leave the forum until his heirs disbursed money to provide for gladiatorial games, Tiberius sent an urban cohort and a cohort from the Cottian Alps to restore order and imprisoned the ringleaders of the disturbance.[3]

Though these superficial matters caught the people's attention and resulted in unpopularity for Tiberius, where the public welfare was genuinely at stake he showed an alert concern. In 15 flooding of the Tiber did serious damage. A new board of five curators of the banks and bed of the Tiber under L. Arruntius was appointed to share the task of dealing with the problem with the existing curators of the water-supply under the great jurist C. Ateius Capito.[4] The boards devised elaborate plans for diverting and damming the rivers and lakes that fed the Tiber. Unfortunately the towns affected protested vigorously on economic, sentimental and religious grounds, and the senate, moved either by these arguments or by the magnitude of the engineering problems involved, used its freedom to vote that no interference with the course of nature should be attempted.[5]

[1] Tac. *Ann.* 1.77, Suet. *Tib.* 34.1.
[2] Tac. *Ann.* 4.14, Suet. *Tib.* 37.2, Dio 57.21.3.
[3] Suet. *Tib.* 37.3.
[4] Tac. *Ann.* 1.76, Dio 57.14.7f.
[5] Tac. *Ann.* 1.79.

Most important of all was the corn supply, for which Tiberius asserted his constant care in 22, in his reply to the sumptuary proposals of C. Bibulus.[1] He had given tangible proof of this concern in 19, when high prices provoked complaints among the people.[2] He had of course already had experience in this field in a subordinate position in his youth.[3] Now he intervened to fix a retail price that the public could afford to pay, and in order that the dealers should not suffer loss in consequence agreed to make up to them the difference between the controlled price and that previously current. This action was joyfully received, and suggests that Tacitus is doing Tiberius justice when he remarks in his summary of the 'good years' that, although the people suffered from the high price of corn, the princeps was wholly blameless in this, for he did all that could be done by hard work and liberal spending to counteract the effects of bad harvests and losses at sea.[4]

But another sphere in which Tiberius made a bad impression when comparisons were made between him and his predecessor was that of public building.[5] Suetonius says roundly that he undertook no works of note, leaving even the two buildings on which operations were started, a temple of Augustus and the restoration of the theatre of Pompey, uncompleted at his death; according to Tacitus, they were finished but not dedicated.[6] A magnificent building programme was expected of the princeps, but was at this time, thanks to the activities of Augustus, quite unnecessary, and, as in the matter of circuses, Tiberius considered the good of the treasury more than his personal popularity.[7] He did, however, as Tacitus and Dio record, complete such buildings as had been left unfinished by Augustus and also repaired others that had grown dilapidated with age or been damaged by fire.[8] These included a temple to Liber, Libera and Ceres dating from the middle of the third

---

[1] Tac. *Ann.* 3.54.
[2] Tac. *Ann.* 2.87.
[3] Suet. *Tib.* 8, Vell. 2.94.1; cf. above, p. 15.
[4] Tac. *Ann.* 4.6, cf. 6.13.
[5] For Augustus, cf. *RG* 19–21.1.
[6] Tac. *Ann.* 6.45, Suet. *Tib.* 47, *Cal.* 21; for adornments in the temple of Augustus, cf. Suet. *Tib.* 74, Plin. *NH* 35.28, 131.
[7] The treasury contained 27,000,000 sesterces at his death (Suet. *Cal.* 37.3).
[8] Tac. *Ann.* 2.49, Dio 57.10.

century, a temple of Flora of similar date, and the temple of Janus commemorating the first Roman naval victory over Carthage in 260. A temple of Spes from the same war, which had been destroyed by fire for the second time in 31, was rebuilt and consecrated by Germanicus. Tiberius did not affix his own name to any of these buildings; only those of the original builders appeared. This emphasis on the maintenance and revival of tradition in preference to self-advertisement is entirely characteristic, but Tiberius' attitude was beyond the comprehension of the naïvely enthusiastic Velleius, who celebrates the number of buildings erected by the princeps both in his own name and on behalf of the members of his family.[1]

In the field of social legislation Tiberius seems to have been chiefly moved by a desire to preserve the traditional dignity of the higher orders in the state. Suetonius cites a number of cases which reveal this motive.[2] Among those against whom the princeps took action were married women of respectable station who had registered as prostitutes and young men of the senatorial and equestrian orders who tried to evade the decree of the senate that banned them from performing as actors or gladiators. Both groups of offenders were exiled. He also demoted a senator who resorted to fraud in the renting of a house and a quaestor who, in order to benefit from the preference given to married men, took a wife on the day before the allotment of posts and divorced her on the day after. Suetonius' category of married whores may represent a generalization from the case of Vistilia in 19.[3] This provoked a decree of the senate that no woman whose grandfather, father or husband had been or was of equestrian rank should be allowed to register as a prostitute. Women of the senatorial order were of course included *a fortiori*. Vistilia herself was from a praetorian family. She had resorted to this ingenious device to escape the usual penalties for adultery. Tacitus remarks that traditionally the shame attaching to such a step had been regarded as sufficient punishment, but Vistilia was exiled to the island of Seriphos.

[1] Vell. 2.130.1, though even he cites only the same two examples as Suetonius; for a possible reference to building activity by Drusus during his second consulate in 21, cf. Tac. *Ann.* 3.37, though *aedificationibus* may be corrupt.
[2] Suet. *Tib.* 35.
[3] Tac. *Ann.* 2.85.

Suetonius also credits the princeps with numerous sumptuary measures controlling meat prices, limiting the activities of food-shops and restaurants, and even forbidding altogether the sale of pastries.[1] That Tiberius was frugal by nature is true, but the Tacitean reports of debates in the senate suggest that his attitude to sumptuary questions was rather more fatalistic. In 16 Q. Haterius and Octavius Fronto passed motions forbidding the use of solid gold dishes at dinner and the wearing of silk by men, but when Fronto was encouraged by this success to demand restrictions on furniture, silverware and slaves, he was opposed by Asinius Gallus and heavily outvoted. Tiberius remarked that he had no wish to play the censor on this occasion, though he promised to step in if matters got really out of hand.[2] He made his position even clearer in 22, when the aediles, led by C. Calpurnius Bibulus, complained to the senate that sumptuary regulations were being ignored and that prices of luxury goods were rising daily. The senate, as always eager to avoid responsibility, especially in so invidious a matter, referred the complaint to Tiberius without making any recommendation. In his letter of reply the princeps explained that he thought legislation on such private matters would be futile and by creating new opportunities for delation would give rise to evils far worse than those it was intended to stamp out.[3]

It is noteworthy that where nothing important was at stake Tiberius was prepared to sanction laxity in the application of the laws, rather than encourage the delators. A similar problem had arisen in 20, when proposals were made to moderate the Augustan *lex Papia Poppaea*, which penalized celibacy.[4] It was argued that the law had failed in its object, the encouragement of marriage and consequent boosting of the birth-rate, while at the same time it caused tremendous hardship by opening up a large and fruitful field for the delators, to whom it offered rewards. Tiberius again placed social welfare above the letter of the law and provided for a commission of fifteen men (five consulars, five ex-praetors and five other senators) to prevent abuses. The situation

---

[1] Suet. *Tib.* 34.1.
[2] Tac. *Ann.* 2.33, Dio 57.15.1.
[3] Tac. *Ann.* 3.52-55; Dio 57.13.3f. probably refers to the same letter of Tiberius.
[4] Tac. *Ann.* 3.25, 28.

resembled that which bedevilled the law of *maiestas*: it was impractic-
able to repeal the law altogether, and so abuses could only be checked
as they arose in individual cases.

3. HONOURS AND TITLES

Tiberius' principal virtue was moderation,[1] and at the outset of his
reign and in subsequent years the servility of senate and people gave
him ample opportunity to exercise it. He refused to accept the title
Imperator as a *praenomen*, in the manner in which it had been used by
Augustus[2] – his position as supreme commander of Rome's armies was
clear beyond challenge without such advertisement. He also rejected
in 15 the title of *pater patriae*, which had been repeatedly offered him by
the people, and although the senate decreed that the oath to observe his
acts should be taken annually, Tiberius himself vetoed the proposal.[3]
Suetonius quotes the reason he gave: the senate should not bind itself
to honour any man's acts, because chance might bring about a change
in him. It was on this occasion that Tiberius gave a promise which was
to prove tragically ironical: 'I shall always be true to myself, nor shall I
ever change my ways, as long as I am of sound mind.'[4] If the senate
ever came to doubt his devotion, he said, the title of *pater patriae*
would not lessen his shame; it would merely serve to condemn the
senators, whether of rashness in conferring the honour upon him or of
inconsistency because they had now changed their minds.[5] By contrast
Tiberius insisted that an oath to observe the acts of Augustus should be
taken by everyone, and took it himself with some degree of ostentation,

[1] Cf. in general Suet. *Tib.* 26–32, Dio 57.7–12. For the celebration of *moderatio* on
the imperial coinage, cf. Rogers, *Studies*, 6off.; Sutherland, *Coinage*, 97f.
[2] Suet. *Tib.* 26.2, Dio 57.8.1. For unofficial usage and provincial errors, cf. *ILS*
152, 8786, 8787 (= *EJ* 93), *CIL* VIII 685, *IG* IV² 599, VII 195, XII 2.205, 206,
539, 3.517, 1116, *SEG* I 286, *IGRR* III 845, *SIG³* 791B, 792, *EJ* 94, 102, 290, 291,
343a, 345; Grant, *Aspects*, 43, 47. For Augustus, cf. Syme, *Historia* 7, 1958, 172ff.
[3] Tac. *Ann.* 1.72, Suet. *Tib.* 26.2, 67.3, Dio 57.8.1, 4. An annual oath of allegiance
was, however, taken later, cf. Dio 58.17.2f. For the absence of *pater patriae* from
Roman coins, cf. Grant, *Aspects*, 43f. The law of Gytheum (*EJ* 102) gives Tiberius
this title as well as the *praenomen imperatoris*.
[4] Suet. *Tib.* 67.3.
[5] Suet. *Tib.* 67.4.

not on New Year's Day when others did, but separately at a later date.[1] In 25 he expelled Apidius Merula from the senate for failing to take the oath.[2] The title of *pater patriae* was offered him again in 19, on the occasion of his intervention to reduce the price of corn; in the decree his occupations were described as divine and he himself was addressed as master. Tiberius protested at the insult, proclaiming that he was master only to his slaves, *imperator* to the armies and princeps to the rest.[3]

His attitude to the name of Augustus was more complex. Dio states that he never allowed it to be voted to him, but did not object to its use by others and used it himself when writing to foreign kings.[4] This might suggest that Augustus was not a part of Tiberius' usual titulature, but such was clearly never the case. Tiberius repeatedly appears on the coinage as TI. CAESAR AVGVSTVS and TI. CAESAR DIVI AVG. F. AVGVSTVS – Tiberius Caesar Augustus, son of the deified Augustus – and these are also standard forms of the name on official as well as unofficial inscriptions.[5] Whatever Tiberius' personal preference and private usage may have been, he must at least have acquiesced in the public use of the title not only throughout the empire but in Rome itself.

To preserve moderation in the matter of honours was not easy. In their eagerness to demonstrate their loyal enthusiasm, distant communities did not stop to consider the complex feelings of the princeps and heaped upon him titles he had already rejected, while the senate's obsequiousness extended into this field too. The most striking example came in 21, when Tiberius in Campania expressed his intention of going to Gaul to supervise the restoration of order after the revolt of Florus and Sacrovir. Not only did the senate vote prayers and supplications for his safe return, which was reasonable; P. Cornelius

---

[1] Dio 57.8.5.
[2] Tac. *Ann.* 4.42.
[3] Tac. *Ann.* 2.87, Suet. *Tib.* 27, Dio 57.8.2.
[4] Dio 57.8.1f., cf. Suet. *Tib.* 26.2; the literal truth of the statements in the sources is defended by Scott, *CP* 27, 1932, 43ff.
[5] Cf. e.g. *ILS* 113, 159, 938, 940, 943, 944, 1514, 2267, 2280, 2281, 2688, 2690, 2691, 3783, 5516, 5829, 5829a, 6080, 6286, 9483 (= *EJ* 82, 85, 208, 210, 212, 213, 158, 256, 265, 267, 246, 245, 228, 215, 348, 292, 293, 133, 229, 209); *EJ* 49–52, 83, 84, 86, 87, 123, 126, 130, 132, 134, 137, 144, 148, 153, 154, 209a, 209c, 216, 218a, 225, 226, 269, 284, 291, 318, 344, 347a; Grant, *Aspects*, 41ff.

Dolabella actually proposed that he should celebrate an ovation on his return from Campania. Tiberius' reply was coldly disdainful. He was not, he said, so desperate for glory, after winning or refusing so many triumphs in his youth, as to crave in his old age an empty reward for a peregrination of the suburbs.[1] A similar display of savage wit had greeted the proposal that the months of September and October should be renamed Tiberius and Livius. 'What,' Tiberius caustically enquired, 'will you do if you have thirteen Caesars?'[2]

4. RELIGION

Both Tiberius and the leading members of his family figured prominently in the cult of Augustus: the new college of *sodales Augustales* comprised twenty-one leading senators chosen by lot, together with Tiberius, Drusus, Germanicus and Claudius.[3] In the provinces too the worship of Augustus was actively encouraged. In 15 permission was granted to Tarraco in Spain to build a temple to the dead princeps, and this served as an example to the other provinces.[4] One case suggests that observance of the cult, once established, might be enforced, for in 25 Cyzicus lost the freedom it had earned by its services in the Mithridatic War, because the shrine of Augustus that the city had begun to build had not been completed and Roman citizens had been imprisoned.[5]

But Tiberius was scrupulous in the matter of divine honours for himself, refusing temples, priests and statues at Rome.[6] Even in Italy, however, his refusals were not always effective. Decrees of the year 18 are preserved from Forum Clodii in Etruria, providing for sacrifices on Tiberius' birthday as well as on those of Augustus and Livia, and for the dedication of statues to Augustus, Tiberius and Livia. A priest of

---

[1] Tac. *Ann.* 3.47.
[2] Suet. *Tib.* 26.2, Dio 57.18.2 (who appears to have said that the name *Tiberius* was to be given to November, the month in which the princeps' birthday fell).
[3] Tac. *Ann.* 1.54, Suet. *Claud.* 6.2; cf. Taylor, *Divinity*, 230. As Taylor remarks (*Divinity*, 231), the attempts of the delators to exploit Augustus' divinity as a source of charges of *maiestas* presuppose Tiberius' interest in the cult.
[4] Tac. *Ann.* 1.78; cf. Taylor, *Divinity*, 281, who suggests that *ILS* 6964 (= *EJ* 105) may refer to a temple of Augustus at Narbo built on the Spanish example.
[5] Tac. *Ann.* 4.36, Suet. *Tib.* 37.3, Dio 57.24.6 (more precise).
[6] Suet. *Tib.* 26.1, Dio 57.9.1f.; cf. Taylor, *TAPA* 60, 1929, 87ff.

Augustus and Tiberius is recorded at Asculum and a priest of Tiberius at Venusia. Statues of Tiberius and Livia were also dedicated at Cumae.[1] Of the western provinces Gaul is the most prolific in dedications. Already in the lifetime of Augustus Tiberius was included in the imperial cult at Lugdunum, and his safe arrival was celebrated at Bagacum Nerviorum. At Vienna there was an altar to Augustus and Tiberius, while Tiberius was linked with Jupiter in Aquitania and perhaps at the altar of the *nautae Parisiaci*. A dedication from Nasicum in Belgica honours not only Tiberius himself but also the 'divine house'.[2] The strategeion at Cyrene had been restored and rededicated to Tiberius between 4 and 14, while from his principate dedications have been found in Africa at Thugga and Mograwa, the latter coupling Tiberius with Rome.[3] In the East the harvest is predictably richer. A Pergamene monument in front of the Stoa of Attalus at Athens was rededicated to Tiberius early in the reign, and numerous inscriptions from Greece and Asia Minor honour him as a god.[4] At Nysa a priest of Tiberius is attested as early as 1 B.C. He also had a priest and an altar at Thera, a priest and temple at Lapethus in Cyprus, and priests at Corinth, Pergamum, Sardis and Iconium.[5]

Divine honours were also paid to other members of the imperial family. Livia appears at Athens as Pronoia and Boulaea, as Vesta and the new Demeter at Lampsacus, where there was a priest of the Augusti, as Diana Pacilucifera at Corinth, as Ceres at Gaulus, and as mother of the world in Spain. She had priests or priestesses also at Atina, Salonae and Vasio, and at Olisipo, where she shared a priest with Germanicus.[6] Germanicus and Agrippina were deified at Mytilene, while Germanicus and Drusus were associated with the

---

[1] *ILS* 154 (= *EJ* 101), 6565, *CIL* IX 6415, *ILS* 6481, *AE* 1927.158.

[2] *CIL* XIII 1769, *ILS* 8898 (= *EJ* 44), *CIL* XII 1844, *EJ* 132, *ILS* 4613d (= *EJ* 341), *EJ* 137. Also a private dedication from Martigues (*AE* 1906.144).

[3] Cf. Polacco, *Volto*, 49ff.; *EJ* 345, *CIL* VIII 685 = 11912.

[4] *Hesperia* 28, 1959, 86ff., *IG* III 455 (Athens: doubtful), VII 195 (Pagae), XII 1.772a (Lindos: doubtful), 2.205 (Mytilene), 3.1058 (Pholegandros), 1116 (Melos), *AE* 1934.89 (Cos), *EJ* 88 (Myra), 115(b) (Ammochostus: doubtful), 352 (Cyzicus).

[5] Cf. Magie, *Roman Rule*, 1297; *IG* XII 3.339, 471, 517, *OGIS* 583 (= *EJ* 134), *Corinth* VIII 2.77, *AM* 32, 1907, 321 (before 4), *Sardis* VII 1.47, *IGRR* III 1473.

[6] *IG* III 461, *EJ* 89, 128, 129, 130, *ILS* 121 (= *EJ* 126), *EJ* 123, 124, *ILS* 9390, 7160 (= *EJ* 347), 6991, 6896 (= *EJ* 131).

worship of Rome and Augustus at Nemausus and shared a posthumous cult in Lycia.[1] At Athens Drusus was the new Ares, and his wife Livia Julia was Aphrodite Anchisias at Troy; their twin sons shared a priest with Tiberius himself at Ammochostus in Cyprus.[2]

Where private individuals and even communities acted on their own initiative, there was little Tiberius could do. To criticize or suppress demonstrations of loyalty would only give rise to puzzled disappointment if not disaffection. His personal pronouncements, however, are always consistent. The first came not long after his accession, perhaps in early summer 15, in response to a law of Gytheum, the port of Sparta.[3] The Gytheates had decided to erect three statues, of Augustus, Livia and Tiberius himself, and to institute a six-day festival, the first day to be sacred to Augustus, the second to Tiberius, the third to Livia as the Tyche of the people and city of Gytheum, the fourth to the Nike of Germanicus, the fifth to the Aphrodite of Drusus and the last to T. Quinctius Flamininus, still revered for his part in the liberation of Greece from Macedonian domination in the early second century. Tiberius' reply was courteous. He thanked the people of Gytheum for their piety towards his father and the honour they intended to himself, but made it known to all men and to Gytheum in particular that divine honours should in his view be reserved for Augustus, who had conferred such great benefits upon the entire world. For himself more modest honours on a mortal scale would suffice. Livia, he added, would make her own answer when she had heard the details of the honours proposed for her.

Nevertheless, in 23 a request came from Asia for leave to build a temple to Tiberius, Livia and the senate as a token of gratitude for the punishment of two oppressors, the governor C. Junius Silanus in 22 and the princeps' procurator Lucilius Capito in 23.[4] Permission was

[1] *ILS* 8788 (= *EJ* 95), *IG* XII 2.208, 213b, 258, *CIL* XII 3180, 3207, *IGRR* III 680. Cf. also *EJ* 130a.

[2] *EJ* 136, *ILS* 8787 (= *EJ* 93), *EJ* 115(b).

[3] *EJ* 102. If the inscription is correctly restored, Tiberius' reply belongs to his sixteenth year of tribunician power – July 14 to July 15 – at a time when he was already *pontifex maximus*, i.e. after 10 March, 15.

[4] Tac. *Ann.* 4.15, cf. 3.66–69. The dispute as to where the temple should be located was still going on in 26, cf. Tac. *Ann.* 4.55f.

given, and this precedent encouraged Hispania Ulterior to send envoys
to the senate in 25 to beg leave to erect a temple to Tiberius and Livia
only.[1] Tiberius decided that the time had come to make his position
fully clear. He realized, he said, that consistency might seem to demand
that he grant to others the licence already conceded to Asia. But Asia
had been a special case. Augustus had allowed the building of a temple
to Rome and himself at Pergamum, and for him every utterance or
action of Augustus had the force of law. The cogency of this precedent
had been reinforced by the fact that in the case of Asia the senate had
had a share in the honour. But if such adulation were to become com-
monplace throughout the empire, the glory of Augustus would be
cheapened by imitation. He himself, Tiberius went on, was a mortal
man, content to perform the duties of a man and satisfied if he could
fulfil his function as princeps in a manner worthy of his forebears:
thoughtful for the commonwealth, constant in dangers, and fearless of
unpopularity incurred for the public good. The only temples and
images he craved were in the minds of men, and he ended with a
solemn prayer that his name and deeds might be remembered with
praise and that the gods might grant him till the end of his life peace of
mind and a knowledge of right, human and divine. The words strike
an ominous note. Tiberius had already been deprived too often of the
peace of mind he had so long desired, and by this time the forces were
already at work that were systematically to undermine it until his grasp
of human and divine justice became first capricious and intermittent
and then utterly warped. It is striking too that his hearers had grown so
accustomed to assuming that Tiberius was never telling the truth that
even this lucid and noble declaration was greeted with distrust. Some
accepted it as a proof of moderation, but others suspected a lack of
confidence, or even took it as evidence of a degenerate spirit, since
good men ought to hope for divine honours. In the face of such a total
lack of understanding it is hardly surprising that Tiberius, naturally
uncommunicative, became ever more taciturn and withdrawn with the
years.

Increasing apathy began to mark his attitude to divine honours both
abroad and at Rome. The flattery heaped on Seianus in 29 and 30

[1] Tac. *Ann.* 4.37f.

suggests that Tiberius had completely abandoned any attempt to stem the tide: the prefect's birthday was publicly celebrated, oaths were taken by his fortune as well as that of Tiberius and men sacrificed at his statues as they already did to those of Tiberius himself. It is true that to check this last practice Tiberius forbade yet again the offering of sacrifices to mortal men, but the prohibition doubtless proved just as ineffective then as it had before. It is noteworthy that after Seianus' fall the senate decreed that oaths should be taken in no man's name except that of Tiberius.[1]

In his general religious policy Tiberius was concerned first to enforce a respect for tradition[2] and secondly to keep religion in its proper place. In 22 the *flamen Dialis*, Ser. Cornelius Lentulus Maluginensis, put in a claim for the governorship of Asia, denying the validity of the rule that the high priest of Jupiter was not allowed to leave Italy.[3] He was opposed by Cn. Cornelius Lentulus Augur, and the dispute was referred to Tiberius as *pontifex maximus* (an office which the princeps had not assumed until 10 March, 15).[4] Maluginensis' plea was eventually rejected on the grounds that the rules established under Augustus permitted prolonged absence from duty only in the case of illness.[5] In the same year Livia was seriously ill. To celebrate her recovery the senate decreed games, to be presided over by the *pontifices*, the augurs, the *quindecimuiri*, the *septemuiri* and the *sodales Augustales*. L. Apronius proposed that the *fetiales* should also have a share in organizing the festivities, but Tiberius spoke against him, distinguishing the functions of the various colleges and citing precedents; the *fetiales*, he said, had never had such a right.[6] The death of Ser. Maluginensis in 23 created a problem.[7] The traditional method of appointing a successor required three candidates, all of them patricians

[1] Celebration of Seianus' birthday: Suet. *Tib.* 65.1, Dio 58.2.7; oaths: Dio 58.2.8, 6.2: worship of his image: Suet. *Tib.* 65.1, Dio 58.4.4, Juv. 10.62; Tiberius' ban on worship of mortals: Dio 58.8.4; decree of 31: Dio 58.12.6. For a dedication to Tiberius' *genius* in 27, cf. *ILS* 6080 (= *EJ* 133). Cf. Taylor, *TAPA* 60, 1929, 95.
[2] Cf. his restoration of ancient temples (Tac. *Ann.* 2.49, Dio 57.10; above, p. 140).
[3] Tac. *Ann.* 3.58.
[4] For the date, cf. *ILS* 154 (= *EJ* 101), F. Prae., F. Vat. (*EJ* p. 47).
[5] Tac. *Ann.* 3.71.
[6] Tac. *Ann.* 3.64.
[7] Tac. *Ann.* 4.16.

whose parents had been married by the obsolete ritual of *confarreatio*. Since qualified candidates could no longer be found in sufficient numbers, Tiberius proposed that the requirements be modified, basing his case on the practice of Augustus, who had brought up to date other antiquated regulations. The rule on confarreate marriage was not in fact changed, but another disputed point was cleared up by the passing of a law that the wife of the *flamen* should come under her husband's power for religious purposes only and in other respects enjoy the normal legal rights of women. Maluginensis was duly succeeded by his son. At the same time, to increase the dignity of priestly office and encourage candidates, a gift of 20,000 sesterces was decreed to Cornelia, a newly appointed Vestal, and a seat among the Vestals was reserved for Livia whenever she attended the theatre.[1] It is significant of the decline of religion and the growth of adulation that this last measure was conceived of more as an honour for the Vestals than for Livia.

But where religion was out of place or subject to abuse Tiberius ruled it out of account. When Asinius Gallus proposed that the Sibylline books should be consulted in connection with the Tiber floods of 15, Tiberius rejected the suggestion.[2] No doubt he felt that the matter was one for engineers. During Drusus' second consulship in 21 steps were taken to prevent the abuse of the right of sanctuary inhering in those who were protected by an image of the princeps – a statue or even a coin held in the hand. Under such cover both verbal and physical attacks might be made, even by slaves upon their masters, with the threat of a charge of *maiestas* if the victim dared to retaliate.[3] The lead was taken by C. Cestius Gallus, himself a sufferer from the slanders and imprecations of Annia Rufilla, against whom he had brought a successful action for fraud. *Principes*, said Cestius, were like gods, but even the gods accepted only the prayers of honest suppliants, while such a situation as now existed made a mockery of the laws. Tiberius himself was in Campania, but Drusus, who of course could act without fear of prosecution, was persuaded to have Annia arrested.

---

[1] On Livia's function in the state religion, cf. Grant, *Aspects*, 120ff.; on Livia and the Vestals in particular, cf. Ov. *Trist.* 4.2.13f., *Pont.* 4.13.29f.
[2] Tac. *Ann.* 1.76.
[3] Tac. *Ann.* 3.36.

In 22 the right of asylum in the provinces was similarly checked after long discussions in the senate.[1] Criminals, debtors and runaway slaves had brought asylum into such disrepute that those cities in which there were temples that granted the right were ordered to send envoys to justify themselves. The senate was left complete freedom of decision, but recoiled from the labour involved and passed the burden to the consuls, with instructions to look into the details of disputed cases and report back. It is probable that the eventual decree of the senate prohibited the creation of new rights of asylum as well as limiting and defining those already in existence.

Tiberius' other noteworthy deeds in the field of religion were all acts of suppression. In 16, following the trial of Libo Drusus, astrologers were expelled from Italy by a decree of the senate, while two of their number, L. Pituanius and P. Marcius, who had no doubt been among those consulted by Libo, were executed. Those who undertook to give up their art were, however, pardoned. The consultation of *haruspices*, who observed the entrails of beasts, was also banned, except in the presence of witnesses, at some time during the reign.[2] In 19 came the turn of the worshippers of the Egyptian goddess Isis and of the Jews.[3] To the Jews at least apostasy was offered as an alternative to expulsion. This choice, which would appeal chiefly to converts, confirms the statement of Dio that the principal motive for the decree was concern at the growth of proselytism in Rome. But four thousand able-bodied Jews of freedman stock were shipped off to Sardinia to be employed in the suppression of brigandage. Tacitus' sour comment no doubt reflects the feeling of the senate: if the climate proved too much for them, good riddance. Finally, at an unknown date, perhaps after the Gallic revolt of 21, Tiberius suppressed druidism, which might serve as a focal point for nationalist feeling.[4]

[1] Tac. *Ann.* 3.60–63; for a similar debate in 23, cf. Tac. *Ann.* 4.14.
[2] Tac. *Ann.* 2.32, Suet. *Tib.* 36, Ulp. *Coll.* 15.2; Dio 57.15.8 suggests that there had been an earlier decree banning astrology. Cf. Rogers, *CP* 26, 1931, 203f. For the *haruspices*, cf. Suet. *Tib.* 63.1.
[3] Tac. *Ann.* 2.85, Suet. *Tib.* 36, Dio 57.18.5a, Jos. *AJ* 18.65–84. Cf. Merrill, *CP* 14, 1919, 365ff.; Heidel, *AJP* 41, 1920, 38ff.; Rogers, *Trials*, 32ff.; above all Smallwood, *Latomus* 15, 1966, 314ff.
[4] Plin. *NH* 30.13.

5. THE LAW OF *MAIESTAS*

Much of the routine work of the princeps was concerned with the interpretation and administration of the law. Tiberius, like Augustus, took an active interest in the workings of the less exalted standing courts as well as in the judicial functions of the senate. Dio records that he dispensed justice himself from a tribunal erected in the Forum[1] – this he must have done by virtue of his *imperium* – but his usual practice was to attend the praetorian courts as an assessor. He would take a seat at the side of the tribunal so as not to make the praetor give up his official chair, which Tiberius' superior *imperium* would have allowed him to claim.[2] Suetonius suggests that he interfered only in cases where the undue influence of a guilty defendant seemed likely to procure an unjust acquittal; at such times he would harangue the jurors on the law, religion and the gravity of the crime. It is far more likely, as Tacitus implies, that Tiberius intervened whenever he saw that corruption or the testimony of powerful men was likely to pervert the course of justice. But even here, where the results of his actions were likely to be good, and despite his effort to respect the rights of the praetor, Tiberius was bound to curtail republican freedom – not merely the freedom of juries to decide for themselves instead of surrendering to the constant temptation to do what the princeps wanted, but the traditional republican freedom of the powerful man to bring the full weight of his influence to bear, in the courts as elsewhere in public life, in support of his own interests and those of his friends and dependants.[3]

But the laws were well administered, in Tacitus' view, throughout the early years of the reign, with the exception of the law of treason, *maiestas minuta*.[4] The first general law on the subject had been introduced by a reforming tribune, L. Appuleius Saturninus, in either 103 or 100, to punish the corruption and incompetence of senatorial commanders. The vagueness of the concept of *maiestas* had made the

[1] Dio 57.7.2; Marsh's rejection (*Tiberius*, 123f.) is without foundation.
[2] Tac. *Ann.* 1.75, Suet. *Tib.* 33, Dio 57.7.6.
[3] It is perhaps the latter that was uppermost in Tacitus' mind.
[4] Tac. *Ann.* 4.6. In general cf. Koestermann, *Historia* 4, 1955, 72ff.; Chilton, *JRS* 45, 1955, 73ff.; Rogers, *JRS* 49, 1959, 90ff.; Allison & Cloud, *Latomus* 21, 1962, 711ff.

law a two-edged weapon, and more popular tribunes were prosecuted for sedition than generals for failure in the field. A new law of the dictator Sulla clarified several questions by specifying a number of actions that constituted *maiestas minuta*, a process continued by the law of Julius Caesar. Whether Augustus introduced a further law is uncertain,[1] but he extended its scope to include written libel.[2]

In his preamble to the first trials for *maiestas* under Tiberius, Tacitus accuses the princeps of reviving the law.[3] This is only the first of many misleading statements in the historian's account of treason-trials throughout the reign. The law of *maiestas* had not been repealed under Augustus, nor had its operation ever been formally or informally suspended. Had Tiberius been prepared to take the risk, he could have proposed the repeal of the law, but in not doing so he was merely leaving the existing situation unchanged.

In 15 he was asked by the praetor Pompeius Macer whether charges of *maiestas* were to be admitted to the courts.[4] Why Macer asked this question is obscure – there appears to be no reason why he should have thought that Tiberius might want the operation of the law to be suspended. Tiberius made the only possible reply: the laws must be administered. In this he was following republican principles: the opportunity to pursue one's enemies ruthlessly in the courts was one of the less appealing aspects of republican freedom. But it was soon to appear that this was yet another field in which under the principate republican procedures could survive only in a warped and stunted form.

Two test cases were quickly brought, foreshadowing the evils to come.[5] Both the prospective victims were *equites* of modest standing. The first, Falanius (or Faianius), was accused before the consuls in the senate because he had admitted to the worship of Augustus a panto-mime-actor and prostitute called Cassius and because, when he had

---

[1] Cf. most recently Bauman, *Crimen*, 266ff.

[2] Tac. *Ann.* 1.72.

[3] Tac. *Ann.* 1.72: *legem maiestatis reduxerat*.

[4] Tac. *Ann.* 1.72, Suet. *Tib.* 58. It is possible that what Macer really wanted to know was whether all cases of *maiestas* were to go to the senate.

[5] Tac. *Ann.* 1.73; Dio 57.24.7 may be a garbled and misplaced allusion to the case of Falanius.

sold some gardens, he had included a statue of Augustus in the sale. The second, Rubrius, was brought to trial for swearing by the divinity of Augustus and then breaking his oath. The consuls, not surprisingly, were unsure whether they should countenance these unprecedented charges and so referred both cases to Tiberius. This, as Tacitus admits, was the first that he had heard of the matter. He intervened decisively on the side of sanity and justice, stating in a written reply to the consuls that the deification of Augustus was not to be exploited to encompass the destruction of citizens and that statues of Augustus, like those of other gods, could legitimately be sold along with the houses or gardens in which they stood. As for the perjury, Augustus was to be left to avenge it, as Jupiter would be: wrongs done to the gods were the gods' concern.

Since Tiberius had shown himself unwilling to give his support to charges involving the divinity of Augustus, the next field for would-be exploiters of the law to experiment in was obviously that of attacks on the princeps himself. Not long after the quashing of the charges against Falanius and Rubrius the governor of Bithynia, M. Granius Marcellus, was charged with extortion and *maiestas* by his quaestor Caepio Crispinus, backed by Romanius Hispo, whom Tacitus presents as the archetypal delator.[1] The charge against Granius was threefold: he had made insulting remarks about Tiberius' personal habits, he had placed a statue of himself on a higher pedestal than the statues he possessed of the Caesars, and he had removed the head from a statue of Augustus, replacing it with that of Tiberius. Tiberius, who was present in the senate, lost his temper and shouted that he too would cast his vote in this case, openly and under oath, so that the rest of the senators would have to do the same. At this Cn. Piso asked the obvious awkward question: did Tiberius propose to vote first to give the senate an authoritative lead, or was he going to vote last, in which case others might find they had imprudently dissented? Tiberius was disturbed and perplexed by this dilemma, but decided that the servile abdication of responsibility which was bound to follow if he voted first would be preferable to a possible miscarriage of justice, and so proposed that the defendant be acquitted on the charge of *maiestas*.

[1] Tac. *Ann.* 1.74, cf. Suet. *Tib.* 58.

Tiberius' loss of temper has been much debated. Apologists have claimed that he was infuriated by the triviality of the charges and intended from the first to vote for acquittal,[1] others that his anger was provoked by the nature of Granius' alleged remarks and that in his rage he was ready to demand condemnation until Piso's timely interruption restored his calm.[2] That the recitation of insulting charges against him was at least in part the cause of his anger is strongly supported by his similar outburst at the trial of Votienus Montanus in 25,[3] but the real puzzle lies in his reaction. If he was merely infuriated by the accusations, it would have been more natural for him to insist, as he did in 25, that he would personally refute these slanders. If on the other hand it was the triviality of the case that had annoyed him, the obvious course was to quash it, as he had done for Falanius and Rubrius. The most likely solution is that Tiberius was angry both because maliciously trivial charges were again being brought despite his stand over Falanius and Rubrius and even more because the prosecutors felt free to insult and embarrass him in public in the furtherance of their unsavoury ends. These motives are in no way mutually exclusive, and in each case the target of Tiberius' anger would be Caepio and Hispo, not Granius. He may have hoped that a solemn personal vote for acquittal might drive home the lesson that his letter on the previous occasion had all too obviously failed to make clear.[4] The evidence for his attitude at the beginning of the reign to insults directed against him confirms that he would hardly have wanted Granius condemned: it was precisely in this connection that he asserted men's right to think and speak as they pleased, and he also warned the senate that, if such charges were admitted, every private quarrel would come before it under this disguise.[5]

---

[1] Cf. Rogers, *Trials*, 10.
[2] Cf. Koestermann, *Historia* 4, 1955, 86.
[3] Tac. *Ann.* 4.42.
[4] This interpretation is acceptable only if the statement of Tacitus, *permotus his quantoque incautius efferuerat paenitentia patiens tulit absolui reum criminibus maiestatis*, does not imply a change of mind on Tiberius' part. There is no reason why it should. The point (sometimes obscured by punctuation) is that Tiberius repented his loss of composure – because it had impaired his dignity and put him in an awkward situation – not any decision that he had taken in his anger. His repentance is therefore no evidence for an originally different intention.
[5] Suet. *Tib.* 28.

The next case of *maiestas*, after the trial of Libo, comes from 17.[1] The defendant, Appuleia Varilla, was, like Libo, of distinguished ancestry – she was a granddaughter of Augustus' half-sister, the elder Octavia – and so a suitable target for delation. As in the case of Granius Marcellus, *maiestas* was urged against Appuleia as a pendant to another charge, this time adultery, though it seems as if the prosecutor tried to claim that because she was a relative of the princeps adultery for her was itself a form of *maiestas*. Despite Augustan precedents for such an approach, Tiberius refused to adopt it and instructed that the charge of adultery should be treated separately under the appropriate law. The grounds for the accusation of *maiestas* proper were that Appuleia had made insulting remarks about Augustus, Tiberius and Livia. Tiberius' response reveals a hardening in his attitude. Four years before in the case of Rubrius he had laid down the principle that wrongs done to the gods were no concern of mortals; now he demanded that Appuleia be condemned if she had in fact blasphemed against Augustus. He still insisted, however, that any utterances against himself were not to be admitted as evidence. The presiding consul asked him – whether maliciously or not it would be rash to conjecture – what his attitude was to the remarks that Appuleia was alleged to have made about his mother. Tiberius gave no reply, but on the next day, presumably after consulting Livia, he requested in her name that remarks directed against her, whatever their nature, should not be taken into account. In fact Appuleia was acquitted of *maiestas*, but condemned for adultery. Tiberius intervened to moderate the legal penalty, proposing that in accordance with tradition her family should be instructed to exile her to a distance of two hundred miles from Rome. The motive for leniency was no doubt political: Appuleia was a woman of high birth and obviously presented no threat to Tiberius' power. Therefore it was as well to treat her gently, since there was nothing to be gained by harshness.[2]

The next prospective victim was of even greater distinction: Aemilia Lepida, who numbered Sulla and Pompey among her forebears and

---

[1] Tac. *Ann.* 2.50. The trial serves to show the injustice of the general statement of Dio 57.19.1.
[2] Thus Koestermann, *Historia* 4, 1955, 91.

had once been the intended bride of Lucius Caesar.[1] She was brought to trial in 20 on a combination of charges. The chief accusation was that Lepida had falsely claimed to have had a child by her rich and childless ex-husband Sulpicius Quirinius, a friend of Tiberius since his time of retirement at Rhodes. To this were added adultery, poisoning and the consultation of astrologers to the detriment of the imperial house. She was defended by her brother, M'. Lepidus. Quirinius was unpopular, and his continuing hostility to Lepida after he had divorced her won her considerable sympathy, even though, according to Tacitus, her reputation was bad and she was guilty – of what he unfortunately does not say.

Tiberius' feelings were difficult to divine: he was not on this occasion ambiguous or inscrutable but inconsistent, veering between clemency and anger. First he asked the senate that the charge of *maiestas* should be quashed, but in his questioning of witnesses, among them the consular M. Servilius, he encouraged them to speak of matters relevant to this accusation. Despite this he handed over Lepida's slaves, who were being kept in custody by the praetorian guard, to the consuls and refused to allow any interrogation on topics relating to his own household. Nor would he permit his son Drusus to give the first opinion, although as consul designate he should by custom have done so. Some interpreted this as a republican gesture, since it left the senate free to make up its own mind, whereas if Drusus had voted first the rest would have felt compelled to follow his lead.[2] Others took it as an indication that Tiberius wanted Lepida condemned but was eager to spare Drusus the odium of making the proposal.

The trial was interrupted by a festival, at which Lepida succeeded in arousing much feeling in her favour and provoking demonstrations against the low-born Quirinius. But the torture of her slaves revealed her crimes – again Tacitus is not precise, but presumably adultery and perhaps also attempted poisoning. She was exiled on the motion of the consular Rubellius Blandus, who had the support of Drusus, though others had voted for a milder penalty. As a concession to her present

---

[1] Tac. *Ann.* 3.22f. (cf. 3.48 on Quirinius), Suet. *Tib.* 49.1. Cf. Townend, *Latomus* 21, 1962, 484ff.; Shotter, *Historia* 15, 1966, 207ff.
[2] Cf. Tac. *Ann.* 1.74.

husband, Mam. Scaurus, who had had a daughter by her, her property was not confiscated. At the very end of the discussion Tiberius announced that his private examination of Quirinius' slaves had confirmed that Lepida had tried to poison her former husband.

The penalty imposed on Lepida was harsher than usual in cases of adultery and was indeed closer to that for *maiestas*, but if Lepida's own slaves had already revealed the attempt to poison Quirinius, this may well have occasioned the abnormal severity. Suetonius somewhat mysteriously quotes this case as an example of Tiberius' avarice. Perhaps the most likely explanation is that Quirinius may eventually have left his estate to Tiberius, so that Lepida's failure to secure it for her child ultimately benefited Tiberius himself.[1] For Suetonius' insinuation that Tiberius contrived Lepida's downfall as a favour to his friend there is no justification whatever.[2] The princeps' vacillation on the charge of *maiestas* was probably the result of a conflict between his sense of justice and his own deep-rooted belief in astrology. The latter will have made him want to ferret out the truth for the sake of his own peace of mind, even though he refused to countenance the charge in court. His unwillingness to interrogate Lepida's slaves in the matter may have been a simple act of self-discipline, or he may have found out enough to calm him from Servilius and the other witnesses.

Several cases are recorded from 21. Two *equites*, Considius Aequus and Caelius Cursor, were punished by a decree of the senate proposed by Tiberius for prosecuting a praetor, Magius Caecilianus, on fictitious charges of *maiestas*.[3] The details are unknown. Popular opinion gave Drusus the credit for his father's action, for no apparent reason.

There followed the prosecution by Ancharius Priscus of Caesius Cordus, the governor of Crete and Cyrene, on a familiar combination of charges, extortion in his province and *maiestas*.[4] Tacitus comments that *maiestas* was now the inevitable accompaniment of all other charges. The nature of Cordus' alleged treason is not recorded, but the account of his eventual condemnation for extortion in 22 implies that

[1] Thus Townend, *Latomus* 21, 1962, 488.
[2] Koestermann (*Historia* 4, 1955, 95) is inclined to take it seriously.
[3] Tac. *Ann.* 3.37.
[4] Tac. *Ann.* 3.38.

the charge of *maiestas* failed.[1] Whether it was quashed or Cordus was acquitted is impossible to conjecture.

More puzzling is the case of Antistius Vetus, a prominent man among Romans resident in Macedonia.[2] Here there was apparently no combination of charges. Antistius was acquitted of adultery, not by the senate but by an ordinary standing court. Tiberius attacked the jury – Tacitus does not say why – and instituted a prosecution for *maiestas*, on the grounds that Antistius was a troublemaker and had been implicated in the plans of Rhescuporis after the murder of Cotys. He was sentenced to banishment, with the rider that his place of detention should be an island well removed from the coasts of Thrace and Macedonia. The charge was a serious one, and there is nothing to suggest that Antistius was unjustly condemned. What is puzzling is the fortuitous way in which he came to be brought to trial for *maiestas* at all. It may be that Tiberius, reluctant to publish the details of Antistius' treasonable dealings in the North, had hoped that the charge of adultery would serve to get rid of him and so was made angry by a verdict that forestalled this design and forced him into the open.

But by far the most famous case in 21 was that of an *eques*, Clutorius Priscus.[3] Clutorius had earned fame and a reward from the princeps for a poem lamenting the death of Germanicus. In this year Drusus was seriously ill, and Clutorius rashly wrote another elegy in anticipation of his death. In his vanity he gave a reading of the work in the house of P. Petronius before Petronius' mother-in-law Vitellia and other ladies of rank. His action was presented, no doubt unjustly, as a piece of black magic intended to hasten Drusus' death. The other members of the audience were frightened into giving a true account of what had happened; only Vitellia bravely maintained that she had heard nothing. Her stand was futile, and the consul designate, D. Haterius

---

[1] Tac. *Ann.* 3.70.
[2] Tac. *Ann.* 3.38.
[3] Tac. *Ann.* 3.49–51, Dio 57.20.3f. The suggestion that Drusus presided as consul at the trial (thus Rogers, *CP* 27, 1932, 75ff.; *Trials*, 63) is excluded by the fact that he had resigned his consulship months before, probably, like Tiberius, at the end of April (cf. Degrassi, *Fasti consolari*, 8). The absence of Drusus' name from accounts of the trial suggests that he was not present; he may already have been in Campania, perhaps convalescing after his illness.

9a Tiberius at about the time of
his adoption by Augustus

9b Tiberius at about the time of
his association with Augustus in
the imperial power

9c Tiberius portrayed as a young
man, with the *corona ciuica*

9d Tiberius at about the time of
his accession

10a Cameo: Germanicus

10b Agrippina

10c Drusus, son of Tiberius

10d Gaius Caligula

Agrippa, proposed the death sentence, an aggravation of the usual penalty of exile. He was opposed by M. Lepidus on the grounds that Clutorius had done no material mischief and that therefore there was cause for moderation, especially as Tiberius himself – who was absent from Rome – had so often shown himself in favour of clemency. Since Clutorius presented no danger, Lepidus argued, he should be allowed to live, under pain of exile and confiscation, as if he were guilty under the law of *maiestas*.[1] But of the consulars only one, Rubellius Blandus, voted for Lepidus' proposal. The others supported Haterius, and Clutorius was removed to prison and executed.

When Tiberius learned what had happened, he was courteously critical – he could hardly attack the senate too severely when for once it had dared to make up its mind for itself, even though the decision was not to his liking. So he commended the senators for their loyalty but deprecated the fact that mere words had been so hastily punished, and though he praised Lepidus, he did not condemn Haterius. For the future a resolution of the senate was passed that decrees, including criminal sentences, should not be conveyed to the treasury until an interval of ten days had elapsed.[2] Tiberius emerges from the incident with some credit.[3] It has been noted that even in Tacitus' account he seems to criticize the severity of the sentence only by implication and to be more concerned with the hasty execution of the verdict, an aspect emphasized by Dio, who attributed Tiberius' annoyance entirely to the fact that he had been deprived of any say in the matter. However, since intervention in such cases was virtually bound to be in favour of clemency, the distinction is largely academic.

The next year saw yet another case in which the charges of extortion and *maiestas* were combined, this time against C. Junius Silanus, the governor of Asia.[4] Silanus was accused of extortion by the provincials; the consular Mam. Scaurus, the praetor Junius Otho and the aedile Bruttedius Niger added the charges of perjury against the divinity of Augustus and insult to the *maiestas* of Tiberius. That senators of note

[1] For this distinction, cf. the similar one of Modestinus, D.48.4.7.3.
[2] Only when deposited at the treasury did laws and decrees of the senate become operative; cf. Suet. *Tib.* 75.2.
[3] Koestermann's attack (*Historia* 4, 1955, 101) is inexplicable.
[4] Tac. *Ann.* 3.66-69.

should degrade themselves in this way was to Tacitus a grave indication of Rome's decline; to make matters worse the accusers were joined by Silanus' quaestor and legate, Gellius Publicola and M. Paconius. Tacitus here states plainly what he more than once implies elsewhere: that the principal purpose of the *maiestas* charge was to deter the defendant's friends and relatives from coming to his aid.[1] Tiberius showed himself openly hostile. He interrogated Silanus ruthlessly and arranged for his slaves to be bought by the state, thus making it legal for their evidence to be used against their former master. Realizing that his situation was hopeless, Silanus begged a few days' grace and abandoned his defence, though he summoned up the courage to write to Tiberius a letter of mingled reproach and supplication.

When the senate debated Silanus' sentence, Tiberius produced a precedent from the reign of Augustus, reading a memorandum by his predecessor on the case of Volesus Messalla, together with the subsequent decree of the senate. This is highly significant, for Messalla had not been accused of *maiestas*, but only of extortion aggravated by atrocious cruelty, and on both these counts, according to Tacitus, Silanus too was undoubtedly guilty. Now the sentence imposed on Silanus was no more than what was normal for *maiestas*, though it was harsher than the usual penalty for extortion. Thus if a precedent of this sort had to be invoked to justify it, it is likely that Silanus too was condemned only for extortion and cruelty and not for *maiestas*, that is, that the charge of *maiestas* had been quashed or Silanus acquitted. It would seem to follow that Tiberius' hostility to Silanus was provoked less by the alleged insults to himself than by legitimate anger at Silanus' conduct in the province.

The sentence of exile was proposed by L. Calpurnius Piso, the *pontifex*, who specified the waterless island of Gyaros. The only modification was suggested by Cn. Lentulus: that the property Silanus had inherited from his mother should not be confiscated but given to his son. This was approved by Tiberius. There followed an abjectly sycophantic motion by P. Cornelius Dolabella: no man of dissolute habits and evil reputation should be allowed to govern a

---

[1] Rogers (*Trials*, 67) misunderstands Tacitus, who attributes this intention to the delators, not to the princeps.

province, and the princeps should have the task of deciding whether or not any applicant was a fit person. Tiberius rejected this dubious privilege, saying that it was impossible to predict what effect the appointment to a governorship might have on a man.[1] His reply embodied two of his deepest political beliefs: respect for established institutions, in this case the principle that the punishment must not precede the crime, and the conviction that the princeps already had enough work and enough power. He ended with a warning against weakening the constitution by an increase in the autocratic power of the princeps at the expense of the laws. More specifically on the subject of Silanus, he suggested the substitution for Gyaros of the rather more civilized island of Cythnos, and this was duly accepted.

The other case of 22, that of the *eques* L. Ennius, is interesting chiefly as an illustration of the malice and stupidity with which Tiberius had to contend in his dealings with the senate.[2] Ennius was prosecuted for *maiestas* because he had melted down a silver statue of the princeps. Tiberius, as might have been expected, flatly refused to admit the charge, only to find himself openly attacked by the jurist C. Ateius Capito for curtailing the freedom of the senate by depriving it of the right to decide for itself. Tiberius, said Capito, might be slow to anger, but he had no right to condone crimes against the state. This ingeniously sordid piece of pedantic hypocrisy was unavailing; Tiberius stood firm.

Such are the recorded cases of *maiestas* from the years before the death of Drusus. No doubt they were not the only ones. Tacitus selected only cases of particular interest: some illustrated the growth of delation and the gradual extension of the law; in most the defendants were persons of distinction and Tiberius himself played a prominent part.[3] Thus, despite the question of Pompeius Macer in 15 and Tiberius' reply, no case that was tried in the standing praetorian court is reported, only those that were for one reason or another important enough to come before the senate.

It is indisputable that the operation of the law was a major source of

---

[1] Cf. his reply to Asinius Gallus (Tac. *Ann.* 2.36).
[2] Tac. *Ann.* 3.70; on Capito, cf. Tac. *Ann.* 3.75, Suet. *Gramm.* 22, Dio 57.17.2.
[3] Cf. Koestermann, *Historia* 4, 1955, 97.

evil. The eagerness of professional informers to exploit its possibilities, the reluctance of their friends and families to assist defendants for fear that they might seem accessories to treason, and the senate's sycophantic readiness not merely to condone but often to initiate abuses of the letter and spirit of the law are symptoms of a diseased society. But the blame must rest on the principate as an institution. Tiberius had not created the situation, nor could he conjure it out of existence. Time after time in individual cases he stepped in to prevent the exploitation or irresponsible application of the law. He could do nothing more. His detractors have complained that despite his several praiseworthy interventions he did not, as he should have done, take any measures to stamp out delation once and for all, without which the delators, however often they were rebuffed, would never give up trying.[1] This criticism is unrealistic. To repeal or suspend the law of *maiestas*, or even to abolish the rewards for successful prosecution, would have been nothing less than an open invitation to conspiracy and assassination.[2] The law had to exist, and rewards for accusers were needed in a society where there was no public prosecutor and the gratuitous exercise of public spirit had long gone out of fashion. It was impossible to check delation in advance: only by allowing a man to bring his accusation was it possible to determine whether he was an honest and loyal citizen or a delator who had spotted a likely victim. Hence no general proleptic safeguard could be devised; all that could be done was to keep a close check on the merits of individual cases and throw out those that were patently malicious or absurd. This, despite the tenacity of the delators and the spinelessness of the senate, Tiberius did to the best of his ability.

6. THE PROVINCES

For Rome's subjects the reign of Tiberius was in the main a time of peace.[3] The bulk of the empire's military strength was spread along the

[1] Cf. Koestermann, *Historia* 4, 1955, 83.
[2] Cf. Tiberius' response to this suggestion when it was made in 24 (Tac. *Ann.* 4.30). Tiberius is defended by Rogers, *Trials*, 83; cf. also Marsh, *Tiberius*, 60.
[3] For the gratitude of the provinces for peace under Tiberius, cf. Philo *Leg.* 141; note also Velleius' peroration (2.137.2).

northern frontier.[1] In Illyricum Pannonia normally had three legions, VIII Augusta, IX Hispana and XV Apollinaris, though IX was temporarily transferred to Africa in 20 to help deal with the rebel Tacfarinas; Dalmatia had two, VII at Delminium and XI at Burnum, and Moesia also two, IV Scythica and V Macedonica. Clearly no major threat was expected from across the Danube, which was held by only five legions, with the Dalmatian legions ready either to reinforce them or to hurry to Italy should some crisis arise. By contrast the Rhine had eight legions, II Augusta at Argentorate, XIII Gemina at Vindonissa, XIV Gemina and XVI Gallica at Moguntiacum on the upper river, I Germanica and XX Valeria at Oppidum Ubiorum, V Alaudae and XXI Rapax at Vetera on the lower. Their task was not only to keep the Germans out but to be ready to put down trouble in Gaul, as is underlined by the siting of bases at Argentorate and Vindonissa. Elsewhere in the West Spain, which had still been troublesome in the time of Augustus, had three legions, IV Macedonica, VI Victrix and X Gemina, the senatorial province of Africa normally only one, III Augusta. Further east the vital territory of Egypt had two, III Cyrenaica and XXII Deiotariana. Only four legions occupied Syria: III Gallica, VI Ferrata at Apamea, X Fretensis at Cyrrhus and XII Fulminata at Raphaneae. Their positioning suggests that their principal function was police work, rather than to guard the frontier against the Parthians, who were unlikely to threaten danger unless provoked. Italy itself had the three urban cohorts as well as the nine cohorts of the praetorian guard, and two of Rome's principal naval bases at Misenum and Ravenna – the third was at Forum Julii in Gaul.

In the North, once the German campaigns had been abandoned, the only source of disquiet was Thrace. This kingdom had been ruled by Rhoemetalces, who had rendered good service to Rome in the Pannonian revolt, but he had died by 12 and Augustus had divided the land between his son Cotys and his brother Rhescuporis. The latter, who had received the less civilized parts of the country, began to encroach on his nephew's territory, slowly at first, while Augustus was still alive, but with increasing rapidity and blatancy after his death.

[1] For the distribution of the legions, cf. Tac. *Ann.* 4.5; Parker, *Roman Legions*, 119ff.

Tiberius was eager to avoid trouble and first of all merely sent a centurion to warn the kings not to resort to force in the settlement of their differences. Cotys at once dismissed his troops, but Rhescuporis lured his nephew to a banquet, ostensibly for the amicable discussion of their affairs, seized him and put him in chains. To Tiberius he wrote that he had thwarted an impending plot against himself, and hurriedly strengthened his forces on the pretext of an expedition against the Bastarnae and the Scyths.

Tiberius' reply was deceptively mild. Rhescuporis, he said, could rest secure in his innocence, if indeed there had been no treachery. Neither he nor the senate would jump to conclusions before they had heard the details of the case. Rhescuporis was instructed to hand over Cotys and present himself at Rome to back up his version of events. This letter was taken to Thrace by Latinius Pandusa, the legate of Moesia, to whom Cotys was to be handed over. When he arrived he found Cotys dead, murdered by Rhescuporis, who put it about that he had committed suicide. Tiberius patiently set another trap. Pandusa died, and to replace him, apparently in 18, the princeps appointed a friend of Rhescuporis, the consul of 17, L. Pomponius Flaccus. Flaccus enticed Rhescuporis into the Roman camp, and there he was arrested and brought to Rome. He was prosecuted in the senate by Cotys' widow Antonia Tryphaena and condemned to exile. Thrace was divided between his son Rhoemetalces II, who was known to have been opposed to his father's designs, and the three sons of Cotys. Since they were minors, their share of the kingdom was put under the charge of a former praetor, T. Trebellenus Rufus. Rhescuporis was taken to Alexandria and there lost his life 'attempting to escape'. Thus for the moment Thrace was again quiet.[1]

Fresh disturbances broke out in 21. Complaints were made against Rhoemetalces II and Trebellenus. The Coelaletae, Odrusae and Dii took up arms, but no leader emerged who was capable of forging a united resistance. The greater part of the rebel forces concentrated on besieging Rhoemetalces in the city of Philippopolis on the Hebrus. The nearest Roman army was that of Moesia, and P. Vellaeus, who had

[1] Tac. *Ann.* 2.64–67, Suet. *Tib.* 37.4, Vell. 2.129.1. For Rhoemetalces II, cf. *EJ* 168; for Rhoemetalces III, son of Cotys, cf. *EJ* 169.

succeeded Pomponius Flaccus as legate, hastened to the relief of Philippopolis with the bulk of his infantry, while his cavalry and light-armed auxiliaries dealt with the remaining marauding bands. His operations were entirely successful, and Thrace was peaceful for a further five years.[1]

But the savage mountain tribes made awkward subjects. They were reluctant to provide men for Roman auxiliary levies, and even when they were willing to serve they refused to obey any commanders but their own or to fight against any opponents except their neighbours. Their patience was finally broken in 26 by a rumour that they were to be split up and combined with troops from other nations and sent to fight in foreign parts. Before taking up arms they sent envoys who promised continuing loyalty if no new and unreasonable demands on them were made but threatened war to the death if they were treated as slaves. The long-serving governor of Moesia, Achaea and Macedonia, C. Poppaeus Sabinus, returned friendly answers until he had assembled his troops, adding to the forces he had on the spot a legion brought up from Moesia by the legate Pomponius Labeo and the Thracians who still remained loyal under Rhoemetalces. Then he marched against the enemy and rapidly reduced them to extreme difficulties. Some took the advice of the aged leader Dinis and surrendered, but the majority of the young warriors fought on and was defeated. However, the early advent of the harsh Thracian winter saved the more remote mountain tribes from subjection. Poppaeus was granted triumphal insignia – not un-deservedly, for despite the escape of the mountain tribes the revolt was crushed and there was no further trouble.[2]

More dangerous because much nearer Rome was the revolt in 21 of a number of Gallic tribes instigated by Julius Florus and Julius Sacrovir – the name may indicate a Druid – among the Treveri and the Aedui.[3] The rising was confined to the provinces of Lugdunensis and Belgica, leaving Aquitania and Narbonensis untouched. Its causes were financial. The burden of a heavy tribute, the exactions of Roman governors and their own love of rich display had drained the coffers of

[1] Tac. *Ann.* 3.38f.
[2] Tac. *Ann.* 4.46–51.
[3] Tac. *Ann.* 3.40–47.

the Gallic nobles and forced them into the clutches of Roman usurers.
The German campaigns of 15 and 16 had put an abnormal strain on the
resources of the country. Now the news of Germanicus' death had
made the armies of the Rhine once more restive. The time therefore
seemed ripe to make a bid for freedom.

The first tribes to rise in open revolt were the Andecavi and the
Turoni. The former were contained by Acilius Aviola, the governor of
Lugdunensis, with the cohort on garrison duty at Lugdunum. Aviola
also defeated the Turoni, this time with legionaries sent by C. Visellius
Varro, Caecina's successor as commander on the lower Rhine. At this
stage Tiberius was consulted, but he offered no advice as to how best
to deal with the revolt.

The rebellion of the Treveri was shortlived. Florus had little success
when he tried to persuade the Treveran cavalry squadron serving with
the Romans to defect and massacre the Roman businessmen in the area.
So, at the head of a band of debtors and dependants, he headed towards
the forests of the Ardennes, but found himself cut off by troops sent by
Varro and C. Silius, who was still at the head of the legions of the upper
Rhine. The Roman advance guard was led by Julius Indus, himself a
man of the Treveri, but an enemy of Florus and so loyal to Rome.
Florus evaded capture, but when he saw that all ways of escape were
blocked he committed suicide. With his death the revolt of the Treveri
collapsed.

The situation among the Aedui was more serious: their resources
were greater and they were not within such easy reach of the Rhine
armies. Sacrovir had occupied their capital, Augustodunum, and
armed a force of forty thousand men. But neither among the Aedui nor
among their neighbours does there seem to have been any great degree
of unanimity. Tacitus speaks of the young men studying at Augustodunum as hostages for the adhesion of their relatives, and there was no
official support from adjacent tribes.

At Rome rumour had magnified the revolt out of all proportion. The
whole of Gaul was thought to be in arms, with German support, and
the Spanish provinces endangered. Tiberius was harshly criticized for
doing nothing and ironic enquiries were made as to when Sacrovir
would be brought to trial in the senate on a charge of *maiestas*. Tiberius,

who knew the real scope of the rebellion, received these gibes impassively and did not even pretend to think of moving north.

After a quarrel between Varro and Silius over which of them should take command, the aged and ailing Varro gave way, leaving Silius in charge. By this time the Sequani had joined forces with the Aedui, and it was they who provided Silius' first objective as he moved west at the head of two legions. Thence he pressed on at full speed towards Augustodunum. Twelve miles from the town Sacrovir drew up his troops to meet him. The Gauls were overwhelmed and Sacrovir fled, first to Augustodunum and then to a nearby estate of his own, where he too committed suicide.

Tiberius at last made his one and only communication to the senate on the subject of the war,[1] praising not only the loyalty and courage of the legates but also his own planning. In answer to the criticisms of himself he reaffirmed the principle he had enunciated in 14, that neither he nor Drusus should leave Rome to deal with a minor revolt in one corner of the empire. He did, however, express the intention, never of course fulfilled, of going to inspect the situation and restore order in Gaul, now that he could no longer be suspected of acting out of fear.

The most troublesome province at this time was Africa. War broke out there in 17.[2] Like other rebels, including the great Arminius, the enemy leader, a Numidian named Tacfarinas, had served in the Roman auxiliary forces and put his experience to good use in organizing his own troops. To his own people, the Musulamii, he joined the neighbouring Mauri under their chieftain Mazippa. To oppose them the governor of Africa, M. Furius Camillus, had only III Augusta and its complement of auxiliaries. Their superior numbers gave the Numidians hopes of victory in a pitched battle, but they were routed by Camillus' men. Tiberius praised Camillus' achievement in the senate and triumphal insignia were voted him.

Nothing more is heard of Tacfarinas until 20, when he progressed from the usual type of predatory raids to the encirclement of a Roman

[1] Tac. *Ann.* 3.47; interpreted by Vell. 2.129.5 as proof of the marvellous speed with which the revolt was crushed.
[2] Tac. *Ann.* 2.52.

cohort in a fortress near the river Pagyda.[1] Despite the courage of their commander, Decrius, the Romans were put to flight. This disgrace spurred Camillus' successor, L. Apronius, who had already won triumphal insignia in Germany,[2] to inflict the obsolete punishment of decimation on the guilty cohort. This salutary lesson inspired the veteran garrison of Thala to repulse Tacfarinas' forces. In the battle one M. Helvius Rufus saved a comrade's life and was decorated by Apronius. Tiberius added the *corona ciuica*, with a rebuke to Apronius for not awarding it himself.[3] Tacfarinas learned his lesson and avoided pitched battles and sieges, confining himself to guerrilla raids in which his vastly superior mobility left the Romans exhausted and frustrated. His attacks on coastal cities brought him so much booty that he established a settled camp. There he was brought to battle by Apronius' son, who commanded a force of cavalry and auxiliaries together with the most mobile of the legionaries, and was driven into the desert.[4]

In the next year he returned, and the senate reluctantly accepted the task of choosing as governor of Africa Seianus' uncle Q. Blaesus.[5] Tacfarinas had by now grown so confident that he sent envoys to Tiberius demanding lands for himself and his troops and threatening unceasing guerrilla warfare if he was refused.[6] Tiberius was enraged that a deserter and a brigand should attempt to negotiate like an honourable enemy. He sent instructions to Blaesus that an amnesty might be offered to Tacfarinas' followers but that Tacfarinas himself must be taken at all costs.

Blaesus set out to beat the Numidian at his own game. He divided his forces into three columns. The first, under P. Cornelius Lentulus Scipio,[7] commander of IX Hispana (transferred from Pannonia to Africa in 20), was to protect Lepcis Minor and cut Tacfarinas off from the Garamantes. The western column, under Blaesus' son, was intended

[1] Tac. *Ann.* 3.20f.
[2] Tac. *Ann.* 1.72; for Apronius in Africa, cf. *EJ* 209a.
[3] Tac. *Ann.* 3.21, Suet. *Tib.* 32.1, Gell. 5.6.14; for Helvius, cf. *ILS* 2637 (= *EJ* 248). It would in fact have been very rash for Apronius to make the award, cf. Bickel, *RhM* N.F.95, 1952, 130f.
[4] For L. Apronius Caesianus, cf. *ILS* 939.
[5] Tac. *Ann.* 3.32, 35; cf. above, p. 131. For Blaesus in Africa, cf. *EJ* 209c.
[6] Tac. *Ann.* 3.73f.
[7] Cf. *ILS* 940.

to guard Cirta. The main column, under Blaesus himself, advanced directly into the territory of the Musulamii. As the march continued, the enemy constantly found themselves trapped between two or three Roman forces and suffered heavy losses. Blaesus then split his three armies up into even smaller groups under the command of reliable centurions, and these continued to harry Tacfarinas throughout the winter of 22. But when Tacfarinas' brother had been captured Blaesus withdrew, even though the guerrillas had not been exterminated. Tiberius treated the war as concluded, although Tacfarinas himself was still at large, and not only granted triumphal insignia to Blaesus but allowed the legions to hail him as *imperator* – the last time that this honour was ever attained by a man who was not a member of the imperial house.[1]

Two trials for *maiestas* arose out of the war in 23.[2] One of the defendants was Carsidius Sacerdos, the other C. Sempronius Gracchus, son of Julia's lover, who had accompanied his father into exile on the island of Cercina off the African coast and had been forced to make a living as a trader between Africa and Sicily. Both men were accused of supplying Tacfarinas with corn, an offence covered by one of the older and more respectable chapters of the law. Both were acquitted, but Gracchus, though innocent, is said to have owed his salvation to the support of two former governors of Africa, L. Aelius Lamia and Apronius.[3] No doubt his father's misfortunes had made him appear a suitable target for delation.

It was not until 24 that the nuisance of Tacfarinas was finally brought to an end.[4] By that time, as Tacitus sourly observes, three laureate statues stood in Rome of men who had won triumphal insignia for victories over Tacfarinas, but Africa was still being plagued and Tacfarinas was stronger than ever, for after the partial success of Blaesus Tiberius had ordered the withdrawal of the ninth legion. Tacfarinas seized on this to spread a rumour that the Romans were about to abandon Africa altogether and to present his cause – apparently

[1] Tac. *Ann.* 3.74, Vell. 2.125.4.
[2] Tac. *Ann.* 4.13.
[3] For Lamia in Africa, cf. Vell. 2.116.3, *EJ* 291.
[4] Tac. *Ann.* 4.23-26.

for the first time – as a war of liberation. He besieged Thuburnicum, but the new governor, P. Cornelius Dolabella, brought up all the troops he could muster and raised the siege, proving yet again that the Numidians were incapable of resisting the Romans in an infantry engagement. He then applied the tactics of Blaesus, using four columns instead of three as well as roving bands of Mauri. He had the good fortune to take the Numidians completely by surprise while they were encamped at the half-destroyed fortress of Auzea. The guerrillas were massacred, Tacfarinas' son was captured, Tacfarinas died fighting and the war was over. Dolabella asked for the triumphal insignia he richly deserved, but Tiberius refused, allegedly out of consideration for Blaesus, in the vain hope that his renown might be saved from eclipse. His dislike of the sycophantic Dolabella may also have influenced his decision.[1]

Tiberius' attitude to provincial revenues is summed up by his message to the prefect of Egypt Aemilius Rectus: 'I want my sheep shorn, not shaved.'[2] It is clear, however, that this maxim was not always followed, for several governors were brought to trial for extortion or cruelty in their provinces.[3] There may well have been others whose cases are not recorded; Tacitus again selected only interesting examples, in particular those where the charge of extortion was linked with one of *maiestas*.

Indeed Tacitus' interest in extortion trials is so small that he does not give the result of the first case he mentions, the prosecution of Granius Marcellus in 15.[4] After Granius had been acquitted of *maiestas*, the proceedings against him for extortion in Bithynia continued, but the verdict is unknown. The next reported case is that of Caesius Cordus, brought to trial in 21 and condemned in 22 for extortion in Crete and

---

[1] Cf. Tac. *Ann.* 3.47, 69. For Dolabella's victory, cf. *AE* 1961, 107.

[2] Suet. *Tib.* 32.2, Dio 57.10.5; cf. Tac. *Ann.* 4.6. Alföldy (cf. next note) probably exaggerates economic exploitation (though not the economic exhaustion of the provinces, a legacy from Augustus); in particular he builds too much on the corrupt passage Vell. 2.38.1.

[3] Cf. Brunt, *Historia* 10, 1961, 189ff., with justified suspicion of the alleged major improvement in administration under the principate. Tiberius' treatment of the provinces is comprehensively attacked by Alföldy, *Latomus* 24, 1965, 824ff.

[4] Tac. *Ann.* 1.74; cf. above, p. 153.

Cyrene.[1] The governor of Hispania Ulterior, C. Vibius Serenus, was condemned for *uis publica*, the arbitrary execution or use of force against Roman citizens, in 23 and exiled to Amorgos.[2] The most striking successes were achieved by Asia in 22 and 23. In the former year the governor C. Silanus was condemned for extortion aggravated by cruelty.[3] This encouraged the provincials to accuse Tiberius' procurator, Cn. Lucilius Capito, whose case was heard by the senate in 23.[4] In collecting money Capito had exceeded his powers and had borrowed troops from the governor to lend weight to his demands. Such behaviour had not been unknown under the republic, when the agents of private individuals might beg a squadron of cavalry from a helpful governor to assist in collecting a debt. But Tiberius, on whom the senate waited for a lead, energetically repudiated the practice. If Capito had usurped the governor's powers and used troops, he had done so, the princeps said, in defiance of his orders; he had been given authority only over slaves and Tiberius' private funds. Capito was duly condemned and exiled, and the cities of Asia, their joy perhaps heightened by surprise, decreed a temple to Tiberius, Livia and the senate.

But in spite of Tiberius' attitude here and his warning to Aemilius Rectus, it must be remembered that two provincial revolts were caused by Roman greed.[5] The burden of debt that had driven the Gauls to rebel in 21 had been largely the result of excessive demands for tribute and the exactions of Roman governors,[6] and the suppression of the revolt brought only increased hardship, since Silius and his wife Sosia Galla both made considerable profits out of his victory.[7] The rising of the Frisii in 28 is even more revealing.[8] They paid their tribute in the form of hides for the army; the number had been fixed by the elder Drusus, but nothing had been done to specify the quality or size until

---

[1] Tac. *Ann.* 3.38, 70; cf. above, p. 157.
[2] Tac. *Ann.* 4.13.
[3] Tac. *Ann.* 3.66–69; cf. above, p. 159.
[4] Tac. *Ann.* 4.15, Dio 57.23.4; for Capito, cf. *EJ* 266.
[5] Cf. Alföldy, *Latomus* 24, 1965, 829f.
[6] Tac. *Ann.* 3.40.
[7] Tac. *Ann.* 4.19.
[8] Tac. *Ann.* 4.72.

the prefect Olennius decided on the aurochs as the standard. This grossly unreasonable demand reduced the Frisii to borrowing first on their cattle, then on their land, and finally on their wives and children. Such a steady decline into debt must have taken some time, but nothing was done to relieve the situation, although the Frisii protested. It was only when their complaints brought no result that the tribesmen rebelled out of sheer desperation and lynched the soldiers who came to collect the tribute. The general situation under Tiberius seems to have been summed up accurately by Philo: extortion was rife, he says, but Tiberius did his best to punish it after it had happened.[1] Undoubtedly, however, more could and should have been done to prevent it.[2]

Only occasionally did Tiberius give the provinces financial help. In 15 Achaea and Macedonia complained about the burden of taxation, and in consequence a decree was passed removing them from the control of the senate and placing them directly under the princeps.[3] This may have brought with it cancellation of the debt outstanding to the treasury; if not, it is hard to see how the provinces would gain, though they may in future have been spared the expense of maintaining separate governors, since both were now attached to Moesia. But the most famous example of Tiberius' generosity – according to Suetonius, the only one – was occasioned by the earthquake of 17, the worst in history, says the elder Pliny, which destroyed twelve cities in the province of Asia and also did damage in Sicily and the country round Rhegium.[4] Sardis, the city worst hit, received a special grant of 1,000,000 sesterces and the tribute of all the towns was remitted for five years. The ex-praetor M. Ateius was chosen to inspect the damage at first hand and superintend the work of restoration; it was thought that if a man of consular rank were sent, problems of precedence might arise between

[1] Philo *Flacc.* 105.
[2] Tiberius' fatalism about human nature, which influenced his outlook on this very issue (Tac. *Ann.* 3.69), was hardly an excuse for the lack of adequate control, even though his reasons for rejecting that particular proposal were sound. It is worth noting that Josephus (*AJ* 18.172–176) thought Tiberius left governors in their posts for many years because he believed that extortion, though inevitable, would thus be moderased: further evidence, if true, of a fatalistic approach.
[3] Tac. *Ann.* 1.76 (cf. Koestermann *ad loc.*), Suet. *Claud.* 25.3.
[4] Tac. *Ann.* 2.47, Suet. *Tib.* 48.2, Dio 57.17.7, Vell. 2.126.4, Strabo 13.4.8, Sen. *NQ* 6.1.13, Plin. *NH* 2.200, Phlegon 257F36.XIIIf.

him and the consular governor of the province. The cities hailed Tiberius as their founder and erected a statue of him at Rome, and the imperial coinage celebrated his liberality.[1] He acted in a similar fashion in 23, when a less serious earthquake damaged Aegium in Achaea and Cibyra in Asia. Both cities had their tribute remitted for three years.[2]

Tiberius has also been criticized for deliberately halting the political and social progress of the provinces, which had begun with Julius Caesar and continued under Augustus.[3] Urbanization, it is said, came to a standstill, colonization, which helped to spread the Roman way of life, was virtually non-existent, and grants of Roman citizenship were few and far between. There was little to stimulate Tiberius to such action. Colonization and citizenship had specific political uses: to secure freshly conquered or troublesome territory, to reward loyal service by communities or individuals in civil war or in the more peaceful furtherance of a politician's ambition, or to guarantee future loyalty to a new régime. It is therefore not surprising that they bulked so large in the policy of the founder of the principate, while in the period of peaceful consolidation that followed there was small need of them. But to say that Tiberius neglected colonization and the extension of the franchise because he did not find them politically necessary is to admit that he cannot have regarded the gradual elevation of the provinces to a status approaching that of Italy as an end desirable in itself. This is perhaps one of the less appealing facets of his adherence to republican tradition. For him, as for statesmen under the republic, the provinces were the estates of the Roman people, to be managed for the benefit of the people.[4] Even when checking the rapacity of an Aemilius Rectus, he was plainly considering the question from the viewpoint of the sheepfarmer, not the sheep.

The most striking characteristic of Tiberius' administration is his habit of leaving governors in their provinces for long periods. In 15

[1] *ILS* 156 (= *EJ* 50), 8785, *CIL* III 7096, *EJ* 49; cf. Sutherland, *Coinage*, 95.
[2] Tac. *Ann.* 4.13.
[3] Cf. Alföldy, *Latomus* 24, 1965, 827, 836ff.; but there is nothing in the passages he cites from Velleius to suggest that the historian was particularly opposed to grants of citizenship, though Velleius' disapproval of overseas colonization is more striking.
[4] Cf. Tac. *Ann.* 3.54.

C. Poppaeus Sabinus had his term as governor of Moesia extended. He had first been appointed by Augustus in 12, and he remained in charge of Moesia, Achaea and Macedonia until his death in 35.[1] Tacitus offers various reasons for this practice, among them the true one: that Tiberius disliked making decisions and saw no reason in change for its own sake when existing arrangements were still satisfactory. His feeling was no doubt intensified by the hazards that attended decisions in this particular field – a brilliant general might be a potential rebel, while a corrupt or incompetent man might bring disaster or disgrace. From Tiberius' point of view there was therefore every reason to leave competent and unambitious men like Sabinus, once they had been found, in the same posts for as long as possible.[2] The suggestion that he took a conscious pleasure in excluding as many as he could from the profits of provincial government need not be taken seriously.

7. TIBERIUS AND THE PRECEPTS OF AUGUSTUS

In a speech to the senate in 25 Tiberius remarked of his predecessor: 'I treat all his actions and words as if they had the force of law.'[3] The early years of his principate offer many examples of his devotion to Augustan precedent in major questions of policy as well as in trivial details of routine administration.

The most important issue on which Augustus had laid down the law for his successor was the doctrine that the boundaries of the empire should not be extended.[4] This Tiberius faithfully observed. The German campaigns of 15 and 16 did not infringe the precept. Augustus had never abandoned the view that the frontier of Roman Germany was the Elbe and it was he who had appointed Germanicus to the Rhine.[5] Nor was the empire being enlarged in any real sense when Cappadocia and Commagene passed from puppet status to direct Roman control. At the very beginning of the reign Tiberius refused to increase the

[1] Tac. *Ann.* 1.80, 6.39.
[2] For the possible dangers, cf. Syme, *Tacitus*, 441; for Josephus' view, cf. above, p. 172, n. 2.
[3] Tac. *Ann.* 4.37; cf. Shotter, *GR*[2] 13, 1966, 207ff.
[4] Tac. *Ann.* 1.11.
[5] Cf. Timpe, *Triumph*, 31f.

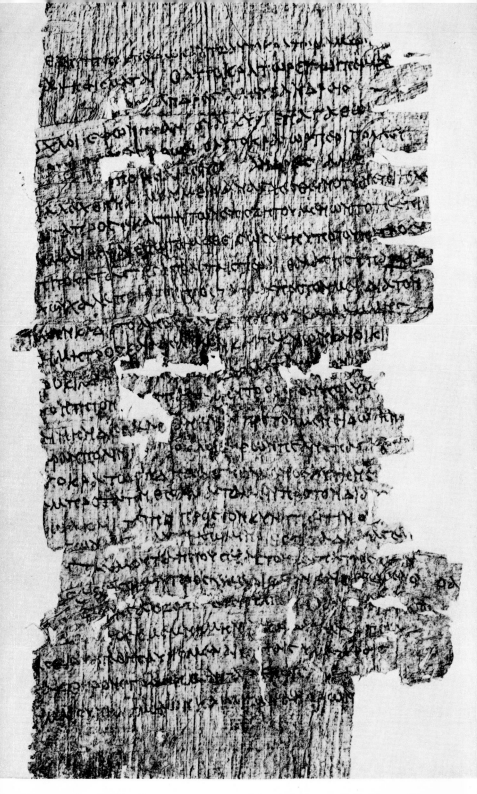

11 Oxyrhynchus Papyrus no. 2435, containing part of a speech by Germanicus on his arrival at Alexandria.

12a Coin of Tiberius: Augustus, with the legend DIVVS AVGVSTVS PATER
12b Coin of Tiberius celebrating the restoration of the cities of Asia after the great earthquake, with legend CIVITATIBVS ASIAE RESTITVTIS.

12c Coin of Tiberius celebrating the birth of his twin grandsons Tiberius Gemellus and Germanicus.
12d Coin of Tiberius honouring Livia as Julia Augusta: a *carpentum* drawn by two mules.

number of praetorships prescribed by Augustus for the following year. That he went so far as to bind himself by oath over such an unimportant and ephemeral matter may itself be significant.[1] In 15 a decision of Augustus saved actors from the risk of corporal punishment.[2] When Germanicus visited Egypt in 19, Tiberius' principal overt objection was that in doing so he had contravened the regulations laid down by Augustus, though here this may have been only a cover for more serious suspicions that Tiberius did not want to publish.[3] The exiled D. Silanus was allowed to return to Rome in 20, but Tiberius was careful to stress that he had not laid aside Augustus' personal grievances or overruled Augustus' wishes.[4] When Germanicus' son Nero was introduced to public life in the same year Tiberius cited as precedent the honours decreed at Augustus' request to himself and his brother Drusus.[5] The severe sentence imposed on C. Silanus in 22 was justified by Augustus' memorandum on the similar case of Volesus Messalla, and in the same year the rules established under Augustus served to deprive the *flamen Dialis*, Ser. Lentulus Maluginensis, of the governorship of Asia.[6]

It has been said that Tiberius departed from the practice of Augustus on one important matter by referring the question of concessions to the mutinous legions in 14 to the senate,[7] whereas Augustus had always regarded military affairs as entirely his private concern.[8] But this is false, since Augustus did in fact consult the senate whenever the terms of military service were in question.[9]

Tiberius has sometimes been criticized for slavish adherence to the policies of Augustus. It is hardly surprising that he made no strikingly original contribution to the development of a constitutional form with which he found himself so little in sympathy. Moreover, his

[1] Tac. *Ann.* 1.14; cf. above, p. 124.
[2] Tac. *Ann.* 1.77; cf. above, p. 137.
[3] Tac. *Ann.* 2.59; cf. above, p. 104.
[4] Tac. *Ann.* 3.24; cf. above, p. 131.
[5] Tac. *Ann.* 3.29; cf. above, p. 119.
[6] Tac. *Ann.* 3.68, 71; cf. above, p. 160, 148.
[7] Tac. *Ann.* 1.25f.
[8] Thus Rogers, *TAPA* 71, 1940, 532ff.; Tac. *Ann.* 1.26 is not evidence for this view.
[9] Cf. Dio 54.25.5f., 55.24.9.

preoccupation with Augustan practice was intended to emphasize the continuity between Augustus' principate and his own and so to assert by implication the legitimacy of his rule. There is no contradiction between this dynastic outlook and Tiberius' democratic treatment of the senate. The latter was the result of his republican view of the duties of his position, but that position, on which his personal security depended, was founded, whether Tiberius liked it or not, on his status as Augustus' adopted son and chosen successor. Tacitus sums up the situation with malicious accuracy in his account of Tiberius' accession: Tiberius, he says, wanted to create the impression that the state had picked him out and summoned him to rule, not that he had crept to power thanks to Livia's pressure and an old man's act of adoption.[1]

That attacks of this kind could be and were made is strikingly illustrated by the sneer of the rebel slave Clemens in 16; when Tiberius asked him how he had become Agrippa, he boldly replied: 'The same way as you became Caesar.'[2] It is in the light of such criticisms that we must regard Tiberius' extreme sensitivity to the acclamation of Agrippina as the sole descendant of Augustus and to Agrippina's own constant harping on her birth.[3] Such behaviour was not merely a studied insult to himself, the adopted son, and to his mother, who was Julia Augusta only by testamentary adoption; it implied a challenge to Tiberius' position. Such a challenge had no basis in logic, for the principate was not a hereditary office, but its emotional appeal was strong enough to make it a source of constant worry and resentment.

How important the matter was to Tiberius is revealed by the coinage.[4] The nomenclature TI. CAESAR DIVI AVG. F. AVGVSTVS and

---

[1] Tac. *Ann.* 1.7.

[2] Tac. *Ann.* 2.40. That is, the liquidation of Agrippa, who should have been the next Caesar, left the place of Caesar vacant for Tiberius to fill – a place to which, according to Clemens, Tiberius had no more right than he himself had to Agrippa's identity, which had also been left open to usurpation by Agrippa's murder. The incident may well be mythical, but is not less significant on that account.

[3] Tac. *Ann.* 1.40, 2.71, 3.4.

[4] Cf. *EJ* 54; Sutherland, *Coinage*, 85f.; Grant, *Aspects*, 92, 96f., 104, who calls attention to the dynastic advertisement of the *gens Iulia* and the *domus*. (Cf. the Cypriot oath published by Mitford, *JRS* 50, 1960, 75ff.; also *EJ* 135, 137, 352.) For emphasis on the Julian connection in honours to Drusus and Livia Julia in Greece, cf. Rogers, *Studies*, 112.

the legend DIVVS AVGVSTVS PATER – the most common of all Tiberian types – both affirm unequivocally Tiberius' dynastic right to the principate. But the legend is more revealing than the name. When Octavian wanted to advertise his own dynastic position as the heir of Julius Caesar, he devised the magnificently arrogant name Imperator Caesar Diui f., to which Augustus was later added.[1] The name Ti. Caesar Diui Aug. f. Augustus is the same in structure, though more moderate, but DIVVS AVGVSTVS PATER deliberately diverts attention towards Augustus and away from Tiberius himself. The practical result is of course the same, as far as Tiberius' place in the dynasty is concerned. But that Tiberius chose to say in effect: 'My position is legitimate because Augustus was my father' rather than 'My position is legitimate because I am Augustus' son' reveals the frame of mind that made his principate a retrospective period of consolidation on past achievement, not one of further development and innovation.[2]

[1] Cf. Syme, *Historia* 7, 1958, 172ff.
[2] Sutherland makes the interesting suggestion (*Coinage*, 88f.) that Tiberius' attempt to work with the senate was conceived as a deliberate improvement on the Augustan system. But although Tiberius, disapproving of the principate, would have considered increased senatorial participation an improvement, he probably saw it as a step backwards towards the republic, not a step forward in the moulding of the principate. His ultimate withdrawal from Rome did contribute greatly to the growth of autocracy and the atrophy of the senate, but it was not a conscious act of policy undertaken with those political consequences in mind.

VI

SEIANUS

1. THE RISE OF SEIANUS

For Tacitus the year 23 marked the major turning-point in Tiberius'
reign. It is at the beginning of this year that he places his brief sketch of
Seianus' early career.[1] Born at Vulsinii in Etruria, he had as a young
man accompanied Gaius Caesar on his ill-fated journey to the East. By
the time of Tiberius' accession he had already won the confidence of the
new princeps, who appointed him to share the prefecture of the
praetorian guard with his father, Seius Strabo; Seianus then continued
to hold the post alone when Strabo became prefect of Egypt in 15.
Tiberius also sent him as Drusus' mentor when the prince set out to
put down the Pannonian mutiny.[2] The significance of this should not,
however, be exaggerated, since Seianus as joint prefect was a natural
commander for such a large praetorian force. He increased the political
potential of the guard by concentrating the cohorts in a single camp
outside the city and gradually secured the allegiance of the troops for
himself.[3] Centurions and tribunes, who should have been chosen by the
princeps, were in fact selected by Seianus – but it would be only
proper for the princeps to accept the prefect's recommendations. At the
same time Seianus worked to extend his influence in the senate,
securing for his adherents magistracies and provinces.[4] Tiberius not
only relied on him, but was not averse to publishing the fact, describ-

---

[1] Tac. *Ann.* 4.1f., cf. Dio 57.19.
[2] Tac. *Ann.* 1.24.
[3] Tac. *Ann.* 4.2, Suet. *Tib.* 37.1, Dio 57.19.6.
[4] Cf. Juv. 10.91ff.; one example was Junius Otho (Tac. *Ann.* 3.66). But Seianus
seems never to have had great influence on the consular elections; cf. above, p. 128.

ing Seianus as the partner of his labours in speeches to both senate and people and allowing the erection of his statues in theatres and public places and in the shrines of the legions.

The first major token of favour had come in 20, when Seianus' daughter had been briefly betrothed to Drusus, the son of Claudius, whose ludicrous death prevented a match that had aroused much adverse feeling.[1] In the next year, when Tiberius forced a reluctant senate to choose between M. Lepidus and Q. Blaesus for the governorship of Africa, Blaesus was picked because he was Seianus' uncle.[2] When the theatre of Pompey was destroyed by fire in 22, Tiberius promised to finance the rebuilding and lavished praise on Seianus for his hard work and vigilance in restricting the damage done.[3] Apparently the praetorians under Seianus' command had fought the fire and, although they had been unable to save the theatre, had at least prevented the blaze from spreading. The senate responded by decreeing that a statue of Seianus should be set up in the theatre itself. The same year brought further honours to Blaesus, who received triumphal insignia and a salutation for his campaign against Tacfarinas.[4] Tiberius stated specifically that these distinctions were granted to Blaesus as a compliment to Seianus.

Blaesus was not the only relative of Seianus to attain the consulship. Velleius credits him with consular brothers and cousins.[5] Their identity has tested the ingenuity of prosopographers.[6] On the most likely interpretation of the evidence the brothers will have been Q. Aelius Tubero, consul in 11 B.C., Sex. Aelius Catus, consul in 4, and L. Seius Tubero, suffect consul in 18, and the cousins the younger Q. Blaesus, suffect consul in 26, L. Cassius Longinus, consul in 30, and C. Cassius Longinus, suffect in the same year.

---

[1] Tac. *Ann.* 3.29, Suet. *Claud.* 27.1, Dio 58.11.5; cf. above, p. 119.
[2] Tac. *Ann.* 3.35; cf. above, p. 131.
[3] Tac. *Ann.* 3.72; for the statue, cf. Dio 57.21.3.
[4] Tac. *Ann.* 3.72; cf. above, p. 169.
[5] Vell. 2.127.3.
[6] Cf. Sumner, *Phoenix* 19, 1965, 134ff., proving that the acephalous inscription *ILS* 8996 (= *EJ* 220) does not refer to Seius Strabo. For earlier views, cf. Cichorius, *Hermes* 39, 1904, 461ff.; Adams, *AJP* 76, 1955, 70ff.; Sealey, *Phoenix* 15, 1961, 97ff.

2. SEIANUS' AMBITIONS

Seianus' career poses two major problems. The first is the question of responsibility: did Tiberius use Seianus as a pawn and prompt his baleful designs against Agrippina and her sons, or did Seianus exploit Tiberius, deluding his master into courses that would guarantee his own advancement? Suetonius confidently asserts the former opinion, while Tacitus is at first content merely to highlight the dilemma: in 23, he says, Tiberius began to be cruel himself or to further the cruelty of others.[1] He does, however, at once go on to state that the initial impetus came from Seianus.[2] This is probably the truth of the matter. Seianus knew Tiberius' character well and directed his steps along paths that by nature he was already only too inclined to take.[3] The essence of Tiberius' guilt in their partnership is formulated with succinct profundity by Tacitus a little later, when he attributes to him an excessive readiness to believe Seianus' allegations.[4] Seianus played with consummate skill on Tiberius' gnawing fears and suspicions, and Tiberius believed, demanding neither proof nor even plausibility, his blind confidence all the encouragement that Seianus needed.

The second problem is Seianus' precise objective. Tacitus speaks of his desire to secure imperial power for himself,[5] but this is too vague to be of much assistance. The key is to be found in the words in which Tacitus describes the situation that confronted Seianus at the beginning of 23.[6] The house was full of Caesars, Tiberius had a son in his prime and adult grandsons: these were the obstacles to Seianus' desires. The emphasis laid on the ages of the princes is vital. Drusus, who was intended to rule as guardian for Nero, was a young man. There was therefore no likelihood that he would die while Nero was still young enough to need a guardian – for Nero and his younger brother Drusus

---

[1] Tac. *Ann.* 4.1, Suet. *Tib.* 55; *Tib.* 61.1 is somewhat nearer the truth.
[2] Tac. *Ann.* 4.1: *initium et causa penes Aelium Seianum.*
[3] Cf. Tac. *Ann.* 1.69.
[4] Tac. *Ann.* 4.67: *credendi temeritas.*
[5] Tac. *Ann.* 4.1. Dio 57.22.4b is absurd: if Tiberius ever believed that Gemellus was a bastard, he can have done so only after Apicata's revelations in 31, as Suet. *Tib.* 62.3 implies. For the suggestion, cf. also Dio 58.23.2.
[6] Tac. *Ann.* 4.3.

too had already reached manhood, though they had as yet no experience of public life.[1] Seianus' ambitions then were blocked by any man who could occupy the place of guardian to a prince and by any prince old enough soon to be able to dispense with the services of a guardian altogether. The station Seianus had conceived for himself must therefore have been that of regent to a prince too young to rule. That is why it was the existence only of adult princes that hindered him.

Such an ambition would be more realistic than a simple desire to replace Tiberius. Seianus was no fool. He knew that he was hated, not only by the aristocracy, who regarded him as an upstart, but also by the people.[2] As princeps he could never be tolerated. The nobility would never accept a man of equestrian birth, no matter how many honours Tiberius heaped on him, while the people and the armies were devoted to the house of the Caesars. But as guardian to a Caesar, his position secured by a suitable marriage to a princess, Seianus might survive to enjoy the realities of power. This was the highest to which he could rationally aspire, and this he ruthlessly set out to achieve.

3. SEIANUS AND THE DEATH OF DRUSUS

The first and greatest stumbling-block for Seianus was Drusus, with whom he had recently quarrelled.[3] Drusus not surprisingly resented Seianus' power and made no attempt to conceal his hostility, complaining bitterly that Tiberius called an outsider his assistant in empire when his own son was alive and well and grimly predicting that Seianus would soon be proclaimed as Tiberius' colleague.[4] Nor had the impetuous and hot-tempered prince been content with words; in one argument he had raised his hand to Seianus and despite the prefect's attempt to parry had struck him in the face.[5] But political considerations more than personal hatred will have made Seianus plan the rapid

[1] Drusus assumed the *toga uirilis* at the beginning of 23 (Tac. *Ann.* 4.4).
[2] Cf. Tac. *Ann.* 3.29, 4.3.
[3] Tac. *Ann.* 4.3.
[4] Tac. *Ann.* 4.7.
[5] Tac. *Ann.* 4.3; Seianus is the aggressor in Dio 57.22.1. Whether the attack narrated under 15 by Dio 57.14.9 is a version of the same incident is uncertain.

removal of Drusus. The shared consulship and the grant of tribunician power did not merely mark out Drusus as Tiberius' immediate successor; seen in the light of Tiberius' increasing withdrawal from public affairs, they strongly suggested that the old man might soon retire and leave his son to rule. For Seianus this prospect was highly alarming. His position depended on the favour of the ruling princeps, but his relations with Drusus were such that, if the prince were allowed to succeed, Seianus' career, if not indeed his life, would certainly come to an abrupt and untimely end. Speed was essential if Seianus was to survive.

To further his plan he secured an invaluable accomplice: Drusus' wife Livia Julia.[1] Her motives are obscure. All that Seianus had to offer her, if the murder of Drusus was safely accomplished, was marriage and a share of the imperial power. Yet Livia Julia's present marriage was far more distinguished than that proposed by Seianus and she was bound in the natural order of things to be empress when Drusus succeeded his father. She was therefore abandoning certain power and prestige for uncertainty and danger with Seianus. The only possible rational explanation of her conduct is that she was acting in the interest of her sons, Tiberius Gemellus and Germanicus.[2] If Drusus followed Tiberius, it was probable that he would respect his father's wishes and hand over power to one or other of the sons of Germanicus, suppressing the claims of his own children just as during Germanicus' lifetime Tiberius had disregarded those of Drusus. But Seianus' plans excluded the succession of Nero and Drusus, and he would hardly be able to establish himself as guardian to Gaius after liquidating that prince's mother and brothers. His target must have been the guardianship of Drusus' sons, for which marriage to Drusus' widow would fit him perfectly.[3] It would therefore be in his own interest to promise her that Gemellus or Germanicus would one day

---

[1] Tac. *Ann.* 4.3. She was also known as Livilla, cf. Dio 57.22.2. Their affair is regarded by Eisenhut (*MH* 7, 1950, 128) as perhaps a fiction based on Seianus' subsequent request for her hand. But in that case Apicata's behaviour would be unintelligible, unless it were assumed that she believed Seianus had left her for Livia Julia but was mistaken in this belief.

[2] Cf. Marsh, *Tiberius*, 163f.

[3] Cf. Charlesworth, *CAH* x, 626.

succeed and this prospect may have tempted Livia Julia, whether she was moved simply by affection for her children or by a desire to fill the social and political rôle to which Livia had attained and Agrippina tactlessly aspired. However, the search for a rational explanation is perhaps futile. It may be just that Livia Julia was in love with Seianus. Speculation about her marriage with Drusus is pointless.[1] Nothing at all is known about Livia Julia herself except that she had been an ugly child who grew into a striking beauty.[2] Drusus, in addition to his love of luxury, had a hasty temper and a streak of cruelty in his nature,[3] but whether he exercised these on his wife and whether, if he did, she found them displeasing is quite beyond conjecture. Yet Seianus could offer as bait a marriage which considered from a social and political viewpoint would appear distinctly unattractive, and this may suggest that Livia Julia's emotions were involved, an impression confirmed by Tacitus' assertion that when Seianus asked Tiberius for her hand in 25 he did so partly in response to her repeated demands that he keep his promise to marry her.[4]

Livia Julia's doctor, Eudemus, was made privy to the plot, and Seianus divorced his wife Apicata, by whom he had had three children.[5] The need for swift action had been underlined at the beginning of 23, when young Drusus assumed the *toga uirilis*.[6] The same honours were bestowed on him by the senate as had been voted to Nero three years before. More significantly Tiberius' speech was largely devoted to praise of Drusus for treating his dead brother's sons with the benevolence of a father. For his weapon Seianus chose poison, the effects of which might be passed off as the symptoms of disease.[7] The draught was administered by a eunuch, Lygdus, probably Drusus' taster. Drusus was ill for several days, during which time Tiberius

---

[1] No weight can be attached to Drusus' public expressions of devotion (Tac. *Ann.* 3.34).
[2] Tac. *Ann.* 4.3.
[3] Cf. Tac. *Ann.* 1.29, 3.23, Dio 57.13.1, 14.9.
[4] Tac. *Ann.* 4.39. According to Dio 57.22.4b Seianus was in love with Livia Julia but did not intend to marry her until Agrippina and her sons had been disposed of.
[5] Tac. *Ann.* 4.3.
[6] Tac. *Ann.* 4.4.
[7] Tac. *Ann.* 4.8, cf. Dio 57.22.2f.

characteristically continued to attend all meetings of the senate, but on 14 September he died.[1] The first stage of Seianus' grand design had been successfully accomplished.

Such is the official story of Drusus' murder, as it was revealed after Seianus' fall in 31.[2] The tale was told in a letter to the princeps from Seianus' divorced wife Apicata. Her motive was revenge on Livia Julia.[3] The letter once sent, Apicata prudently committed suicide, but her allegations were confirmed by the statements of Eudemus and Lygdus under torture. There is, however, room for doubt. It is striking that until Apicata's disclosures there had never existed the slightest suspicion that Drusus had not died a natural death. He himself cannot have claimed in his last illness that he had been poisoned, and Tiberius remained convinced for eight years that his son had died of ill-health and excessive self-indulgence.[4] Moreover, it seems almost incredible that Seianus and Livia Julia should have left Eudemus and Lygdus alive to tell their tale.[5] Problems are also raised by Apicata's letter. She was not in Seianus' confidence, and the plan was still in its infancy when he divorced her: in particular Lygdus had not yet come upon the scene. What then could she have known and how did she come to know it? There are three basic possibilities. First, Drusus was murdered and Apicata either discovered this by some means beyond conjecture or deduced it from her knowledge of Seianus' ambitions. Second, Drusus was not murdered, but her knowledge of Seianus' ambitions led Apicata sincerely to believe that he had been. Third, Drusus was not murdered and Apicata had no reason to believe that he had been but invented her story from beginning to end to destroy Livia Julia. If either the first or the second of these possibilities is correct, a further question arises: did Apicata, although she knew or thought she knew that Drusus had been murdered, nevertheless invent part of her story,

---

[1] For the date, cf. *F. Opp.*, *F. Ant.* (*EJ* p. 52).

[2] Tac. *Ann.* 4.11, Suet. *Tib.* 62.1; cf. Balsdon, *CR* 65, 1951, 75; Meise, *Untersuchungen*, 55ff., 63ff.

[3] Dio 58.11.6; despite Dio, Apicata committed suicide before the execution of her two younger children, though her elder son had been put to death two days before, cf. *F. Ost.* (*EJ* p. 42).

[4] Suet. *Tib.* 62.1.

[5] Cf. Spengel, *SB München* 1903, Heft 1, 59; Eisenhut, *MH* 7, 1950, 127.

including the parts played by Eudemus and Lygdus?[1] If Apicata
believed, rightly or wrongly, that Seianus and Livia Julia had had
Drusus poisoned, she might have felt the need for circumstantial detail
to give her charges plausibility and so imagined the rôles of Eudemus
and Lygdus: Livia Julia's apothecary and Drusus' taster would be
obvious ingredients with which to thicken the plot. She would not even
have had to know their names; it would be sufficient to specify their
occupations. But it is not really necessary to assume that Apicata mentioned Eudemus and Lygdus at all. She may have claimed only that
Drusus had been poisoned by Seianus and Livia Julia, without naming
their accomplices. When Tiberius acted on this information, their professional duties at the time of the alleged murder would ensure that the
unfortunate Eudemus and Lygdus stood at the head of the list of
candidates for the rack. The time-lag of course presents no problem,
no matter which explanation is correct – it was not until after Seianus'
fall that Apicata had any hope of being believed.

Certainty is impossible, but the total lack of suspicion in a poison-
conscious age and the failure of Seianus and Livia Julia to liquidate
their supposed accomplices remain powerful arguments against the
presumption of murder. In a sense the question is purely academic.
The logic of Seianus' schemes undoubtedly demanded that Drusus
should die and die quickly, and his seduction of Livia Julia must have
been intended as the first step towards the prince's murder. If Drusus
died a natural death in 23, as he had almost done in 21, nature merely
forestalled Seianus.

In public Tiberius wore an impassive mask.[2] When Drusus was
dead he came to the senate and found that the consuls, as a token of
mourning, had abandoned their usual places and gone to sit among the
mass of senators. The princeps rebuked them for neglecting the dignity
of their office and checked the tearful manifestations of the senate. He
was aware, he said, that some might think it unnatural for him to visit
the senate at a time when most men could hardly bear the company
even of their family and friends. It was not for him to condemn the

[1] The fact that Eudemus and Lygdus confessed proves of course only that their
torturers were competent.
[2] Tac. *Ann.* 4.8, Dio 57.22.4a.

weakness of others, but he preferred to seek a more potent consolation by immersing himself in affairs of state. He went on to point to the gap left by Drusus' death: he was an old man and his grandsons were still untried. At this point he asked for Nero and Drusus to be brought in. The consuls obeyed, and Tiberius solemnly commended the youths, who had lost first their father and now their uncle, to the care of the senate and reminded them that their good or bad fortune was a matter of concern to the state.

So far Tiberius had kept control of himself. Despite the lacuna in his plans caused by Drusus' death he clearly still intended that power should eventually pass to Nero or to both the princes. But at the end of his speech he could not keep himself from showing how the loss of Drusus had shattered his most cherished dream, for he spoke of restoring the republic and asked that the consuls or anyone else should relieve him of his power.[1] Tacitus sneers at what he calls these futile and ludicrous words, but they reveal with terrible clarity the state of Tiberius' mind. In practice of course his appeal was futile, as unrealistic as his attempts at evasion in 14, and now as then he will have known that this was so. But once again he was too deeply moved to accept his fate without protest, however vain. To suggest that the consuls should resume control of the state was at least rational, though quite impractical, but 'or anyone else' is not a constitutional proposal, simply a cry of despair. Tiberius had been on the point of retiring. The peace he had craved for almost ten years had at last seemed to be within his grasp. Now Drusus' death had destroyed his hopes and there lay before him only the indefinite prolongation of his labours until Nero was sufficiently experienced to take over or death relieved him of his burden.

Drusus' memory was honoured with the same decrees as had been passed for Germanicus.[2] Indeed adulation went even further. His funeral was of great magnificence, adorned by the images of Julii and Claudii, and Tiberius and Nero delivered speeches before the Rostra, where Drusus' body had lain in state. Senate and people made a show of grief, but in their hearts they were not sorry that Drusus was dead,

[1] Tac. *Ann.* 4.9: *de reddenda re publica utque consules seu quis alius regimen susciperent.*
[2] Tac. *Ann.* 4.9, 12, Dio 57.22.4a, *EJ* 94b.

for although the prince had not been unpopular his demise seemed to herald an early resurgence of the house of Germanicus, at which there was widespread though secret delight. Agrippina, incautious as ever, did nothing to conceal the revival of her hopes. The succession of Nero and Drusus seemed certain, and with it their mother's long-awaited rise to power. For Seianus the task ahead was clear. While Tiberius tried to bury his grief under the routine of public business, he slowly and carefully began to work towards the downfall of Agrippina and her sons.

4. FROM DRUSUS' DEATH TO TIBERIUS' WITHDRAWAL TO CAPREAE

Seianus was now compelled to adopt different methods from those he had been preparing to use against Drusus. It was impossible to poison all three of his intended victims, for their retainers were loyal, and Agrippina's notorious chastity excluded any prospect of seduction. But time was now on Seianus' side. With Drusus dead there was no longer any immediate danger of Tiberius' retirement, and so Seianus could afford to develop his campaign at leisure. His first target was Agrippina, against whom he stirred up Livia – domineering herself, she had always found Agrippina's arrogance difficult to bear – and Livia Julia. Prompted by Seianus they complained to Tiberius that Agrippina was eager for power and that she had the support of the people: charges that hardly exaggerated the facts and were also skilfully calculated to exacerbate Tiberius' already deep-rooted suspicions of the proud and ambitious widow. Seianus did not rely only on his own influence but suborned others to reinforce his charges. Among them was Julius Postumus, the lover of Livia's close friend Mutilia Prisca; it was Mutilia's task to play upon Livia's own craving for power and to increase her dislike of Agrippina. Even Agrippina's friends were tampered with and instructed to provoke her to further rash displays of ambition.[1]

Tiberius devoted himself to public business,[2] but the death of Drusus was not to be his only loss in 23. Drusus' son Germanicus died

[1] Tac. *Ann.* 4.12.
[2] Tac. *Ann.* 4.13.

at the age of four, leaving his twin brother Tiberius Gemellus as the princeps' only direct male descendant, and Tiberius also lost an old friend, Lucilius Longus, the only senator who had accompanied him to Rhodes. Despite his lack of noble ancestry, the senate voted him a state funeral and a statue at the public expense in the Forum of Augustus.[1] Young Nero made another well-received public appearance in the course of the year. When permission was granted to the cities of Asia to build a temple to Tiberius, Livia and the senate, Nero delivered a speech of thanks on their behalf to the senate and the princeps.[2] His performance delighted his hearers, reviving their memories of his father. Seianus' ill-will towards the prince was common knowledge and his danger increased his popularity. But every expression of popular favour will have provided Seianus with fresh fuel to stoke the fires of Tiberius' suspicions.

During 23 Seianus had worked quietly – there had been no public attack on Agrippina or any of her friends. But just how effective his insinuations had been was strikingly revealed on 3 January, 24.[3] When the *pontifices* and the other priests offered the customary vows for the safety of the princeps, they took the liberty of including Nero and Drusus in their prayers. Ironically, if Tacitus is to be believed, they did so chiefly to flatter Tiberius, presumably encouraged by his speech of the previous September to express in this way their approval of his plans for the succession. But Tiberius objected and objected strongly. That he regarded it as an insult to his years for the youthful princes to be treated as if they were his equals is not surprising, and his speech to the senate merely gave a salutary warning against tempting young men to arrogance by premature honours. But he had previously summoned the *pontifices* in private and had asked them angrily whether Agrippina had used supplications or threats to persuade them to such a course. Their denials calmed him – they were after all among the leading men in the state and several were actually related to him. But his outburst is indicative of the weight of suspicion that thanks to his own temper and Seianus' devices now constantly burdened his mind.

[1] Tac. *Ann.* 4.15.
[2] Tac. *Ann.* 4.15; cf. above, p. 146.
[3] Tac. *Ann.* 4.17, Suet. *Tib.* 54.1; for the date, cf. Gaius D.50.16.233.1.

Seianus was quick to follow up his advantage and bring forward accusations that were graver, though less plausible. The state, he claimed, was torn in two as if by civil war.[1] There were those who called themselves the party of Agrippina, and unless they were checked their numbers would grow. Only the removal of the leaders of this group could prevent the spread of discord. The image was well chosen to work on Tiberius. He hated the feuds and intrigues of palace politics and his tumultuous childhood had left him with a lasting horror of civil strife.

The two most obvious victims were C. Silius and the *eques* Titius Sabinus.[2] Both had been friends of Germanicus and had stayed faithful to the interests of his widow. Silius had other advantages: seven years as commander on the upper Rhine and his victory over the Gallic rebel Sacrovir had made him arrogant, and he was accustomed to boast that his legions had remained loyal when the others had mutinied and to claim that Tiberius could not have maintained himself in power if they too had chosen to revolt. Tiberius was naturally resentful of this and he also disliked Silius' wife, Sosia Galla, because she was a friend of Agrippina. For Seianus the destruction of so prominent a man as Silius would serve as a useful deterrent to the chivalrous and so contribute to the isolation of Agrippina. Sabinus was set aside for future reference and the consul L. Visellius Varro was persuaded to prosecute Silius and Sosia. Varro made a plausible agent, since his father had been Silius' rival for the command against Sacrovir.[3] Silius made the not unreasonable request that the trial should be postponed until Varro's term of office as consul came to an end. Tiberius opposed the plea, with striking reasons.[4] It was the custom, he said, for magistrates to appoint the day for the hearing of charges against private citizens and it was the duty of the consuls to see that the state came to no harm. Both arguments appeal to republican tradition.[5] Yet neither had the slightest relevance to the present situation. This ominous phenomenon becomes

[1] Tac. *Ann.* 4.17.
[2] Tac. *Ann.* 4.18–20; cf. Shotter, *Latomus* 26, 1967, 712ff.
[3] Cf. Tac. *Ann.* 3.43.
[4] Cf. Bauman, *Historia* 15, 1966, 423f.
[5] The second cites the wording of the *senatus consultum ultimum*, which gave the consuls extraordinary powers in emergencies.

increasingly frequent. Tiberius' principles never changed: he had always been guided by respect for republican practice and the authority of the consuls. But as his mind became ever more enmeshed in suspicion and fear his beliefs tended more and more to find expression in warped and twisted forms that made a mockery of their original significance.

The charges were treason and extortion: Silius was accused of complicity in the revolt of Sacrovir and of depredations after his victory, in which Sosia was said to have played a part. Tacitus admits that the accusation of extortion was justified, but the entire proceedings took place under the rubric of *maiestas*, until Silius anticipated certain condemnation by committing suicide. His property was confiscated, even though the Gauls had not dared to put in any claim for compensation so soon after their rebellion. Sosia was exiled on the motion of Asinius Gallus, though M. Lepidus prevented the confiscation of her property, except for the quarter that was due by law to the successful prosecutors as their reward. The session closed with a motion by Cotta Messallinus that governors should be liable for crimes committed by their wives in the provinces, even though they themselves might be not only innocent but ignorant of the offence.

There followed the prosecution for *maiestas* of L. Piso.[1] Eight years before he had threatened to withdraw from public life because of the activities of the delators in the senate and had dared to defy Livia by taking her friend Urgulania to court.[2] Tiberius had persuaded him to stay in Rome but he had not forgotten or forgiven the embarrassment that Piso had caused him. It does not, however, appear that he played any part in initiating the proceedings. The prosecutor was Germanicus' friend Q. Veranius, one of the accusers of Lucius' brother Gnaeus in 20[3] – hardly a likely agent of Tiberius or of Seianus. The attack is probably to be seen as a further act of revenge against Cn. Piso's family, a by-product of the enmities of five years before. The charges were that Piso had used treasonable language in private, that he kept poison at home, and that he had entered the senate wearing a sword.

[1] Tac. *Ann.* 4.21.
[2] Tac. *Ann.* 2.34; cf. above, p. 133.
[3] Tac. *Ann.* 3.10, 13; cf. above, p. 113.

This last accusation was discarded as excessively absurd, but plenty of evidence was brought on the other two points, and so the case was admitted. The only complaint that might be brought against Tiberius here is that contrary to his earlier practice he was now prepared to regard insults to himself as *maiestas*. There can be no doubt that during the twenties his attitude did harden on this point.[1] But it is not certain that Piso's utterances consisted merely of insults, nor is it possible to tell how large a part was played by the accusation of intended poisoning in determining Tiberius' attitude. What the outcome of the trial would have been is hard to conjecture; Piso's death prevented it from being brought to a conclusion. Tacitus is so ambiguous that it is impossible even to be sure whether or not Piso committed suicide.

In fields where his judgment was not clouded by his fantasies or Seianus' promptings Tiberius was still alert and competent. For reasons unknown a praetor, M. Plautius Silvanus, threw his wife Apronia out of their bedroom window.[2] Brought before Tiberius by her father L. Apronius, the former legate of Germanicus and governor of Africa, he announced in some confusion that his wife had committed suicide while he had been half asleep and unaware of what was going on. Tiberius at once went to inspect the room, where signs of a struggle indicated that Apronia was pushed. Arrangements were duly made for the trial. But Silvanus' grandmother Urgulania thought it hardly worth while to wait upon the outcome and sent Silvanus a dagger. This was interpreted as a hint from Tiberius because of Urgulania's friendship with Livia, but Urgulania is hardly likely to have looked to Tiberius or to any man for her cue.[3] Silvanus committed suicide at the second attempt; his ex-wife Fabia Numantina was accused of rendering him insane by spells and drugs but was acquitted. The efficiency shown by Tiberius in ascertaining the truth in this case was also displayed in another field when the slave revolt organized by T. Curtisius, a former member of the praetorian guard, was swiftly and economically suppressed.[4]

[1] Cf. Tac. *Ann.* 4.34, where Cremutius Cordus in 25 takes it for granted that verbal insults to the princeps are covered by the law of *maiestas*.
[2] Tac. *Ann.* 4.22.
[3] Cf. Tac. *Ann.* 2.34 for her character.
[4] Tac. *Ann.* 4.27.

There followed a further example of the increasing tendency towards harshness in interpreting the law of *maiestas*. Tiberius pardoned an *eques*, C. Cominius, who had been condemned for producing a lampoon on the princeps, in response to the pleas of Cominius' brother, a member of the senate.[1] This was in itself commendable, but it is perhaps more significant for the change in Tiberius' outlook that the charge against Cominius must have been admitted and that Tiberius cannot have indicated during the trial that a verdict of guilty would displease him. The princeps showed a similar severity in dealing with Germanicus' former quaestor P. Suillius, who was condemned to exile from Italy for accepting bribes while serving on a jury. It is not known why Tiberius felt so strongly, but he insisted that Suillius be confined to an island, even going so far as to bind himself by an oath that this was in the interests of the state. Also condemned in the first instance to be removed to an island was Firmius Catus, for bringing false charges of *maiestas* against his sister. This time, however, Tiberius intervened to save Catus from exile, though he did not oppose his expulsion from the senate. It was Catus who had planned and executed the downfall of Libo Drusus, and according to Tacitus it was in memory of this service that Tiberius interceded for him now, though he put forward other pretexts. However, Tacitus' own account of the Libo affair makes it clear that Catus was an opportunist acting on his own initiative, not an agent of Tiberius,[2] and since he gives no details of the reasons that Tiberius brought forward, it is impossible to pass judgment on the princeps' motives.

But perhaps the most striking trial of 24, apart from that of Silius and Sosia, was that of Vibius Serenus, exiled in the previous year.[3] Serenus was brought back in chains from his island to face charges preferred by his son. Young Serenus alleged that his father had plotted against the princeps' life and had sent agents to stir up the recent revolt in Gaul. He added that the project had been financed by a former praetor, M. Caecilius Cornutus. Cornutus added colour to the charge, despite his innocence, by promptly committing suicide, but Vibius put up a

[1] Tac. *Ann.* 4.31.
[2] Cf. Tac. *Ann.* 2.27f.
[3] Tac. *Ann.* 4.28–30, cf. 4.13; on Lentulus, cf. Dio 57.24.8.

spirited defence and challenged his son to produce further names, pointing out that he was hardly likely to have planned such a scheme with only a single accomplice. The prosecutor obliged in striking fashion by accusing two consulars, Cn. Cornelius Lentulus and L. Seius Tubero. Tiberius was acutely embarrassed. Both were men of considerable distinction, both were close friends of his own. Moreover Tubero was Seianus' adoptive brother. But Lentulus was a very old man and Tubero a cripple, and the charges against them were dismissed at once. Indeed, Lentulus is said to have burst out laughing at the accusation, while Tiberius remarked that he deserved to die if he had really earned Lentulus' hatred. When the elder Serenus' slaves were examined, their evidence supported the defence, and the mob threatened to lynch his son, who fled from the city. But on Tiberius' instructions he was brought back from Ravenna and forced to continue with the case. Tiberius made no secret of his hostility to the defendant. Eight years before Serenus had been one of the prosecutors of Libo. Unsatisfied with his reward, he had been incautious enough to write to Tiberius complaining that his services had not been acknowledged. Tiberius seems actually to have alluded to this behaviour in the course of the trial. Certainly, if Tacitus' account of the case against Serenus is adequate, Tiberius behaved with a pettiness and self-centred malice that are by no means redeemed by his subsequent mitigation of Serenus' sentence. First of all he vetoed the death penalty, then, when Asinius Gallus suggested banishment to either Gyaros or Donusa, he pointed out that both these islands were waterless. Serenus was therefore sent back to Amorgos.

Even more important than the trial was an incident arising out of it. Because of the suicide of Cornutus it was proposed that, if a defendant on a charge of *maiestas* committed suicide before the conclusion of the trial, the rewards for the prosecution should be abolished.[1] The motion would have been passed, if Tiberius had not spoken with unusual frankness, complaining that the laws were being set at nought and the foundations of the state undermined. It would be better to do away with the laws, he said, than to deter their guardians. Tacitus fumes at this open encouragement to the pernicious breed of delators, yet Tiberius

[1] Tac. *Ann.* 4.30; cf. above, p. 162.

was right. But in his outburst here there is a note of hysteria revealing the growing irrational fears and suspicions that beset Tiberius' mind and deterred him from exercising the vigilant restraint he had imposed in the early years, so that the evil inherent in the system was soon to be free to run wild without curb.

After his success against Silius and Sosia Galla Seianus again bided his time. His one important victim in 25 was the historian A. Cremutius Cordus, whose fate was not connected with the prefect's campaign against the house of Germanicus. Cordus' alleged crime was that in his *Annals* he had praised the assassins of Julius Caesar, speaking highly of Brutus and calling Cassius the last of the Romans. But the prosecutors Satrius Secundus and Pinarius Natta were Seianus' clients and the real cause of Cordus' downfall was the enmity of Seianus.[1] Like many others, Cordus resented Seianus' predominance, but unlike them he was rash enough to express his resentment. In particular he remarked that the ruin of the theatre of Pompey had taken place, not when it was destroyed by fire in 22, but when Seianus' statue was erected in it,[2] lamenting that the monument of a great commander was being degraded with the image of a disloyal soldier.

No doubt these insults to his favourite made Tiberius hostile to Cordus, but he may have had other reasons too. Brutus and Cassius had fought and died for the republic. Tiberius' father had not only lived but had surrendered his wife to the new autocrat Octavian. Tiberius himself had betrayed his republican beliefs, accepting the principate with its hypocrisy and compromise. Acutely sensitive, constantly brooding, always ready to see in the most innocent action or remark a covert attack on himself, Tiberius may well have come to torment himself with the question – if Cassius was the last of the Romans, then what was Ti. Claudius Nero, and what was Tiberius Caesar? It is true that he must have been familiar with Cordus' work for many years and had hitherto shown no sign of resenting it. It may have been the insulted Seianus who discreetly turned his thoughts to the possible implications of Cordus' words. He had had a golden

---

[1] Tac. *Ann.* 4.34f., Suet. *Tib.* 61.3, Dio 57.24.2ff., Sen. *Marc.* 1.3, 22.4ff.; the responsibility of Seianus is heavily stressed by Seneca and Dio.
[2] Cf. Tac. *Ann.* 3.72.

opportunity at the end of 22 with the death of Junia, Brutus' sister and Cassius' widow, whose will recorded legacies for almost every man of distinction in the state – except Tiberius.[1] Ten years had passed since Tiberius had declared that in a free state men must be free to speak their minds.[2] Then his belief in freedom and justice would have triumphed, reducing his petty resentment to its proper perspective, but now, as he grew more withdrawn and self-obsessed, he could no longer escape from the labyrinth of his mind into the light of rational values.

Cordus, already determined on suicide, spoke cogently in defence of free speech.[3] He pointed out that he had said nothing against the princeps or any of the princeps' relatives, who alone were covered by the law of *maiestas*, and cited many republican, Caesarian and Augustan precedents. Then he left the senate and starved himself to death. Seneca paints a depressing picture of the prosecutors running to complain to the consuls when they heard the news and demanding that Cordus be forcibly prevented for fear that they might lose their rewards. The senate decreed that Cordus' books should be burnt by the aediles, but copies survived and they were published again by his daughter Marcia early in the reign of Gaius.[4]

Perhaps this success made Seianus over-confident, perhaps he had to act to silence Livia Julia's demands for marriage. At all events he now composed a letter to Tiberius.[5] Unctuously he recalled the benefits he had received, first from Augustus and then from Tiberius himself, though he had never sought the splendour of high office, deeming it sufficient reward to serve such a master. The fairest honour granted him had been the promise of a marriage-tie with the house of the princeps, and it was this that had inspired his present hope. He had heard that Augustus, when looking for a husband for his daughter, had considered the claims of men of equestrian rank: so, if a husband were required for Livia Julia, he begged that Tiberius would remember his

---

[1] Tac. *Ann.* 3.76; at the time Tiberius showed no resentment.
[2] Suet. *Tib.* 28.
[3] His speech is presumably an invention of Tacitus, but the contents are plausible enough.
[4] Suet. *Cal.* 16.1, Sen. *Marc.* 1.3.
[5] Tac. *Ann.* 4.39.

friend. He was not trying to escape the burden of his duties – for himself he would be well satisfied to live and die under such a princeps as Tiberius – but for the sake of Livia Julia's children he would be happy if the imperial house were strengthened against the attacks of Agrippina.

The letter gives a fascinating insight into Seianus' political skill and the height of his ambition.[1] His picture of himself as the hardworking faithful servant illuminates the official version of his place in the state,[2] and his appeal to the practice of Augustus was calculated to impress Tiberius. But his principal justification for his request was that Livia Julia needed a husband to protect her children against Agrippina's machinations. This confirms that the position at which Seianus was aiming was that of guardian to Tiberius Gemellus. It is striking that he seems to take it for granted that Nero, Drusus and Gaius were to be excluded, provided that Agrippina's plans could be thwarted; it is as if the house of Germanicus no longer formed a part of the dynasty at all. Yet in 23 Tiberius had still thought of Nero and Drusus as the ultimate heirs to his power. But the most intriguing puzzle in the letter is the reference to Livia Julia's children, for Gemellus seems to be the only one to whom Seianus' words could apply. The only other surviving child of Drusus, Julia Livilla, was betrothed to Nero and so could hardly be supposed to be in danger from Agrippina. Perhaps for a moment Seianus had allowed himself to dream that instead of Gemellus a son of his own might one day inherit the power.

Tiberius was clearly taken aback. For the moment he sent only a brief note in reply, praising Seianus' loyalty.[3] Then, when he had had time to think the matter over, he wrote at considerable length. Other men, he began, need take into account only their own advantage in making their decisions, but the princeps had to allow for public opinion. He would not resort to the obvious evasive answer – that Livia Julia could decide for herself whether she wanted to marry again and that, if she needed advice, Antonia and Livia were more fitted to give it

---

[1] The substance of the correspondence is accepted as genuine by Koestermann, *ad loc.*; Syme not only dismisses the letters as a Tacitean invention (*Studies*, 5) but also doubts the authenticity of Seianus' request (*Tacitus*, 404).

[2] For the image that Seianus tried to project, cf. Vell. 2.127.3 (favourable, despite Sumner, *HSCP* 74, 1970, 292ff.).

[3] Tac. *Ann.* 4.40.

to her. Instead, Tiberius said, he would speak openly, and first of all of the hostility of Agrippina, which would become much more bitter if Livia Julia made a marriage that split the house of the Caesars into factions. The rivalry between the princesses would be heightened and the struggle might spread to embrace the princeps' grandsons. Another objection was Seianus' rank: Livia Julia, who had been the wife first of Gaius Caesar and then of Drusus, would never consent to grow old with an equestrian husband. Even if he himself were to give his consent, the leading men in the state would not tolerate such a match. Seianus might not want promotion, but there were those who made no secret of their belief that already he had risen far beyond the permissible limits of equestrian advancement, and their resentment of Seianus was a criticism of himself. Augustus might have contemplated giving his daughter to an *eques*; it was more significant that he had not actually done so, but had instead married her first to Agrippa and then to Tiberius himself. Friendship had made him speak plainly. Nevertheless he would not oppose any plans that Seianus and Livia Julia might make. For the time being he preferred to keep to himself the future that he had in mind for Seianus and the ties by which he proposed to bind them together. But there were no heights to which Seianus might not attain by his virtues and loyal service, and in due course Tiberius would publish his intentions.

This letter has been hailed as a masterpiece of deception, by which Seianus, cunning as he was, was outwitted and deluded by the deeper guile of his master, as he was to be again in 31.[1] Tiberius certainly proved himself superior in argument, but there is every reason to suppose that at this time his trust in Seianus was still unflawed and that his promise of further advancement, though vague, was perfectly sincere. It was nevertheless prudent to issue a timely reminder that, hated as he was by everyone else, Seianus owed his present position entirely to Tiberius' favour, while his future depended on his continuing loyalty. There is also an implication that Seianus had gone too far in discounting completely the claims of Nero and Drusus; Tiberius would not have such decisions made for him. It is clear that he knew nothing at all of Seianus' affair with Livia Julia, but his objections to

[1] Thus Syme, *Tacitus*, 320, followed by Koestermann on Tac. *Ann.* 4.40.

the marriage are cogent enough, with no hint of duplicity. Agrippina would undoubtedly have made herself an even greater nuisance if the match had taken place, and this prospect will have filled Tiberius with repugnance. As far as the social aspects of the proposal were concerned, he was presumably wrong about Livia Julia's feelings, but certainly right about the reaction of the upper classes. The hostility aroused by the shortlived betrothal of Junilla to Drusus the son of Claudius indicated how unpopular this much more important alliance between Tiberius' family and the equestrian upstart would have been.[1]

The one major difficulty in the letter is Tiberius' announcement that he would not stand in the couple's way. Although this comes as a distinct surprise after such telling arguments against the marriage, it cannot be dismissed lightly,[2] for Tiberius always weighed his words and is unlikely to have let his pen run away with him at so important a juncture. But he hated to be forced to unveil his intentions in plain language; he expected men to proceed from guarded hints to an intuitive perception of his wishes. Here he allowed himself two contradictory statements: there were overwhelming objections to the marriage; he would not oppose the designs of Seianus and Livia Julia. He stopped short of resolving the contradiction by bringing the two statements into a logical relationship with one another. This is characteristic, but the relationship is simple enough: Tiberius would have no objection to the marriage if the obstacles he had indicated did not exist. The letter was not meant to be a final discouraging answer. It was rather a pointer to further action, an implied answer to the question that Seianus was bound to ask himself: what should he do next? In practical terms this question could now be rephrased: how could he overcome Tiberius' objections to the marriage? These were in essence two: Seianus' equestrian status and Agrippina. To remedy the former Seianus himself could do nothing. Only Tiberius could help him here, and he had duly promised at the end of his letter to attend to the matter in the fullness of time. To the second problem Tiberius had offered no solution, but it would not be hard for Seianus to bridge the gap in his master's thought. If Agrippina stood in his way, then now more than

[1] Cf. Tac. *Ann.* 3.29.
[2] As it is by Koestermann *ad loc.*: 'sachlich ohne Bedeutung'.

ever Agrippina must be destroyed. There was no other conclusion that he could possibly draw. This is not, however, to say that Tiberius was cynically using Seianus to get rid of Agrippina without actually giving him direct instructions to do so, with the conscious intention of allowing Seianus to take the blame as a means of liquidating him in his turn when he had served his purpose. Always reluctant to make decisions, more hesitant and cautious now than ever before, he may well have avoided pursuing the logic of his desires to so concrete a conclusion even in his own mind.

Seianus, alarmed, wrote again to placate Tiberius.[1] It was at this point, according to Tacitus, that he conceived the plan of persuading Tiberius to leave Rome for good. Again he showed his consummate skill in turning to his own advantage Tiberius' natural inclinations. The princeps' protracted absence from the city in 21 and 22 told its own story. All that Seianus had to do was to encourage him discreetly to take the decisive step. The benefits for the prefect would be immense. He would control not only personal access to the princeps but to a large extent also communications by letter, for the imperial post was in the hands of the praetorians. So Tiberius would come to see the outside world entirely through Seianus' eyes, knowing only what Seianus thought it fit that he should know and relying on Seianus in all his dealings with the senate and with individuals. He would no longer need to keep up appearances and so he would be ready to surrender more and more power to Seianus. Seianus would have to deprive himself of the flattering manifestations of his creatures, but in so doing he might lessen his unpopularity and he would be amply compensated by the gain in real power. So Seianus began to inveigh against the humdrum business of the city and to extol the delights of peace and solitude, in which Tiberius could concentrate on the essentials of government, free from the boredom and pinpricks of routine.

Tiberius still hesitated, but an embarrassing incident in the latter part of 25 encouraged his thoughts in the direction that Seianus wanted them to take.[2] The rhetorician Votienus Montanus was brought to trial for insulting Tiberius, and one of the witnesses, Aemilius, a military

[1] Tac. *Ann.* 4.41.
[2] Tac. *Ann.* 4.42.

man,[1] was carried away by his eagerness to substantiate the charge. Despite the efforts of tactful senators to keep him quiet, he insisted on repeating in detail exactly what Votienus was alleged to have said. Tiberius was deeply shaken, as on a similar occasion in 15,[2] and shouted that he would prove the accusations against him false. The efforts of his friends and flatterers finally restored his customary calm, but this fiasco stimulated him to shun meetings of the senate. Votienus was condemned and exiled to the Balearic Islands, where he shortly died.[3]

It was not until the following year that Seianus, who had learned a patience to match Tiberius' own, took a further step in his campaign against Agrippina by attacking one of her closest friends, her cousin Claudia Pulchra.[4] The prosecution was noteworthy for the first appearance of the notorious Cn. Domitius Afer, praetor in the previous year, who accused Claudia of a familiar combination of crimes, adultery and *maiestas*, the latter consisting in the casting of spells against Tiberius and attempts to poison him. Anger and fear at the danger threatening her friend made Agrippina even less cautious than usual. Without even waiting till she could see Tiberius in private, she approached him while he was sacrificing to Augustus. Her speech suggests that she had lost her head completely. It ill befitted Tiberius, she declared, to sacrifice to Augustus while persecuting his descendants. The spirit of Augustus had not passed into statues: it was she who was the living image of the first princeps, the scion of the divine blood. She was aware of her danger and knew that Claudia's only crime was the folly of showing her too much respect, despite the fate that such behaviour had already brought on Sosia Galla. Tiberius, angered by this public scene, seized her and quoted at her a line of Greek: the fact that you are not a queen does not mean that you are being persecuted.[5] This brief response reveals yet again how Tiberius' distrust and loathing of Agrippina's limitless arrogance and ambition had destroyed in

[1] He had perhaps served under Germanicus (cf. Tac. *Ann.* 2.11) and may now have been – significantly enough – a tribune in the praetorian guard (cf. *ILS* 2686).
[2] Tac. *Ann.* 1.75; cf. above, p. 153.
[3] Cf. Koestermann on Tac. *Ann.* 4.42.
[4] Tac. *Ann.* 4.52.
[5] Tac. *Ann.* 4.52, Suet. *Tib.* 53.1.

him any capacity he might ever have had to understand her position and give her complaints a fair hearing. Claudia and her lover Furnius were condemned, apparently for adultery only; the charge of *maiestas* against Claudia may have been allowed to drop.

Shortly afterwards Agrippina fell ill, but sickness did nothing to make her less provoking. When Tiberius came to visit her, she wept for a long time without speaking and then began to beg him to take pity on her loneliness and give her a husband.[1] She was still capable of bearing children, and marriage was the only legitimate consolation for an honest woman. There must be men in Rome, she ingenuously remarked, who would be proud to give a home to Germanicus' widow and children. Tiberius was only too well aware of the political implications of her request. The imperial widows were a constant potential menace, and to marry either or both of them while both were still alive could only raise to fever pitch the jealousies and dissensions that Tiberius feared and abhorred. The considerations that had made him reluctant to let Livia Julia marry Seianus, his most trusted friend, will have left him even less inclined to provide Agrippina with a husband who might be tempted to encourage and abet her ambition in the hope of profit for himself. Not wishing to reveal these thoughts to Agrippina and unable or unwilling to devise a pretext, Tiberius said nothing and despite her repeated pleas left her without an answer.

Seianus for his part could not tolerate the slightest risk that Agrippina might be allowed to marry again, and worked hard to strengthen Tiberius' distrust and hatred.[2] He had his agents even among those whom Agrippina thought to be her friends, and these now warned her to avoid the princeps' table as Tiberius was plotting to poison her. With a gullibility almost incredible in one so politically active, Agrippina walked straight into the trap: her opinion of Tiberius was apparently such that she found no difficulty in believing the accusation. Yet again her behaviour was as inept as it could have been. The next time Tiberius invited her to dinner she did not even attempt to find some excuse not to attend (her health would have been the obvious one) but came – and ostentatiously ate nothing. Inevitably Tiberius noticed

[1] Tac. *Ann.* 4.53.
[2] Tac. *Ann.* 4.54, cf. Suet. *Tib.* 53.1.

this and decided to make sure of the reason. Some apples were brought to the table, and before they were touched by any of the other guests the princeps with his own hand offered them to Agrippina. Agrippina, her suspicions increased, refused. To her Tiberius said nothing, but turning to Livia he remarked that it was hardly surprising if he adopted an unfriendly attitude to a woman who pretended that he was trying to poison her. Though his view of the problem constituted by Agrippina was distorted, her conduct will again have made him feel that his behaviour was completely justified. For Seianus, another brilliant success. An interesting sidelight on Tiberius' unpopularity is thrown by public reaction to the incident when the story of it spread: it was rumoured that Tiberius would gladly poison Agrippina if he could find a way of doing so secretly, though he did not dare to commit such a crime openly.

In the same year Tiberius at last made the decision that he had meditated for so long and left the city.[1] As in 21, Campania was his first destination, and the official reason for his journey was the dedication of two temples, one at Capua to Jupiter, the other at Nola to Augustus. In recording his departure Tacitus raises yet again the problem of the attribution of responsibility to Tiberius or Seianus. He chose to follow the majority of his sources in ascribing the princeps' withdrawal to the wiles of Seianus, but he did not fail to notice the obvious fact that for six more years after Seianus' fall Tiberius remained in voluntary exile and indeed never returned to Rome. So he came to wonder if reasons should not rather be sought in Tiberius' own character. Those he excogitates are not impressive: a yearning to practise secret vices already contracted at Rhodes, embarrassment at his increasingly bizarre physical appearance, or an inability to endure any longer the burden of Livia's craving for power. The dilemma is to a large extent a false one. Tiberius' longing for retirement was not created by Seianus; it had existed before Seianus rose to power. Seianus played upon it, exploited it and brought it to fulfilment, but there was nothing in the circumstances of his fall to allay it – rather the contrary – and so it persisted for the remainder of Tiberius' life.

[1] Tac. *Ann.* 4.57, Suet. *Tib.* 39f., Dio 58.1.1.

5. THE SUPREMACY OF SEIANUS

Tiberius' exhaustion and weariness with public business are reflected in his choice of companions to share his retirement.[1] Only one senator was included in the party, the distinguished jurist M. Cocceius Nerva, grandfather of the emperor. This is not surprising: even if he felt well disposed towards individual senators, Tiberius could hardly decimate the senate by carrying its most valued members away from their duties. Nerva, as a jurist, was probably not deeply concerned with the day-to-day routine of public life; he had been a *curator aquarum* since 24,[2] but his retention of this post throughout his absence from Rome suggests that he may have played no great part in the activities of the board during the two years he was able to attend its meetings. Similarly only one distinguished *eques* – apart of course from Seianus himself – accompanied Tiberius: Curtius Atticus, a former friend of the poet Ovid. The rest of the princeps' retinue consisted largely of scholars, most of them Greeks, in whose discourse he found relaxation. His departure provoked much activity among soothsayers of all kinds. Many of them came to grief, for although they predicted, rightly as events were to show, that Tiberius would never again return to Rome, some were rash enough to announce that his death was imminent, since none could believe that the old man – he was nearly sixty-seven – would live for over ten more years.

Before Tiberius had even left Campania a remarkable incident made Seianus' hold over him even greater than it had been before.[3] The party was dining in a villa called Spelunca, the cavern, carved into the living rock. Suddenly a rockfall blocked the mouth of the cave, burying some of the attendants, and panic seized the diners. Seianus kept a cool head. Crouching above Tiberius, he used his own body to shield the princeps from danger and was careful to stay in position until the military rescue-party arrived on the scene to serve as independent witnesses of his heroism. This display of devotion finally earned him the complete confidence of the princeps.

Seianus was not slow to take advantage of this piece of good fortune.

[1] Tac. *Ann.* 4.58.
[2] Frontin. *Aq.* 102.
[3] Tac. *Ann.* 4.59, Suet. *Tib.* 39.

He decided that the time was now ripe for a direct attack on the family of Germanicus, with Nero, the nearest to the succession, as the principal target.[1] His agents brought accusations against the prince to which colour was given by Nero's behaviour. Most of his companions were freedmen and clients, who hoped to profit from his early accession and improvidently encouraged him to act with all the confidence of an heir apparent. He was the choice, they assured him, of the people and of the armies, and Seianus would not dare to try to dispossess him: his present power was as much the result of Nero's lethargy as of Tiberius' complacence. No doubt his mother's blood in him made it difficult for Nero to resist such blandishments. Though there was nothing in his words or behaviour to suggest that he would ever attempt revolution, he sometimes allowed his tongue to get the better of him. Any indiscreet remark was of course exaggerated before being reported to Tiberius, and Nero's side of the story was never heard. Gradually men began to avoid the prince, turning aside as soon as they had returned his greeting and breaking off conversations that had hardly been begun. Only Seianus' agents still displayed a treacherous amiability, and even Nero's most secret complaints were retailed by Julia Livilla to her mother Livia Julia, who faithfully passed them on to Seianus. Seianus also engaged the sympathies of Nero's brother Drusus, tempting him with the hope that he might gain the principate for himself if his elder brother, whose position had already been weakened, were removed. This prospect appealed to the young Drusus, whose innate greed for power was aggravated by jealousy of his brother, Agrippina's favourite. Seianus had no hesitation in using Drusus for the moment, realizing that the youth's fierce nature would make him an easy victim when his turn came.

The year 27 began in disaster. First the collapse of a jerry-built amphitheatre at Fidenae, to which a huge crowd had flocked from Rome because of the paucity of entertainments in the city, resulted in death or injury for fifty thousand people, then a major fire broke out in

---

[1] Tac. *Ann.* 4.59f. Tacitus remarks that in Nero's presence Tiberius put on a sullen face or a hypocritical smile. Presumably Nero had accompanied the princeps on his journey to Campania; since he did not follow him to Capreae, Seianus must have begun his campaign before the party left the mainland.

Rome itself, sweeping the Caelian Hill.[1] Tiberius paid compensation to all who had suffered, in proportion to their losses, and the senate added to its vote of thanks the proposal that the Caelian should be renamed *mons Augustus*. In the courts too events were ominous.[2] Inspired by his success against Claudia Pulchra, Domitius Afer now attacked her son, Quinctilius Varus, whose father had been the author of the *clades Variana*. He had the assistance of P. Cornelius Dolabella, a relative of the accused. It is not known what the charge was, nor to what degree it was provoked by the fact that Varus was engaged to one of Germanicus' daughters. The senate, however, resisted Afer and refused to make any decision, voting to wait for the return of the princeps. There is no further mention of the case in the sources, but the absence of Varus' family from subsequent history makes it likely that he was later condemned or committed suicide.[3]

The senate's reluctance to decide Varus' fate foreshadows one of the most baleful results of Tiberius' retirement from Rome. The effect of his withdrawal on the conduct of business in the senate and on the rôle of the senate in government was to be disastrous. It had proved virtually impossible to instil in the senators any consciousness of their responsibilities, even when Tiberius had been there in person to bestow encouragement and reproof. Henceforth the senate was afraid to take any decision on its own initiative for fear that it would incur the absent princeps' disapproval. Every matter had to be referred to Tiberius by letter. Delays were inevitable, misunderstandings probable, especially over matters in which Tiberius expected the senate to deduce his wishes from ambiguous hints. Consultation between senate and princeps was at an end, senatorial debate was virtually meaningless.[4] There is no reason to suppose that Tiberius' motives for leaving Rome included the desire to secure greater power for himself. Nevertheless his retirement brought about a major increase in secrecy and

---

[1] Tac. *Ann.* 4.62–64, Suet. *Tib.* 40, 48.1, *Cal.* 31, Dio 58.1.1a. Tacitus implies that both disasters took place before Tiberius withdrew to Capreae; Suetonius' statement that he had already retired to the island, but returned briefly to the mainland in response to public demand when he heard of events at Fidenae, may be correct.
[2] Tac. *Ann.* 4.66; on Varus, cf. Sen. *Contr.* 1.3.10.
[3] Cf. Koestermann *ad loc.*
[4] Cf. Charlesworth, *CAH* x, 632; Koestermann on Tac. *Ann.* 4.57.

despotism in government that was totally at odds with his republican principles. He can hardly have hoped, in the light of past experience, that the senate would recover its independence in his absence. He must simply have accepted the inevitable: he had tried to give the senate a chance, but the senate had refused to take it, and now he had ceased to care.

On his journey through Campania Tiberius had issued an edict forbidding anyone to disturb his quiet and had used his bodyguard to keep away the crowds in the towns through which he passed.[1] For his retirement he scorned the mainland and chose the island of Capreae, which had once belonged to the city of Neapolis but had been secured by Augustus in 29 in exchange for the much more valuable island of Aenaria.[2] It was not only his desire for peace and solitude that dictated the princeps' choice. Tacitus and Suetonius are agreed that what appealed most to Tiberius about Capreae was its inaccessibility.[3] The rocky island had only two landing-places; even more important, no boat could approach it unobserved by the lookout. The weight Tiberius attached to these considerations shows how much he was already a prey to the fear of conspiracy and assassination, a fear that constantly increased, encouraged at first by Seianus but in no way abating after Seianus' fall.

Seianus was now free to work on Tiberius as he pleased, stimulating the princeps' ready suspicions and exploiting his excessive readiness to believe his loyal helper's accusations.[4] No longer concealing his designs against Agrippina and Nero, he used troops to keep a detailed record of their movements and utterances. It may well have been at this time that Agrippina was put under house-arrest at Herculaneum and preparations were made to proceed against Nero, while Gaius went to live with his grandmother Antonia.[5] Seianus sent his agents to urge Agrippina and Nero to take refuge with the German armies or to seek sanctuary at the statue of Augustus in the Forum and appeal to the

[1] Tac. *Ann.* 4.67.
[2] Cf. Koestermann on Tac. *Ann.* 4.67.
[3] Tac. *Ann.* 4.67, Suet. *Tib.* 40.
[4] Tac. *Ann.* 4.67.
[5] Sen. *De Ira* 3.21.5, Plin. *NH* 8.145, Suet. *Cal.* 10.1; cf. the excellent discussion of Meise, *Untersuchungen*, 237ff.

senate and people for protection. These suggestions, though rejected by them, were represented to Tiberius as their plans.

Meanwhile Seianus made his long-delayed attack on Titius Sabinus.[1] Four ex-praetors had combined to work Sabinus' downfall: Lucanius Latiaris, M. Porcius Cato, Petilius Rufus and M. Opsius. Their aim was the consulship, the surest qualification for which, according to Tacitus, was Seianus' favour.[2] Latiaris, as an acquaintance of Sabinus, was cast for the principal rôle in the plot, while the others were to act as witnesses. The pattern was familiar: Latiaris praised Sabinus' constancy, spoke with respect of Germanicus, and pitied the fate of Agrippina. Sabinus, thus encouraged, was unable to conceal his feelings: he launched into a tirade against the cruelty, ambition and arrogance of Seianus and even went on to attack Tiberius himself. Latiaris agreed with him and so became Sabinus' confidant. Then one day the three accomplices hid themselves between the ceiling and the roof in Sabinus' house while Latiaris went off to find Sabinus and bring him home. There ensued a conversation even more incriminating than those that had gone before. A prosecution was promptly brought, and the four wrote a letter to Tiberius, revealing the details of their scheme.[3]

Tiberius struck swiftly and without warning, as he always did once he had decided to act.[4] A letter reached the senate on 1 January, 28, beginning with the traditional prayers and then going on without a break to attack Sabinus. The charges are striking: Tiberius claimed that some of his freedmen had been corrupted and that a plot had been formed against his life. This goes far beyond the material accumulated by Latiaris and his friends. It may be that Tacitus has failed to give sufficient detail or that the prosecutors added these embellishments in court; it is possible that Seianus passed the news to Tiberius in this form. But it is likely that Tiberius' accusations rested on no evidence at all, real or forged, and were simply chimeras of his imagination. The princeps' demand for action was clear. The senate instantly condemned Sabinus to death and he was dragged off to prison, shouting, despite

---

[1] Tac. *Ann.* 4.68, Dio 58.1; cf. Tac. *Ann.* 4.18f.

[2] Cf. Juv. 10.91ff.; it is striking, however, that as far as is known, only Cato ever became consul – in 36!

[3] Tac. *Ann.* 4.68f.

[4] Tac. *Ann.* 4.70.

the efforts of his guards to keep him quiet, that he was a New Year's sacrifice to Seianus. Terror spread through the city, enhanced by the reflection that all this was happening on a day of prayer and religious rites, when good omens should be sought. A letter of thanks came from Tiberius, expressing his gratitude to the senate for punishing an enemy of the state and adding that he went in fear of his life because of the plots laid against him by his enemies. These were not mentioned by name, but it was universally assumed that he meant Agrippina and Nero.

The two letters reveal in alarming fashion how much weaker Tiberius' grasp on reality had become in the past few years. His own fancy now conjured up the kind of charges that he had once thrown out in *maiestas* trials on account of their grotesque implausibility, and his inclination to scrutinize every word and action for an attack on himself had by now been magnified and distorted into an ever present terror of assassination. Asinius Gallus made matters worse by proposing that the senate should beg the princeps to confide his fears to it and allow it to dispel them.[1] Tiberius was angry – unwilling to be burdened with the responsibility that speaking openly would involve, he would have preferred the senate to act upon his hints. But Seianus calmed him, not out of affection for Gallus, but because he thought it wise to let Tiberius' resentment simmer, knowing that it would grow all the more violent with the passage of time.

The pernicious effects of Tiberius' departure from Rome were made manifest in the course of 28, when a revolt broke out among the Frisii.[2] The senate was too frightened and demoralized to do anything but beg princeps and prefect to grace Rome with their presence. Altars were decreed to Clementia and Amicitia, statues to Tiberius and Seianus. Tiberius and Seianus crossed to the mainland but did not condescend to leave Campania. Senators, *equites* and many of the common people flocked to greet them, and Seianus held court in the most arrogant manner while men of nominally higher rank laboured day and night to win the favour of his doorman. Tiberius seized the opportunity to betroth the younger Agrippina, Germanicus' eldest

[1] Tac. *Ann.* 4.71.
[2] Tac. *Ann.* 4.74.

daughter, to Cn. Domitius Ahenobarbus, giving instructions that the marriage was to be celebrated at Rome.[1] Their son, born nine years later, was to be the emperor Nero.

In 29 Livia died at the age of eighty-six.[2] During the last years of her life her relations with Tiberius had become more and more strained. Indeed Suetonius claims that the princeps had spoken to her only once since his retirement from Rome.[3] Her funeral was modest and the provisions of her will were long left unexecuted.[4] Tiberius pleaded pressure of work to excuse his absence from her obsequies and rejected many of the honours decreed her by the senate, in particular refusing to allow her deification on the grounds that she would have preferred it so. He had been plagued for so long by his mother's craving for power that he may have taken a perverse satisfaction in depriving her of the fruits of her labours after her death.[5] The funeral oration was delivered by Gaius, making his first public appearance at the age of seventeen.

For Tacitus the death of Livia removed the last obstacle to tyranny. While she was still alive, he claims, Tiberius was held in check by his respect for her and Seianus too did not dare to oppose her authority. Only when she was dead did they feel free to make an open attack on Agrippina and Nero.[6] Though Tacitus' chronology may be correct, there is nothing to be said for his logic. There is no evidence that Livia had exerted herself to save anyone from Seianus or Tiberius since her notorious intervention on behalf of Plancina in 20.[7] Nor is it likely that she would have protected Agrippina, whom, as Tacitus himself repeatedly states, she detested.[8] It was commonly believed that Livia had intercepted and delayed Tiberius' letter attacking Agrippina and

[1] Tac. *Ann.* 4.75; Ahenobarbus' character makes him a curious choice, cf. Suet. *Nero* 5.
[2] Tac. *Ann.* 5.1, Suet. *Cal.* 10.1, Dio 58.2. Attempts to challenge the Tacitean order of events (cf. Charlesworth, *CP* 17, 1922, 260f.; Pippidi, *Tibère*, 61 n.2) are refuted by Meise, *Untersuchungen*, 237ff.
[3] Suet. *Tib.* 51.2.
[4] Tac. *Ann.* 5.1, Suet. *Tib.* 51.2, *Cal.* 16.3, Dio 58.2.3a.
[5] Cf. Tac. *Ann.* 1.14, 2.34, 3.17, 64, Suet. *Tib.* 50.2–51, Dio 57.12.
[6] Tac. *Ann.* 5.3.
[7] Tac. *Ann.* 3.17.
[8] Cf. Tac. *Ann.* 1.33, 2.43, 4.12.

Nero, which was read in the senate shortly after her death, but no weight should be attached to this extremely implausible tale.

Tiberius was open yet guarded in his accusations: he did not charge the prince with plotting armed rebellion but merely with leading a dissolute life, while against Agrippina he had nothing to urge but her arrogant manner and contumacious spirit.[1] The senate listened to the letter in frightened silence, for although the charges were clear, Tiberius had characteristically given no indication of what action he expected the senate to take. But some of the more disreputable members began to demand that a motion be brought, with Cotta Messallinus prominent on the side of severity, though others, including the magistrates, still hesitated. Then Junius Rusticus ventured the opinion that the consuls should not bring any motion, for Tiberius might come to regret the ruin of the house of Germanicus.[2] Rusticus had been appointed by Tiberius as editor of the *acta senatus*, the official record of senatorial proceedings, and so it was believed that he might have some special knowledge of Tiberius' intentions. His advice was therefore taken. Meanwhile outside the senate-house a major demonstration was in progress. The crowd, carrying images of Agrippina and Nero, shouted that the letter was a forgery and that the destruction of the princeps' family was being planned against his will. Pamphlets attacking Seianus were circulated, forged over the signatures of men of consular rank.

These events gave Seianus ample material with which to confront the princeps. The senate, he claimed, had spurned the princeps' just anger and the people were in revolt. All that remained was for them to take up arms and hail as their commanders those whose images they had already chosen as their standards. So Tiberius wrote again, rebuking the plebs in an edict, repeating his charges against Nero and Agrippina, and complaining that thanks to one senator's trick his *maiestas* had been publicly mocked.[3] Nevertheless he demanded that any decision should be left entirely to him. Faced with this paradoxical document the senate

[1] Tac. *Ann.* 5.3.

[2] Tac. *Ann.* 5.4.

[3] Tac. *Ann.* 5.3; for the behaviour of the senate, cf. Gaius' comment in Suet. *Cal.* 30.2.

could do no more than reply that it would have been ready to apply the extreme penalty had it not been expressly prevented from so doing by Tiberius' instructions.

It is at this point that the narrative of Tacitus breaks off, to be resumed only after Seianus' fall in 31. To make matters worse Dio too is preserved for the years 29 and 30 only in fragmentary excerpts. Only from scraps in Suetonius and elsewhere is it possible to reconstruct a skeleton account of the proceedings against Nero and Agrippina. How the impasse between Tiberius and the senate was resolved is unknown, but one of the leading figures in the eventual prosecution was L. Avillius Flaccus, who became prefect of Egypt in 32.[1] Nero was declared a public enemy by the senate and both he and his mother were removed from the court in conditions of maximum security – chained, in a closed litter, under heavy guard. Nero was confined on the island of Pontia, Agrippina on Pandateria, which had once been the place of exile of her mother Julia.[2] There she seems to have been the first imperial exile to suffer physical ill-treatment, for which Tiberius must bear at least passive responsibility. On one occasion she was so badly beaten by a centurion, apparently for insulting Tiberius, that she lost an eye. Later she attempted to starve herself to death, but was prevented by forcible feeding.

In 30 Tiberius at last satisfied his longstanding grudge against Asinius Gallus.[3] He had never forgiven the man who had married Vipsania after Augustus had forced him to divorce her, and Gallus' frequent provocative behaviour in the senate had done nothing to assuage his anger.[4] Gallus had, it seems, decided to move with the times and had emerged in 29 as one of the leading flatterers of Seianus. Tiberius acted with consummate hypocrisy. To Gallus he was unprecedentedly friendly, even inviting him to visit Capreae and entertaining him with lavish hospitality. But on the same day that Gallus dined at Capreae, the senate received a letter from the princeps complaining that Gallus was envious of his friendship with Seianus. This was enough to make

[1] Philo Leg. 3.
[2] Suet. Tib. 53.2, 54.2, 64, Cal. 7, Plin. NH 8.145.
[3] Dio 58.3.1ff.
[4] Cf. Tac. Ann. 1.12, 2.35, 36, 4.71.

that now completely servile body condemn him, but Tiberius would not allow the execution, despite Gallus' readiness to commit suicide when he heard of the decree, but instructed that Gallus be kept under open arrest until he himself returned to the city. So Gallus spent four years in solitary confinement, being forcibly fed when necessary, until his death from starvation in 33.[1] Dio is confident that Tiberius' sole motive for keeping Gallus alive was to make his sufferings as atrocious as possible, and it is hard to follow apologists in dismissing this suggestion out of hand. Tiberius could be cruel to those he hated, and his cruelty increased in his last years as his reason weakened. The cat-and-mouse game with Gallus before his arrest, prefiguring that which Tiberius was soon to play with such protracted virtuosity against Seianus, tells its own story. It is probable that Tiberius' behaviour in such cases was in part the result of the difficulty he found in forcing himself to any irrevocable decision, but to suggest that nothing else but this reluctance determined his attitude here is perverse. Tiberius' suffering through the years of Gallus' marriage to Vipsania may also help to account for his readiness to make Gallus suffer at length when he had the chance, but nothing can explain away the facts.

Fufius Geminus, the consul of the previous year, also fell victim to a *maiestas* charge in 30.[2] The substance of the accusation is unknown. Geminus committed suicide, and his wife Mutilia Prisca followed suit, stabbing herself in the senate with a dagger she had smuggled in. Geminus, it seems, had charmed Livia and had owed his success to her favour, but he had also been in the habit of making malicious jokes about Tiberius. Tiberius had already hinted at his hostility in his letter to the senate after Livia's death, and the loss of her protection may have hastened Geminus' fate. Mutilia too had been one of Livia's closest friends and had helped Seianus by fostering her dislike of Agrippina, but her services to the prefect did not help her now.

To Seianus the time seemed ripe to dispense with Nero's brother Drusus.[3] Just as he had used Livia Julia against Tiberius' son, so now

[1] Tac. *Ann.* 6.23, Suet. *Tib.* 61.4.
[2] Dio 58.4.5f.; cf. Tac. *Ann.* 5.2 on Geminus, Livia and Tiberius, 4.12 on Mutilia, Livia and Seianus.
[3] Dio 58.3.8; there is unfortunately no way of knowing whether L. or C. Cassius is meant.

he enlisted the aid of Drusus' wife Aemilia Lepida.[1] The charges he brought against the prince are unknown: presumably the usual ones of contumacious speech and excessive ambition. The prince was himself on Capreae at the time, and at first Tiberius' only action was to send him to Rome. Seianus, not yet satisfied, suborned the consul Cassius Longinus to raise the matter in the senate. Drusus, like his brother, was declared a public enemy,[2] but instead of being removed to an island like Nero and Agrippina he was imprisoned in the dungeons of the palace at Rome.[3] Only two heirs of the Julio-Claudian line were still at liberty: Germanicus' surviving son Gaius, now eighteen but with no administrative experience, and Drusus' son Tiberius Gemellus, a boy of ten.[4]

Seianus now stood at the height of his power. His birthday was officially celebrated, oaths were taken by his fortune, and sacrifices offered to his statues, as they were to those of Tiberius himself.[5] He was at last betrothed to Livia Julia: the rivalry of Agrippina was no longer a source of danger and Tiberius was by this time sufficiently devoted to Seianus to defy opinion.[6] He was publicly saluted by Tiberius as the partner of his counsels.[7] Finally, despite his equestrian status, came full recognition of the place he had acquired in the princeps' trust: in 31 Tiberius was to take his fifth consulship, with Seianus as his colleague.[8] To celebrate his success Seianus apparently

[1] Cf. Tac. *Ann.* 6.40.

[2] Suet. *Tib.* 54.2, *Cal.* 7.

[3] Tac. *Ann.* 6.23.

[4] Claudius entered into no one's calculations. Tiberius is said to have granted him consular ornaments, but refused to admit him to the senate, which had offered him a seat among the consulars (Suet. *Claud.* 5, 6.2).

[5] Suet. *Tib.* 65.1, Dio 58.2.7f., 4.4, 6.2, Juv. 10.62.

[6] Cf. Tac. *Ann.* 5.6, 6.8, Suet. *Tib.* 65.1. Dio 58.3.9 says Seianus was engaged to Drusus' daughter, but note the silence of Tac. *Ann.* 6.27. Cf. Sumner, *Phoenix* 19, 1965, 144 n.44; *HSCP* 74, 1970, 295 n.214. The references to Seianus as Tiberius' son-in-law in Tac. *Ann.* 5.6 and 6.8 are more comprehensible if he was betrothed to Livia Julia; sister of Tiberius' adopted son Germanicus and widow of his son Drusus, she could reasonably be considered his daughter. Against Drusus' daughter, note the precision of Tac. *Ann.* 6.45. Cf. Meise, *Untersuchungen*, 57ff. That opinion was hostile is shown not only by the tone of Tac. *Ann.* 5.6, 6.8, but above all by Vell. 2.127f., written in 30 and quite clearly an apology for Tiberius' attitude to Seianus; cf. Sumner, *HSCP* 74, 1970, 292.

[7] Dio 58.4.3.

[8] Suet. *Tib.* 65.1; cf. *EJ* 50a, 358a.

arranged some form of popular election, not in the traditional place, the Campus Martius, where the people still assembled to give formal approval to the lists of candidates prepared by the senate, but on the Aventine, a spot with longstanding popular associations.[1]

The moment of triumph must have seemed very near as Seianus set off for Rome to take up office. Twice during his principate Tiberius had held the consulship, and each time it had been with his acknowledged successor: first with Germanicus in 18, then with Drusus in 21. Only one proof of his intentions was still lacking – the tribunician power.

6. THE FALL OF SEIANUS

At the beginning of 31 Seianus was supreme, openly hailed as the partner of Tiberius' labours, feared and fawned upon even by those who hated him most. Before the year was out he and all his family were dead, his statues thrown down, his name erased from the public records. Two problems, inextricably entwined, confront the historian. Why did Tiberius destroy the man he had raised above all others, the one man he had trusted in his loneliness and fear? And was there a conspiracy of Seianus, and if so what was its object: did Seianus' ambitions at the last vault too high and the patience that had served him so well desert him, was there a last desperate attempt at self-preservation when he realized too late that his master was planning his downfall, or was the plot nothing but an invention of Tiberius' guile or a figment of Tiberius' imagination?[2]

In his brief autobiography Tiberius stated that he punished Seianus on discovering that Seianus had plotted against the children of his son Germanicus.[3] Suetonius indignantly rejects this excuse, pointing out that Nero was executed only after Tiberius had begun to suspect Seianus, and Drusus not until Seianus was already dead. But for official purposes Seianus was guilty of conspiring against the state by planning

[1] *ILS* 6044 (= *EJ* 53); cf. Syme, *Hermes* 84, 1956/7, 257ff.
[2] For various views on the 'conspiracy of Seianus', cf. Marsh, *Tiberius*, 304ff.; Syme, *Tacitus*, 405f., 752f.; Koestermann, *Hermes* 83, 1955, 350ff.; Boddington, *AJP* 84, 1963, 1ff.; Meise, *Untersuchungen*, 77ff.; Bird, *Latomus* 28, 1969, 85ff.
[3] Suet. *Tib.* 61.1.

to assassinate Tiberius and Gaius.[1] The contemporary Valerius Maximus describes his intended crime as parricide, since in his eyes Tiberius was *princeps parensque noster*, and accuses him of wanting to take over the reins of empire.[2] What Tacitus himself believed we do not know, but his account of the upheavals that followed Seianus' fall throws some light upon the official version. The conspiracy was revealed by Satrius Secundus.[3] P. Vitellius was accused of offering to support the *coup* with funds from the military treasury, of which he was prefect.[4] The consul Memmius Regulus threatened his colleague Fulcinius Trio with an enquiry to establish that he had been a party to the plot.[5] In his defence the *eques* M. Terentius spoke of a plot against the state and a plan to murder the princeps.[6] As for Gaius, Seianus' choice to dispose of him was alleged to have been Sextius Paconianus.[7] The poet Juvenal too saw Seianus as aiming to kill Tiberius and replace him. Sneering at the fickleness of the mob, he claims that the men who smashed Seianus' statues and insulted his body would have hailed him as Augustus if he had succeeded in his design against the aged princeps.[8] Even Suetonius accepts that Seianus was plotting revolution, though he offers no details.[9]

Yet it is impossible to believe that Seianus would ever of his own accord have murdered Tiberius. His position depended on Tiberius' favour as much as it had ever done, and his only hope of ultimate power was still as the guardian of Tiberius Gemellus, appointed by Tiberius himself. If Tiberius had been assassinated and Seianus had attempted to seize the principate, the people of Rome, despite Juvenal's gibes, would not have accepted him. Nor would the aristocracy – it is significant that no army commander was involved in Seianus' fall, and

---

[1] Cf. *ILS* 157, 158, 159 (= *EJ* 51, 52, 85).
[2] Val. Max. 9.11. ext. 4; the charge of parricide may also have had its literal sense, cf. Meise, *Untersuchungen*, 59.
[3] Tac. *Ann.* 6.47.
[4] Tac. *Ann.* 5.8.
[5] Tac. *Ann.* 5.11.
[6] Tac. *Ann.* 6.8; Terentius' admissions do not of course prove that there was a *nouissimum consilium*, merely that by this time it was futile, if not fatal, to deny it.
[7] Tac. *Ann.* 6.3.
[8] Juv. 10.74ff.
[9] Suet. *Tib.* 65.1.

only one consular, his uncle Blaesus.[1] Without military backing Seianus would have been helpless, and the readiness with which the praetorians transferred their allegiance to Macro suggests that even they honoured their prefect only as the representative of Tiberius and would not have followed him against his master.[2] The fact that no governor fell with Seianus may show that Tiberius was afraid to challenge their power, but that a man like Lentulus Gaetulicus was strong enough to utter thinly veiled threats against Tiberius himself merely underlines that the provincial commanders could not have been forced to tolerate Seianus.[3]

If then the story of a plot against Tiberius is not pure fiction, it can only have been a desperate measure undertaken not as part of a rational plan but as a last hope of survival when Seianus found out that Tiberius had turned against him. A plot against Gaius on the other hand is much more likely. If Seianus' plans were to succeed, Gaius would have to be removed sooner or later, and it may be that with Agrippina and her other sons already out of the way Seianus decided that the time had come to take action. It was a letter from the prince's grandmother Antonia that first aroused Tiberius' suspicions against Seianus.[4] What, if anything, she had discovered is obscure. She may even have acquired no information at all, merely deducing from recent events that Gaius was marked as Seianus' next victim. Tiberius summoned the young man to Capreae at some time after 31 August, 30.[5] His opinion of Gaius at this time is hard to determine. No honours accompanied Gaius' assumption of the *toga uirilis*, yet early in 31 he was granted a

---

[1] Note Tac. *Ann.* 13.45: the fate of his son-in-law T. Ollius did not endanger Poppaeus Sabinus. Cf. Syme, *Tacitus*, 406. On Seianus' lack of distinguished support, cf. Bird, *Latomus* 28, 1969, 76ff., a useful corrective to some earlier views.

[2] This despite Dio 58.18.2; cf. Dio 58.12.2, which seems something more than just a politic demonstration to assure Tiberius of their loyalty after the event (and the donative).

[3] For Gaetulicus, cf. Tac. *Ann.* 6.30.

[4] Jos. *AJ* 18.181f. An epigram of Honestus (*BCH* 26, 1902, 153ff.) honours an Augusta whose intelligence saved the entire world; this is referred to Antonia's part in the unveiling of Seianus' designs by Cichorius (*Römische Studien*, 362ff.).

[5] Suet. *Cal.* 10.1: Gaius was in his nineteenth year; he was born on 31 August, 12, cf. *F. Val.*, *F. Pigh.* (*EJ* p. 51), Suet. *Cal.* 8.1.

priesthood.[1] But that Seianus wanted to be established as the guardian of Gemellus cannot have been news to Tiberius – Seianus himself had virtually admitted as much as long ago as 25. A moment's reflection would make it plain that this design must involve the exclusion of Gaius, though Tiberius' mind may have shunned this implication. But, apart from all other considerations, the assassination of Gaius by Seianus would take the decision out of Tiberius' hands in a manner as presumptuous as it was definitive, and that, as Tiberius had made quite clear when putting Seianus in his place in 25, the princeps was not prepared to tolerate. If Antonia succeeded in turning him against Seianus, she is most likely to have done so by convincing him that he had been duped by the man he thought his friend. Tiberius needed to believe that it was always he who was the guiding force in the partnership, that Seianus was his minister, acting only in his interests. Antonia implanted in his mind the suspicion that Seianus had tried to outsmart him and exploit his favour entirely for his own profit. From that moment Seianus' days were numbered.

Dio, who says nothing of any conspiracy of Seianus, presents an account of Tiberius' motives that is roughly consistent with what has been suggested above.[2] Seianus' power had grown so great, he says, that both senate and people looked up to him as if he were their ruler. When Tiberius realized this, he feared that they might go so far as to proclaim Seianus princeps. This may seem implausible: Seianus was undoubtedly despised and hated by the vast majority of high and low alike, the exaggerated honours paid to him were entirely the result of Tiberius' unprecedented favour, and Tiberius had shown himself well aware of these facts in 25, when he rejected Seianus' first application for the hand of Livia Julia.[3] But by now Tiberius may not have felt so sure, especially as he had had no direct contact with Rome for so long. The extreme caution with which he proceeded, seeking by various devices to sound the opinions of senate and people,[4] tends to confirm Dio's diagnosis. Dio may have exaggerated and oversimplified, but his

---

[1] Dio 58.7.4, 8.1.
[2] Dio 58.4.1ff., 5.1; cf. Koestermann, *Hermes* 83, 1955, 360ff.
[3] Tac. *Ann.* 4.40; cf. above, p. 197.
[4] Dio 58.6.2f.

narrative contains the fundamental truth that at some point Tiberius became convinced that Seianus, far from being his faithful servant, was using him for his own ends, and he may well be right in claiming that Tiberius decided in 30 to bring Seianus down and that the consulship and the flattering allusions alike were snares to lull him into a false sense of security.[1]

Seianus' consulship began with ill omens, but his power was so great that men did not take them seriously and still continued to swear by his fortune.[2] Tiberius meanwhile deluged Seianus and the senate with letters more bewildering than ever before. At one moment he would claim that his death was at hand, only to announce a short while later the imminence of his arrival in Rome. Seianus himself was now praised, now criticized, till he found himself in complete confusion, too worried to pursue his plans with confidence yet not alarmed enough to resort to desperate measures.[3] He and his son Strabo were granted priesthoods at the same time as Gaius, and like Agrippa and Tiberius before him he was given proconsular *imperium*, presumably when he resigned his consulship.[4] But the appointment of Gaius had been accompanied not only by public rejoicing at this sign of favour for the son of the ever popular Germanicus, but also by hints from Tiberius that he saw in Gaius a likely successor.[5]

The trial of L. Arruntius added to Seianus' worries. Arruntius had always been his opponent, and Seianus now engineered an attack on him. But Tiberius put a stop to the proceedings and Arruntius' accusers, Aruseius and Sangunnius, were punished.[6] Nero, it is true,

[1] Dio 58.4.3. If Gaius was summoned to Capreae in response to Antonia's letter, autumn 30 is the most likely date for the beginning of Tiberius' suspicions. Seianus' designation as consul will then have been sincere, but Tiberius will already have been planning his destruction at the time he took up office. Boddington (*AJP* 84, 1963, 5) objects that such a tactic would deceive not only Seianus but the senate and people as well. This is true, as Dio admits (58.4.4, cf. 6.5, 7.4), but senate and people were only waiting for Tiberius to change his mind, which was all he needed to ascertain.
[2] Dio 58.5.5–6.2.
[3] Dio 58.6.2ff.
[4] Dio 58.7.4. Tiberius and Seianus resigned the consulship on 8 May (*ILS* 6124); 15 May for Tiberius' resignation in Suet. *Tib.* 26.2 is probably corrupt.
[5] Dio 58.8.1f.
[6] Dio 58.8.3, cf. Tac. *Ann.* 6.7, 48, 11.6. D.48.2.12 pr. may be connected with the trial, but it does not prove that a Lentulus defended Arruntius.

was finally put to death at about this time,[1] but in a letter to the senate
on the subject Tiberius referred to Seianus somewhat coldly, without
any of his usual honorifics.[2] To prevent the offering of sacrifices to
Seianus, he once more banned all sacrifices to mortals and forbade the
proposal of honours for himself in order to check the heaping of them
on Seianus.[3]

To calm Seianus' growing fears, Tiberius let the rumour get about
that his favourite was soon to receive the tribunician power.[4] Then
with lightning rapidity he struck. From Capreae came Q. Naevius
Cordus Sutorius Macro, armed with his commission as praetorian
prefect.[5] Entering the city by night, he made his presence known to the
consul Memmius Regulus, who unlike his colleague Trio was reliable,
and the prefect of the *uigiles* (the night-watch), P. Graecinius Laco.[6]
At dawn on 18 October he went to the Palatine, where the senate was
to meet in the temple of Apollo. Outside he encountered Seianus, who
was worried at the lack of any message from Tiberius. Macro assured
him in strict secrecy that he bore with him the news of Seianus' tribunician power. Delighted, Seianus went into the temple, which was
guarded by a detachment of praetorians. These Macro now dismissed
and sent back to camp, revealing that he was their new commander and
carried a letter from Tiberius granting them a donative. In their place
he surrounded the temple with *uigiles* and then delivered Tiberius'
letter to the consuls. Without waiting to hear it read, he hurried to the
camp of the praetorians, leaving Laco in command on the Palatine.

Inside the temple the letter was read.[7] It was long and wordy, full of
irrelevant matter interspersed with trivial complaints against Seianus.
Seianus sat puzzled, as did the mass of senators who had cheered him
when he entered the building. In pathetic terms Tiberius confessed his
fears for his own safety, begging the senate to send one of the consuls

[1] Suet. *Tib.* 54.2, 61.1.
[2] Dio 58.8.4.
[3] Dio 58.8.4.
[4] Dio 58.9.2, cf. Suet. *Tib.* 65.1.
[5] Dio 58.9.2ff. The inscription *AE* 1957.250 reveals not only the correct form of
Macro's name but also the fact that he had been *praefectus uigilum*. For the donative
to the praetorians, cf. Suet. *Tib.* 48.2, Dio 58.18.2.
[6] For Laco, cf. *ILS* 1336f. (= *EJ* 222f.).
[7] Dio 58.10, cf. Suet. *Tib.* 65.1, Juv. 10.71f.: *uerbosa et grandis epistula.*

to Capreae with a military guard to escort him, in his old age and solitude, to Rome.[1] Then at the end he demanded that two friends of Seianus be punished and Seianus himself arrested. Seianus still sat, surrounded now by praetors and tribunes ready to seize him if he tried to escape. Three times Memmius called him forward; at the third call Seianus rose, to find Laco beside him. Despite the storm of abuse that now broke over the fallen favourite, Memmius did not propose the death penalty or risk a general vote. Instead he asked one senator only whether Seianus should be imprisoned.[2] The answer was affirmative, and so, accompanied by Laco and the other magistrates, he led Seianus out and to prison.

In the streets the crowd ran wild, clamouring for revenge, mocking the ruin of Seianus' hopes, tearing down his statues and smashing them to fragments.[3] The reaction of the people and the absence of any sign of trouble from the praetorians gave the senate courage. On the same afternoon it met again, this time in the temple of Concordia, and condemned Seianus to death. The sentence was carried out without delay and the body was dragged to the Gemoniae, where for three days it suffered the insults of the mob and of Seianus' former satellites, who earnestly proclaimed that they had never really liked the man and hurried ostentatiously to trample Caesar's enemy, taking with them as witnesses their slaves, who might otherwise have initiated proceedings against them. What was left was thrown into the Tiber.[4]

A welter of decrees followed the execution.[5] Seianus' death was to be left unmourned, a statue of Liberty was to be erected in the Forum, and an annual festival presided over by the members of all the great priestly colleges was to mark the anniversary of the prefect's fall. For the future excessive honours to any man were forbidden, while oaths were to be taken only in Tiberius' name. Praetorian ornaments were

---

[1] Tac. *Ann.* 6.2, Suet. *Tib.* 65.1: *mitterent alterum e consulibus, qui se senem et solum in conspectum eorum . . . perduceret*; Dio 58.10.2.
[2] This extreme caution may well have been enjoined by Tiberius himself in his instructions to Macro.
[3] Dio 58.11.1ff., cf. Juv. 10.54ff.
[4] Dio 58.11.4f., Juv. 10.66ff., 81ff.; for the date, cf. Tac. *Ann.* 6.25, F. Ost. (*EJ* p. 42), *ILS* 158 (= *EJ* 52).
[5] Dio 58.12.4ff.

voted to Macro, quaestorian to Laco, as well as monetary rewards and
other honours, but both men refused, as did Tiberius when he was
once more offered the title of *pater patriae* and games to celebrate his
birthday were proposed. In reply he merely reaffirmed his veto on all
honours for himself.

Tiberius had been on tenterhooks. Ignorant for so long of the state of
affairs at Rome, he had had no idea whether Macro would succeed in
his mission. In case he failed, Tiberius had had ships at the ready to
take refuge with one of the provincial armies. As a last resort he had
even given Macro orders to release Drusus from prison and proclaim
him princeps if Seianus attempted a *coup*. But Macro's success did
little to ease Tiberius' mind. He refused to receive not only the
deputation that came from senate, *equites* and people to congratulate
him, but even the unquestionably faithful Memmius, who had gone to
Capreae in answer to the princeps' own summons.[1] Suetonius even
claims that for nine months he did not dare to set foot outside his
residence, the Villa Ionis, but this is a gross exaggeration.[2]

Meanwhile at Rome the witch-hunt was on, as Seianus' former
followers turned on one another in a frantic effort to save their own
skins.[3] Some had been lynched by the crowd in the days of disorder
that followed his death, when the praetorians rampaged through the
city, burning and looting, not out of resentment at the fate of their
former commander but in rage at the slur that had been cast on their
loyalty.[4] Many others were condemned or committed suicide.[5] But the
only consular to fall was Seianus' uncle Blaesus, against whom Tiberius
gave vent to many vile accusations.[6] The narrative of Tacitus resumes
after the great lacuna with the trials of P. Vitellius and P. Pomponius
Secundus.[7] Vitellius, who was prefect of the military treasury, was

---

[1] Tac. *Ann.* 6.23, Suet. *Tib.* 65.2, Dio 58.13.

[2] Suet. *Tib.* 65.2. But Tiberius crossed to the mainland early in 32 (Tac. *Ann.* 6.1).

[3] The atmosphere is well conveyed by Dio 58.14, 16.4f., though his suggestion
that Tiberius cynically exploited the situation is unjust. Cf. Tac. *Ann.* 6.7 on the
following year, also Sen. *Ben.* 3.26.1.

[4] Dio 58.12.1f.

[5] Cf. the fragmentary speech in Tac. *Ann.* 5.6. Bruttedius Niger (cf. Tac. *Ann.* 3.66)
was probably one of the victims (Juv. 10.81ff.).

[6] Tac. *Ann.* 5.7.

[7] Tac. *Ann.* 5.8, Suet. *Vit.* 2.3.

accused of offering Seianus financial aid. Pomponius' only offence was his friendship for Seianus' kinsman Aelius Gallus, who when Seianus was executed had taken refuge in Pomponius' gardens. Vitellius, despite the loyal support of his brothers, put an end to his burden of hope and fear by suicide. But Pomponius survived, though he spent the remainder of Tiberius' reign in prison, to be released by Gaius, and under Claudius attained the consulship and triumphal ornaments.[1]

Towards the end of the year Asia and Greece were briefly troubled by the appearance in the Cyclades of a young man claiming to be Germanicus' son Drusus.[2] Men believed that he had escaped from prison and was now on his way to his father's armies to invade Syria or Egypt. Poppaeus Sabinus, the governor of Moesia, Achaea and Macedonia, eventually encountered the pretender at Nicopolis. He said he was a son of M. Silanus, suffect consul in 15, and was about to sail to Italy. Sabinus wrote to Tiberius, relating what he had learned; Tacitus could discover nothing more, but Dio tells us that the false Drusus was arrested and brought before Tiberius.

Seianus' elder son Strabo had been executed not long after his father, on 24 October. Two days later, after writing to Tiberius that Seianus and Livia Julia had murdered Drusus, Apicata committed suicide.[3] Then in late November or early December, though popular fury had by this time died down, the senate decreed the execution of Seianus' two remaining children, Capito Aelianus and Junilla.[4] Capito was old enough to know what was in store, but Junilla asked over and over again where she was being taken and what she had done wrong, promising not to be naughty again and begging to be let off with a whipping, as she was dragged to prison, there to be raped by the executioner – ancestral custom forbade the execution of a virgin – before she was strangled and her body exposed on the Gemoniae along with her brother's.

Whether Tiberius ordered this hideous climax to the terror and degradation that had ravaged Rome in the weeks since Seianus' fall,

[1] Cf. Koestermann on Tac. *Ann.* 5.8.
[2] Tac. *Ann.* 5.10, Dio 58.25.1 (under the year 34).
[3] Dates in *F. Ost.* (*EJ* p. 42), showing that Dio 58.12.6 misdates Apicata's suicide.
[4] Tac. *Ann.* 5.9, Suet. *Tib.* 61.5, Dio 58.12.5; the approximate date is given by *F. Ost.* (*EJ* p. 42).

Coins of Tiberius celebrating his virtues:
13a obverse Tiberius; reverse shield with the legend CLEMENTIAE.

13b obverse Augustus with the legend DIVVS AVGVSTVS PATER; reverse
altar with the legend PROVIDENT(IAE).

14a Coin of Tiberius: obverse Tiberius; reverse seated female figure with legend PONTIF(EX) MAXIM(VS).

14b Coin of Smyrna celebrating the building of the temple to Tiberius, Livia and the senate: obverse busts of Livia and the senate; reverse the temple, with statue of Tiberius.

14c Coin of Gaius commemorating the victories of his father Germanicus and the recovery of the standards lost by Varus, with legend SIGNIS RECEP(TIS) DEVICTIS GERM(ANIS).

whether indeed he even knew in advance of the senate's intention is uncertain.[1] He can hardly have cared. For seven years he had lived in the belief that Seianus was the one man he could trust: only Seianus' vigilance had guarded him against the unceasing machinations of his enemies, foremost among them Agrippina, only Seianus' tireless energy had helped him to bear the burden of power that Drusus' death had forced him to retain when the peace of retirement had at last seemed within his grasp. From Antonia he had learned that Seianus too had betrayed him, and so he had destroyed Seianus. Now he was utterly alone: as long as he lived, he could never trust any man again. Then came Apicata's letter, implanting in his mind the appalling conviction that his only friend had been his cruellest enemy, that Seianus, not drink, had killed Drusus and so robbed him for ever of the rest he craved. All those years, instead of the constant torment of suspicion and fear, he could have known the quiet of retirement, if Drusus had lived. But he had not listened to his son, he had chosen to trust Seianus. Apicata could have been well satisfied with her revenge. Not only had she brought about Livia Julia's death,[2] she had shattered what slender hope Tiberius had had of ever again knowing any peace of mind.[3]

[1] Koestermann (on Tac. *Ann.* 5.9) is overconfident in accusing Tiberius. The senate had sentenced Seianus himself to death without specific instructions from the princeps (Dio 58.10.2).
[2] According to one story she was starved to death by her mother Antonia (Dio 58.11.7); at all events she was dead before the end of 31 (Tac. *Ann.* 6.2).
[3] In the circumstances the story of the Rhodian visitor (Suet. *Tib.* 62.1) is only too credible.

VII

THE LAST YEARS

1. TIBERIUS AND ROME AFTER SEIANUS' FALL

Early in 32 Tiberius crossed to the mainland, but though he repeatedly came close to Rome, even visiting the gardens on the banks of the Tiber, he could not bring himself to enter the city. Instead he returned to his island fastness, where it is said that he showed such imagination in the invention of unprecedented sexual pastimes that eager chroniclers found themselves constrained to devise a whole new terminology.[1]

Meanwhile at Rome the senate had taken the annual oath of loyalty, in which Tiberius must at some time have acquiesced, individually instead of as a body.[2] Its most distinguished members exercised their talents in condemning the memory of Livia Julia, and Seianus' confiscated wealth was transferred from the treasury to the personal chest of the princeps, from which no doubt the greater part of it had issued.[3] A more remarkable proposal came from Togonius Gallus, who begged the princeps to compile a list of senators, twenty of whom, chosen by lot, should act as an armed guard whenever he entered the senate.[4] Tiberius answered calmly in a familiar fashion, indicating his lack of enthusiasm for the proposal by cataloguing the difficulties it would involve.[5] The choice itself would be complex, he wrote: he would not know whether to select experienced men or the young, magistrates or men not at present holding any office. Moreover, once he had chosen,

[1] Tac. *Ann.* 6.1; not very exciting details in Suet. *Tib.* 42–45.
[2] Dio 58.17.1ff.
[3] Tac. *Ann.* 6.2.
[4] Tac. *Ann.* 6.2, Dio 58.17.3–18.1.
[5] Cf. his reply to Asinius Gallus in Tac. *Ann.* 2.36.

should he rely on the same men all the time, or should he change them later? Besides, it would be an unseemly spectacle to see senators girding on arms at the door of the house. If his life could be guaranteed only by such measures, he could not feel that it was worth preserving.

In sharp contrast to this moderate reply was his response to the proposal of the rhetorician Junius Gallio, whose wit had once pleased him, that veterans of the praetorian guard should have the privilege of sitting in the first fourteen rows of the theatre.[1] This innocent suggestion prompted a hysterical outburst. What, Tiberius asked, was Gallio's interest in the army, whose rewards were the concern of their commander and no one else? Had he thought of something that had never occurred to Augustus? Or was this perhaps an attempt at sedition by a henchman of Seianus, trying to corrupt the simple minds of the troops? The distorted echo of the principles that had guided Tiberius throughout his reign – respect for tradition and loyalty to the example of Augustus – makes his fear of conspiracy tragic as well as grotesque. The unfortunate Gallio paid dearly for his attempt at adulation. He was expelled first from the senate and then from Italy, choosing as his place of exile Lesbos. But Lesbos was judged to be too pleasant for him, and so he was brought back to Rome and kept under house arrest.

In the same letter in which he attacked Gallio Tiberius demanded that action be taken against Sextius Paconianus, who was named as the agent chosen by Seianus for the liquidation of Gaius.[2] The senators were delighted, for Sextius was a notorious intriguer. The news of his alleged designs against Gaius fanned their hatred, and Sextius would have been condemned to death had he not turned informer. His victim was the equally hated Lucanius Latiaris, ringleader of the plot that had destroyed Titius Sabinus.[3]

After Latiaris had been condemned, Haterius Agrippa tried to stir up further trouble. He criticized the consuls of the previous year, Memmius Regulus and Fulcinius Trio, for not pursuing the accusations they had brought against each other in the last weeks of 31.[4] Their

[1] Tac. *Ann.* 6.3, Dio 58.18.3ff.; for Gallio and Tiberius, cf. Sen. *Suas.* 3.6f.
[2] Tac. *Ann.* 6.3.
[3] Tac. *Ann.* 6.4, cf. above, p. 207.
[4] Tac. *Ann.* 6.4, cf. 5.11.

silence, he suggested, showed that both had a guilty conscience, and the senate could not be expected to ignore what it had heard. Memmius replied that he would take his revenge in due time, when Tiberius was present; Trio, less sure of himself, claimed that any hasty remarks exchanged between colleagues were best forgotten. Haterius insisted, but was opposed by another consular, Q. Sanquinius Maximus, who urged the senate not to increase the princeps' burden by kindling fresh resentments: Tiberius himself could provide any remedy required. So the incident closed, with Memmius and Trio unscathed, Haterius universally detested.

The next prospective victim was the consular Cotta Messallinus, whose harshness had long since earned him many enmities.[1] He was said to have cast doubts on Gaius' virility and to have made a joke about Tiberius' refusal to grant Livia divine honours after her death. He had also clashed with M. Lepidus and L. Arruntius and had remarked: 'The senate may protect them, but my little Tiberius will look after me.' The senate's most prominent members joined in the attack, but when Cotta appealed to the princeps his confidence was justified. In his letter from Capreae Tiberius spoke of the origins of their friendship and recounted Cotta's many services. Moreover he insisted, as he would have done twenty years before, that remarks taken out of their context and anecdotes recounted at the dinner-table should not be treated as grounds for a prosecution.

But despite this breath of sanity from the past the opening words of the letter revealed with a terrible clarity the anguish in which Tiberius now lived: 'What I am to write to you, or how I am to write, or what indeed I should not write at this time, may the gods and goddesses make me suffer worse than I suffer already every day if I know.'[2] With Cotta safe, the senate duly turned on his principal accuser Caesilianus and decreed that he should suffer the same penalty as Aruseius and Sangunnius, the accusers of Arruntius in the previous year.[3]

[1] Tac. *Ann.* 6.5, cf. 2.32, 3.17, 4.20, 5.3.
[2] Tac. *Ann.* 6.6, Suet. *Tib.* 67.1. Tacitus is obviously right in not limiting the reference of this outburst to the immediate problem of Cotta Messallinus; contra, Rogers, *Trials*, 134.
[3] Tac. *Ann.* 6.7.

The next to be charged were Germanicus' friend Q. Servaeus and an *eques*, Minucius Thermus, whom Seianus' friendship had not made arrogant.[1] Their case aroused general sympathy, but Tiberius denounced them strongly and ordered Cestius Gallus to repeat to the senate the charges he had made in a letter sent to Capreae. So Cestius undertook the prosecution. Tacitus exclaims in just despair at the utter degeneracy of the senate, whose leading members readily descended to the most abject delation, both openly and in secret, so that no man knew who his friends were and the most trivial utterances became the excuse for a charge.[2] Servaeus and Minucius were condemned, but joined the ranks of the informers; their victims were Julius Africanus and Seius Quadratus.

Sometimes a voice was raised in the wilderness, as when the *eques* M. Terentius defended himself in the senate and refused to pretend that he had always hated Seianus.[3] He admitted not only that he had been an adherent of Seianus but also that he had consciously sought Seianus' friendship and had been delighted when he gained it. He had seen Seianus' success as praetorian prefect, first as his father's colleague, then alone, and the advancement of Seianus' kinsmen; friends of Seianus had enjoyed Tiberius' friendship too, while his enemies had lived in fear and affliction. Therefore he too had cultivated not an upstart from Vulsinii but a member of the Julian and Claudian houses, betrothed to Tiberius' daughter Livia Julia, Tiberius' colleague in the consulship: it was not for men such as he to question the princeps' taste in friends. The senate should take into account not just the last day of Seianus' life but the previous sixteen years, during which men had honoured Seianus' henchmen and it was counted an honour to be recognized even by his freedmen and doorkeepers. So, he concluded, let those who had harboured designs against the state and had plotted to assassinate Tiberius be punished, but as for those who had only been Seianus' friends, let Tiberius reckon them as guiltless as he was himself. Terentius' courage in daring to speak what every senator

[1] Tac. *Ann.* 6.7.
[2] Cf. Dio 58.14 on the previous year, Sen. *Ben.* 3.26.1 and Gaius' comment in Suet. *Cal.* 30.2.
[3] Tac. *Ann.* 6.8f., Dio 58.19.3ff.

knew to be the truth won the reward it deserved: not only was he acquitted, his accusers were put to death or exiled.

Tiberius' next letter was directed against a former praetor, Sex. Vistilius, who had once been a close friend of his brother Drusus.[1] Vistilius was said to have criticized Gaius' morals, and Tiberius had barred the old man from his company, which prompted Vistilius to suicide. Nevertheless he had bound up his veins and written to the princeps begging forgiveness, but Tiberius' reply was stern, so he removed the bandages. The inconsistency with Tiberius' treatment of Cotta is striking, as is the fact that Vistilius, like several others who fell during these years, was an old friend of the princeps.

There followed the prosecution for *maiestas* of four consulars, C. Annius Pollio, Ap. Silanus, Mam. Scaurus and C. Calvisius Sabinus, with Pollio's son L. Annius Vinicianus. The senate was panic-stricken, since many of its members were linked by marriage or friendship with the accused. But a witness, Julius Celsus, a tribune in one of the urban cohorts, exculpated Calvisius and Silanus, while Tiberius wrote postponing the other three cases until he himself could investigate them in the senate, though he permitted himself some ominous remarks about Scaurus.

Tacitus then gives full reign to his indignation.[2] Since women could not be accused of conspiracy against the state, he says, they were brought to trial for their tears: the aged Vitia, mother of Fufius Geminus, was put to death because she had mourned her son. According to Suetonius, Tiberius introduced this ban on mourning,[3] but that this was not the case is suggested by an apparent reference to it in the *Ibis* of Ovid, written in or shortly after 8.[4] Such a measure may seem intolerably harsh, but it must be remembered that mourning for the

---

[1] Tac. *Ann.* 6.9.

[2] Tac. *Ann.* 6.10.

[3] Suet. *Tib.* 61.2. The prohibition is referred to in D.3.2.11.3, but with no indication of date.

[4] Ov. *Ibis* 163ff.: *nec tibi continget funus* lacrimaeque *tuorum*, indeploratum *proicere caput, carnificisque manu populo plaudente traheris infixusque tuis ossibus uncus erit.* The parallel between these lines and Tac. *Ann.* 6.19 is very striking. For the date of composition, cf. *Ibis* 1. (Ovid was born on 20 March, 43 B.C.)

victim of a charge of *maiestas* might easily take on the character of a political demonstration.

Heads rolled on Capreae as well as at Rome.[1] Two of Tiberius' oldest friends, Vescularius Flaccus and Julius Marinus, were executed, though both had been with him during his exile on Rhodes and had enjoyed his special favour at Capreae. Their fall was not regretted, for Vescularius had played a leading part in the downfall of Libo Drusus, while Marinus had abetted Seianus in the destruction of Curtius Atticus.

At about this time Tiberius lost an old friend and drinking companion, L. Calpurnius Piso the *pontifex*, who had been *praefectus urbi* throughout the reign.[2] Piso received the honour of a state funeral. He was succeeded by L. Aelius Lamia, who had been appointed as governor of Syria presumably in succession to Cn. Sentius Saturninus but had never been allowed to take up his post.[3]

Where he did not believe that his personal safety was threatened, Tiberius' mind was as precise as it had been in the past. The *quindecimuir* L. Caninius Gallus had demanded a decree of the senate to add a new Sibylline book to the existing corpus, and so a motion was brought by the tribune Quintilianus and duly passed.[4] But a letter came from Tiberius, gently critical of Quintilianus, whose ignorance of ancient custom was excused by his age, but much more severe towards Gallus, who as a priest of long experience should have known better than to raise such a matter without consulting his colleagues in a poorly attended meeting of the senate. Since many bogus Sibylline books were current at the time, the princeps issued a reminder that Augustus had imposed a time-limit, within which newly-discovered prophecies must be handed to the urban praetor, and had forbidden the keeping of them in private. Gallus' new book was duly subjected to quindecimviral scrutiny. Tiberius' interest in the niceties of sacral procedure, guided by his respect for ancestral tradition and the rulings of Augustus, is

---

[1] Tac. *Ann.* 6.10.
[2] Tac. *Ann.* 6.10f., Dio 58.19.5. Tacitus says Piso was *praefectus urbi* for twenty years, but Suet. *Tib.* 42.1 and Plin. *NH* 14.145 show that he was first appointed by Tiberius. For their friendship, cf. Sen. *Ep.* 83.14.
[3] Dio 58.19.5.
[4] Tac. *Ann.* 6.12.

entirely consistent with his attitude to religious questions earlier in the reign.

In the same year the price of corn provoked riots and unusually virulent and sustained attacks on Tiberius in the theatre.[1] Sensitive as ever to scurrilous personal abuse,[2] Tiberius berated the magistrates and the senate for failing to use their authority to curb the people. He added a list of the provinces from which he imported corn and pointed out how much more corn now came to Rome than in the time of Augustus.[3] A decree of the senate and a consular edict followed: it is noteworthy that Tiberius still clung to his desire that the senate and magistrates should perform their proper functions without relying on him.

At the end of the year three *equites*, Geminius, Celsus and Pompeius, were executed for complicity in Seianus' conspiracy.[4] No details are known. The tribune Julius Celsus, whose evidence had saved Ap. Silanus and Calvisius Sabinus, contrived to commit suicide in prison by breaking his neck with his own chains. One Rubrius Fabatus, who had so despaired of life at Rome that he set out to seek sanctuary with the Parthians, was arrested at sea in the straits of Messina and brought back when he could give no plausible reason for his journey abroad. However, he came to no harm, though this, according to Tacitus, was a proof not of Tiberius' mercy but merely of his forgetfulness.

In 33 Tiberius again visited the mainland and came within four miles of the city.[5] He devoted considerable thought to the question of husbands for the remaining daughters of Germanicus, a pressing matter, since Drusilla was now sixteen and Julia fifteen.[6] Eventually he chose for Drusilla L. Cassius Longinus, consul in 30, and for Julia M. Vinicius, Cassius' colleague, the patron of Velleius Paterculus. Tiberius wrote to the senate, offering vague excuses for his absence and asking, in view of the enmities he had incurred on behalf of the state, for permission to bring Macro and a small guard of tribunes and centurions

[1] Tac. *Ann.* 6.13.
[2] Cf. Tac. *Ann.* 1.74, 4.42.
[3] For his concern for the corn supply, cf. Tac. *Ann.* 2.87, 3.54.
[4] Tac. *Ann.* 6.14.
[5] Dio 58.21.1.
[6] Tac. *Ann.* 6.15, Dio 58.21.1.

whenever he entered the senate.[1] The senate naturally granted the request, even adding a clause that its members should be searched on arrival. Tiberius' suggestion may seem surprising in the light of his response to the proposal of Togonius Gallus, but the differences are striking. Gallus' system would, as Tiberius remarked, have aroused jealousy and resentment; it would also have burdened the princeps with guards he could not trust. But insofar as Tiberius now trusted any man, he trusted Macro, and if he could feel safe at all it would be with Macro and a few handpicked officers of the guard.

Measures against the practice of usury gave the senate fresh cause for alarm.[2] Breaches of Julius Caesar's law on the subject had given rise to a number of prosecutions, and the praetor who presided over the court raised the matter in the senate. Few of its members were guiltless, and so they threw themselves on the mercy of the princeps, who granted them a period of eighteen months to put their accounts in order. This, however, led to a shortage of liquid capital, as all illegal loans were called in simultaneously, and the situation was aggravated by confiscations of the property of the condemned, whose wealth thus disappeared from circulation. The senate attempted a remedy, decreeing that two-thirds of all debts must be repaid at once and the money thus recovered invested in Italian land. This measure satisfied neither side: creditors demanded repayment in full, while debtors were afraid that their credit would be ruined if they dared to take advantage of the decree. While debtors desperately tried to raise cash, the usurers turned to buying land instead of lending money. Men unable to borrow were forced to sell their land on a buyer's market and many were ruined. Finally Tiberius stepped in and made 1,000,000 sesterces available from the treasury for interest-free loans of three years' duration, on condition that the borrower could give the state security for double the sum borrowed. This led to a general restoration of credit and a gradual revival of lending by private individuals.

Prosecutions for *maiestas* continued.[3] Considius Proculus was dragged to the senate on his birthday, condemned and executed, while

[1] Tac. *Ann.* 6.15, Dio 58.18.5f.
[2] Tac. *Ann.* 6.16f., Suet. *Tib.* 48.1, Dio 58.21.4f.
[3] Tac. *Ann.* 6.18.

his sister Sancia was exiled. The prosecutor was Q. Pomponius, who thus avenged Considius' attempt to destroy his brother Pomponius Secundus.[1] Also exiled was Pompeia Macrina, whose husband and father-in-law, both leading men in Greece, had already been punished by Tiberius – how, when and why we do not know. When it became clear that she would be condemned, her father, a distinguished *eques*, and her brother, perhaps that Pompeius Macer who as praetor in 15 had asked Tiberius whether charges under the law of *maiestas* should be admitted, both committed suicide. The alleged charge against Pompeia was that her great-grandfather Theophanes of Mytilene had been a close friend of Pompey and had been deified after his death. It is incredible that these can have been the only grounds for the prosecution, but it is remarkable that Theophanes' son, procurator of Asia under Augustus, had been a close friend of Tiberius.[2] He now tended to strike more and more at those whom he had once trusted, and so his isolation grew ever greater.

Another old friend to fall in 33 was Sex. Marius, the richest man in Spain thanks largely to Tiberius' favour.[3] He was accused of incest with his daughter, though according to Dio his real offence was an attempt to protect her from Tiberius' unwelcome attentions. Tacitus gives Marius' wealth as the motive, citing as proof the fact that Marius' gold and copper mines in Spain were seized by Tiberius when his property was confiscated. The reason, however, as in the case of Seianus, was probably that Marius' riches had originated in gifts from the princeps.

In August there followed something close to a clean sweep of those accused of complicity with Seianus who were still held in prison await-ing trial.[4] Tiberius is said to have ordered that they should all be executed. If this is true, his orders were inefficiently carried out: Pomponius Secundus certainly survived, as did Sextius Paconianus – though not for long – and there may have been others.[5] Nevertheless

---

[1] Cf. Tac. *Ann.* 5.8.
[2] Strabo 13.2.3.
[3] Tac. *Ann.* 6.19, Dio 58.22. For Marius, cf. Tac. *Ann.* 4.36. This case may perhaps be the basis of the remarkable generalization in Dio 58.16.7.
[4] Tac. *Ann.* 6.19; for the date, cf. *F. Ost.* (*EJ* p. 43).
[5] Cf. Tac. *Ann.* 5.8 (Pomponius), 6.3, 39 (Sextius).

Suetonius' figure of twenty executions in a single day, which probably refers to this occasion, goes some way towards justifying Tacitus' rhetoric.[1]

But the final extinction of the supposed conspiracy of Seianus brought no comfort to Tiberius' other enemies. The first to succumb was Asinius Gallus, who had been in solitary confinement since 30.[2] That he died of starvation was not disputed, but men were uncertain whether or not it had been enforced. When asked for permission to bury the body, Tiberius acceded but complained that fate had carried off Gallus before he had been proved guilty in his presence. The remark is somewhat oracular: apologists claim that Tiberius was regretting only that Gallus would now inevitably be enrolled among the martyrs of the reign, others that he resented being deprived of the pleasure of condemning Gallus himself. These interpretations are not mutually exclusive and both may well be true.

Germanicus' son Drusus too was starved to death, though some had believed that Seianus' fall might mean that he and his mother would be spared.[3] But Tiberius' hatred for Agrippina and her son remained unaltered – though even if he had come sometimes to wonder whether Seianus had not deceived him as to their intentions, no man, even one far less worried for his own safety than Tiberius, could have risked restoring Agrippina to public life after the treatment he had inflicted on her. But Tiberius' reaction to Drusus' death shows that his convictions on this point had not changed. He attacked the dead man for his immorality, his hostility to his brother Nero and his enmity towards the state, and ordered the reading of a day-to-day record of Drusus' words and actions, spanning all the years since Tiberius first conceived his suspicions and culminating in Drusus' last desperate pleas for food and his solemn dying curses against the princeps. Shattered by this document, the senate marvelled that Tiberius, who had once been so cunning in the concealment of his crimes, should now with such confident unconcern draw back the veil and reveal in detail the atrocities he had committed against his grandson. But it was not overconfidence or

---

[1] Suet. *Tib.* 61.4; *F. Ost.* say only *complures*.
[2] Tac. *Ann.* 6.23, Dio 58.23.6; cf. Suet. *Tib.* 61.4, Dio 58.3.
[3] Tac. *Ann.* 6.23f., Suet. *Tib.* 54.2, Dio 58.22.4f., 25.4.

lack of concern that made Tiberius act in this manner. Despite his scant interest in the vagaries of public opinion, he had always hated to be misjudged, though he had often provoked misinterpretations by failing to make himself clear. Now, by publishing all the facts, he hoped, in vain of course, to convince the senate of what he still believed to be the truth – that Drusus had been an enemy to him and to the state – and to prove this he was ready to bear all the hatred and scorn that sympathy with Drusus' sufferings might inspire.

The death of Agrippina came soon after that of her son.[1] Seianus' fall had at first given her hope, but when it brought no improvement in her condition she starved herself to death. By chance or design she died on 18 October, the anniversary of Seianus' execution. Tiberius' letter to the senate was even more fantastic than that which had greeted the death of Drusus. He accused Agrippina of adultery with Asinius Gallus and claimed that it was only Gallus' death that had made her tired of living. She was lucky, he added, that she, unlike Seianus, had not been strangled and exposed on the Gemoniae. Bewildered and terrified, the senate could do no more than thank Tiberius for his clemency towards Agrippina and decree an offering to Jupiter in celebration.

Agrippina's suicide was followed by that of Plancina.[2] Why she was prosecuted now is unknown, but Tacitus and Dio agree that it was as much the hatred of Agrippina as the friendship of Livia that had saved her in 20, and Dio claims that Tiberius would have removed her long before were it not that her fall would have given Agrippina pleasure. Such speculations, however bizarre they may sound, cannot be dismissed out of hand: Tiberius' patience was infinite and his mind by now cruelly warped.

Meanwhile the jurist M. Cocceius Nerva, the only senator to share Tiberius' retirement, had also decided to commit suicide.[3] Tiberius was profoundly disturbed. He tried to find out Nerva's motives and begged him to change his mind, admitting that it would burden his conscience as much as it would damage his reputation, if his closest

---

[1] Tac. *Ann.* 6.25, Suet. *Tib.* 53.2, Dio 58.22.4f.
[2] Tac. *Ann.* 6.26, Dio 58.22.5.
[3] Tac. *Ann.* 6.26, Dio 58.21.4 (with a curiously legalistic reason). For Tiberius' attitude, cf. Tac. *Ann.* 2.34.

friend killed himself without giving any reason. But Nerva refused to discuss his decision and carried out his plan of starving himself to death. Those in whom he had confided reported, according to Tacitus, that a close acquaintance with the ills of the state had determined him to take his own life while his honour was still uncompromised and his welfare still unthreatened from without.

Public opinion was also distressed by the marriage of Drusus' daughter Julia, who had formerly been married to Germanicus' eldest son Nero, to the consular Rubellius Blandus, whose grandfather had been a mere *eques* from Tibur.[1] In December Lamia's brief tenure of the urban prefecture ended with his death; he was replaced by an old friend of the princeps, Cossus Lentulus, consul in 1 B.C.[2] But another old friend, L. Pomponius Flaccus, who had succeeded Lamia as governor of Syria, also died, prompting a letter from Tiberius in which he complained of the reluctance of qualified men to govern provinces – this despite the fact that he had not only prevented Lamia from taking up his post in Syria, but had also kept Arruntius from going to Spain, to which he had been appointed ten years before.[3]

In 34 the consuls, Paullus Fabius Persicus and L. Vitellius, celebrated the twentieth anniversary of Tiberius' accession and the grant of his provinces was renewed by the senate. Tiberius did not on that account come to Rome, though he was again on the mainland, in the neighbourhood of Tusculum, nor did the celebrations interrupt the succession of prosecutions, for Macro was sedulous in extracting confessions.[4] Pomponius Labeo, the former legate of Moesia, committed suicide and was imitated by his wife Paxaea.[5] He apparently faced a charge of extortion, and Tiberius had formally renounced his friendship. In his letter to the senate Tiberius claimed, as he had done years before after the suicide of Cn. Piso, that by killing himself Pomponius

---

[1] Tac. *Ann.* 6.27, cf. 3.29.
[2] Tac. *Ann.* 6.27, Sen. *Ep.* 83.15; for the date, cf. *F. Ost.* (*EJ* p. 43).
[3] Tac. *Ann.* 6.27, Suet. *Tib.* 41, Dio 58.8.3, 19.5. Tiberius' treatment of Lamia and Arruntius is an unsolved mystery: cf. Koestermann on Tac. *Ann.* 6.27; Pippidi, *Tibère*, 114ff. For his friendship with Pomponius, cf. Suet. *Tib.* 42.1.
[4] Dio 58.24.1f., cf. 58.21.3.
[5] Tac. *Ann.* 6.29, Dio 58.24.3; cf. Shotter, *Latomus* 28, 1969, 654ff.

had tried to shift the burden of guilt onto the princeps.[1] As for Paxaea, though guilty, she had been, he insisted, in no danger.

Mam. Scaurus was then prosecuted again for *maiestas* and adultery with Livia Julia.[2] His prosecutors, Servilius and Cornelius, claimed that he had consulted soothsayers, but the real cause of Tiberius' hostility was Scaurus' tragedy *Atreus*, in which, borrowing a line from Euripides, he had declared that it was necessary to bear with the follies of one's rulers. Tacitus asserts that it was Macro who hated Scaurus and first drew Tiberius' attention to the play; Dio says that Tiberius decided of his own accord that the line was aimed at him and remarked with typically savage wit, 'If I'm Atreus I'll make him Ajax' – for Ajax's folly had been fatal to himself. The princeps' self-centred and hypersensitive nature makes Dio's account highly plausible, but Tacitus too may be right: Macro would merely have to suggest that Tiberius read the play and leave his master's imagination to do the rest. Scaurus and his wife both committed suicide, but Servilius and Cornelius did not gain: both were exiled to islands for accepting a bribe in return for dropping a charge against Varius Ligus.

A last attempt to exploit the 'conspiracy' of Seianus was made by the former aedile Abudius Ruso.[3] He had commanded a legion under Lentulus Gaetulicus and now tried to attack Gaetulicus because he had been going to marry his daughter to one of Seianus' sons. But Gaetulicus was in an impregnable position. Commander of the legions of the upper Rhine, he was very popular with his troops, while the other Rhine army was under his father-in-law L. Apronius. So he could afford to write to Tiberius in terms that barely cloaked the potential threat he presented. He and Tiberius, he said, had made the same mistake; it was therefore unjust that others should suffer while Tiberius himself did not. But his loyalty was unimpaired and would remain so – provided that no snares were laid for him. Recall he would regard as tantamount to a sentence of death. Therefore, he suggested, they should come to an agreement: Tiberius could do as he would with

---

[1] Tac. *Ann.* 6.29: *culpam inuidia uelauisse*; cf. 3.16.
[2] Tac. *Ann.* 6.29f., Suet. *Tib.* 61.3, Dio 58.24.3ff., Sen. *Suas.* 3.22.
[3] Tac. *Ann.* 6.30; the family's military strength perhaps encouraged Tiberius to condone the behaviour of Apronius' son Caesianus (Dio 58.19.1f.).

the rest of the empire, but he would keep his province. Tiberius was only too well aware of the force of these arguments. Gaetulicus, his influence undiminished, remained at the head of his army; Abudius was condemned and expelled from the city.

In 35 Fulcinius Trio was again threatened with prosecution, but committed suicide before proceedings could begin.[1] He left behind him a will in which he attacked not only Macro and the princeps' leading freedmen but also Tiberius himself, calling him a victim of senile decay, no better than an exile. Trio's heirs tried to suppress this document, but Tiberius, who was again in the neighbourhood of Rome, ordered it to be read in the senate. Tacitus suggests two possible motives: either Tiberius wanted to parade his tolerance of freedom of speech in others and his indifference to their opinion, or his experience with Seianus had made him prefer that the truth should always be published, no matter what the cost to his feelings and reputation. The latter is almost certainly near the mark – Tiberius will have wanted to convince the senate of what he believed to be the truth about Trio, just as he had insisted on demonstrating at length the 'truth' about Drusus.

There followed the suicide of Granius Marcianus, prosecuted for *maiestas* by C. Gracchus, and the execution of the former praetor Tarius Gratianus; no details of either case are known. Another suicide was Trebellenus Rufus, the former regent of Thrace.[2] The informer Sextius Paconianus, who had survived the purge of August 33, was now strangled because he had whiled away his time in prison by writing lampoons on Tiberius.[3]

For the next year too Tacitus found little to record but a catalogue of condemnations and suicides.[4] An *eques*, Vibullius Agrippa, poisoned himself in the senate, but was dragged to prison and strangled, so that his suicide would not protect his property from confiscation.[5] The ex-king of Armenia, Tigranes IV, was condemned and executed; nothing is known of the details of the case. Three suicides vividly

[1] Tac. *Ann.* 6.38, Dio 58.25.2ff.
[2] Tac. *Ann.* 6.39, cf. 2.67, 3.38.
[3] Tac. *Ann.* 6.39, cf. 6.3, Suet. *Tib.* 61.6.
[4] Tac. *Ann.* 6.40, cf. Dio 58.21.4, who gives Agrippa's *nomen* correctly, but dates the incident to 33.
[5] Cf. Tac. *Ann.* 6.29.

illustrate the demoralization of the ruling class. C. Galba, the consul of 22, took his own life because Tiberius forbade him to put his name forward for the governorships of Africa or Asia.[1] Q. Blaesus, suffect consul in 26, and his brother had been promised priesthoods before their father's fall, but now the places were granted to others as if they had become vacant. The brothers interpreted this as a sign that they were presumed to be dead and acted accordingly. Aemilia Lepida, the former wife of Germanicus' son Drusus, also committed suicide to escape condemnation. She had disgraced herself by joining in the attacks on her husband, but had escaped retribution while her father M. Lepidus was alive. But his death in 34[2] had left her vulnerable, and she was now accused of adultery with a slave. Since her guilt was beyond doubt, she abandoned her defence and anticipated the verdict.

Despite the increase in confiscations Tiberius could still be generous when there was cause. On 1 November, 36, a fire broke out in the Circus Maximus and swept the Aventine.[3] Tiberius made 1,000,000 sesterces available to compensate for damage to houses and blocks of flats. A commission of five was set up to deal with claims: the husbands of Tiberius' four granddaughters – Domitius, L. Cassius, Vinicius and Rubellius Blandus – and P. Petronius, who was nominated by the consuls. The senate predictably heaped honours on Tiberius, but his death made it difficult for Tacitus to discover whether or not he accepted them.

The last year of Tiberius' life began with more prosecutions.[4] Acutia, the former wife of P. Vitellius, was prosecuted for *maiestas* by D. Laelius Balbus and condemned, but the decree rewarding her accuser was vetoed by the tribune Junius Otho. Soon afterwards Laelius was expelled from the senate and deported to an island. Then Albucilla, former wife of the informer Satrius Secundus, was charged with impiety towards the princeps and adultery. The roll of her alleged lovers added interest to the case: Domitius Ahenobarbus, Vibius

---

[1] Cf. Suet. *Galba* 3.4.
[2] Cf. Tac. *Ann.* 6.27.
[3] Tac. *Ann.* 6.45, Dio 58.26.5; for the date, cf. *F. Ost.* (*EJ* p. 43).
[4] Tac. *Ann.* 6.47–49, Dio 58.27.2ff. According to Suet. *Nero* 5.2 Domitius was also accused of incest with his sister Domitia Lepida. He was still in prison when Tiberius died.

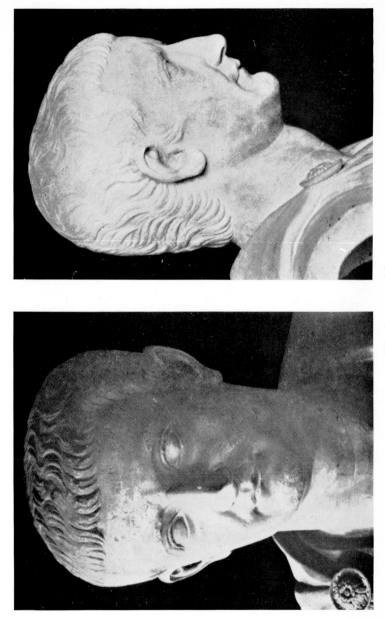

15 Tiberius as an old man

16a Squeeze of the epitaph of Agrippina (*ILS* 180), set up under Gaius.

16b Squeeze of the epitaph of Tiberius Gemellus (*ILS* 172).

Marsus and Arruntius. The senate was suspicious: the papers presented to it showed that Macro had presided at the interrogation of witnesses and the torture of slaves, while no letter had been received from Tiberius himself. This suggested that Macro might be acting entirely on his own initiative, for his hatred of Arruntius was common knowledge. So Domitius and Vibius refrained from suicide, but Arruntius, despite the arguments of his friends, persisted in opening his veins. His life, he said, had been guiltless, yet his old age had been a time of constant fear. He had been hated by Seianus, now he was hated by Macro, and after Macro there would be another. No doubt he could put off his trial till Tiberius died, but how could he escape the youthful Gaius – and Gaius, with Macro to guide him, would be worse, just as Macro had proved to be more evil than Seianus. All that could lie ahead was a servitude more harsh than he had already endured, from which there was only one way of escape. Albucilla attempted to stab herself, but was carried off to execution by order of the senate. Of her accomplices, the ex-praetor Carsidius Sacerdos was banished to an island and Pontius Fregellanus was expelled from the senate. Still more lurid was the case of the mother of Sex. Papinius, probably the son of the consul of the previous year. Papinius had been driven to suicide to escape her incestuous advances; she was brought to trial in the senate and expelled from the city for ten years, by which time it was thought that her other son would be old enough to defend himself.

Tiberius' last years have been called a reign of terror. Apologists have disputed the label, pointing out that by modern standards at least the number of victims was small and trying to prove that all or most of them were guilty. This counting of heads misses the point. There was a reign of terror in the most literal sense. Sketchy though Tacitus' narrative is, it reveals all too plainly the hysteria, the panic that prevailed at meetings of the senate. Delators could conjure accusations out of thin air and the outcome depended not on justice or reason but on the whim of one lonely and terrified old man. An honest and courageous defence might bring its reward to a Terentius, but there was no guarantee that another man would be as lucky, when at one moment Tiberius was capable of dismissing ridiculous charges against Cotta Messallinus, but at another of inventing grievances even more absurd against

Scaurus. Even abject servility was no warrant of safety, as the fate of Junius Gallio underlined. It is this element of uncertainty, of unpredictability, of unreason governing matters of life and death that created an atmosphere in which men were ready to commit suicide at the slightest hint of the princeps' displeasure and fully justifies the term 'reign of terror'.

2. THE EASTERN FRONTIER

In 35 fresh trouble came to a head in the East, where fifteen years of peace had made Artabanus overconfident.[1] When Artaxias of Armenia died, he seized the chance of placing on the throne his own eldest son Arsaces, and also sent envoys to Tiberius demanding the return of the treasure abandoned by Vonones in Syria and Cilicia. At the same time he boasted that he would reconquer all the lands that had ever formed part of the Persian empire: his first target seems to have been Cappadocia. But the Parthian's arrogance had displeased some among his own people, led by the wealthy noble Sinnaces and the eunuch Abdus. This party sent an embassy to Rome, requesting that Phraates, son of Phraates IV, should be placed on the Parthian throne: his Arsacid birth and the authority of Rome would suffice, they claimed, to ensure success.

Tiberius found the plan attractive, for it would restore a favourable situation in the East without recourse to the hazards and expense of military intervention. Meanwhile Artabanus got wind of the plot and reacted vigorously: Abdus was poisoned, Sinnaces kept busy. Fortune too seemed to be on his side, for Phraates fell ill and died in Syria before he had the chance to claim his inheritance.

But despite this setback Tiberius did not give up hope. To replace Phraates he chose Tiridates and to recover Armenia he called in Mithridates the Iberian, whom he reconciled with his brother King Pharasmanes. Control of operations on the spot was entrusted to L. Vitellius as governor of Syria. Mithridates set about his task with great

[1] Tac. *Ann.* 6.31–37, Suet. *Tib.* 41, 66, Dio 58.26.1ff., Plin. *NH* 15.183, Jos. *AJ* 18.96–105. Suetonius' version of Artabanus' letter must be grossly exaggerated. Cf. Anderson, *CAH* x, 747ff.

energy. Arsaces' retainers were bribed to poison him, and a large
Iberian army swept into Armenia and occupied Artaxata. But Artabanus did not resign himself to defeat and sent out a force under his
son Orodes. Pharasmanes acquired reinforcements from the Albani and
Sarmatae; some of the latter tribe supported the Parthians, but the
Iberians garrisoned the Caspian passes and so were able to prevent
them from interfering. Pharasmanes constantly provoked the weaker
Orodes to battle, till the Parthians could no longer bear his insults and
forced their commander to fight. In the battle Pharasmanes and Orodes
met in single combat and Orodes was wounded. The rumour quickly
spread that he had been killed, and this false belief hastened the
Parthian defeat.

In 36 Artabanus mounted a major expedition, but despite their
numerical inferiority the knowledge of the terrain they had gained in the
previous year gave the Iberians the upper hand. This would not have
deterred Artabanus, had not Vitellius mustered his legions and put
about a tale that he was on the point of invading Mesopotamia. The
ruse was entirely successful. Artabanus came hurrying back to defend
his kingdom and the Parthian threat to Armenia was at an end. Vitellius
at once attempted something more ambitious, plotting to overthrow
Artabanus himself. The king's military failures had weakened his
position at home, and Sinnaces brought over his father Abdagaeses and
others, till only Artabanus' mercenary guards remained loyal. But in
spite of these defections at court Artabanus knew that he could still
find support in the regions where he had grown up, the distant
satrapies of Hyrcania and Carmania. So he withdrew to the boundaries
of Scythia, there to plan the recovery of his power.

Vitellius urged Tiridates to seize his chance and moved his forces
across the Euphrates to give the pretender moral support. At first all
went well. The satrap of Mesopotamia, Ornodaspes, who when in
exile had served under Tiberius at the time of the Pannonian revolt
and had been rewarded with Roman citizenship, put his numerous
cavalry at Tiridates' disposal, while Sinnaces and Abdagaeses soon
followed, the latter bringing with him the royal treasure and regalia.
Vitellius decided that his show of force had been sufficient, and after
encouraging Tiridates to remember the example set by his father

Phraates and his guardian Augustus and warning the Parthian dignitaries to show loyalty to their king and respect to Rome, he led his legions back to Syria.

There he sent the legate M. Trebellius to deal with a rebel tribe, the Cietae in Cilicia Aspera.[1] Objecting to the Roman system of tribute, they had withdrawn into the Taurus and there defied the efforts of local troops to dislodge them. Trebellius, however, was able to reduce them without undue difficulty.

Meanwhile Tiridates marched by way of the Greek cities of Anthemusias and Nicephorium to the Parthian towns of Halus and Artemita, receiving an enthusiastic welcome from the people, who hoped that his Roman upbringing would make him a milder ruler than Artabanus.[2] He was also rapturously received by the masses in the great city of Seleucia on the Tigris, which still retained its Hellenic form of government.[3] In the internal politics of the city Artabanus had favoured the aristocracy, so Tiridates naturally restored the people to power. He then turned his mind to the choice of a day on which to celebrate his coronation. But the two most powerful satraps, Phraates and Hieron, wrote requesting a brief delay, which their importance forced Tiridates to grant. Crossing the Tigris to Ctesiphon he duly waited, but as time went by and the satraps still did not arrive, he had himself crowned by Surena amid general rejoicing.

But instead of devoting his attention to the interior of his realm in order to secure the loyalty of waverers, Tiridates wasted time in besieging a fortress to which Artabanus had consigned cash and concubines.[4] This prompted Phraates, Hieron and others who had not been present at the coronation to go over to Artabanus: some were afraid that Tiridates would resent their absence, others objected to the power of Abdagaeses, whose influence over Tiridates was great. They succeeded in convincing the wily Artabanus that the time was ripe for him to reclaim the throne, and Hieron began to attack Tiridates for his youth, his subservience to Abdagaeses, and his effete foreign ways.[5]

[1] Tac. *Ann.* 6.41.
[2] Tac. *Ann.* 6.41.
[3] Tac. *Ann.* 6.42.
[4] Tac. *Ann.* 6.43.
[5] For the last point, cf. Tac. *Ann.* 2.2.

Artabanus moved quickly and his troops were soon close to Seleucia while Tiridates was still hesitant and unprepared.[1] Some of his counsellors advised him to strike at once, with Artabanus' army still weary from its march and unstable in its loyalties. But Abdagaeses spoke in favour of withdrawing into Mesopotamia in the hope of Armenian and Roman aid. Tiridates adopted this misguided scheme, but the withdrawal soon became a rout as his forces deserted to Artabanus or quietly slipped away home.

Tiberius accepted Tiridates' failure philosophically and instructed Vitellius to make peace with Artabanus.[2] Artabanus had learned his lesson and was happy to comply. The meeting of the governor and the king on the Euphrates probably belongs after Tiberius' death, but Tiberius deserves the credit for preserving all that was vital to Roman interests after the collapse of Tiridates. Mithridates remained on the Armenian throne, Artabanus, who sent his son to Rome as a hostage, had been taught to respect Roman claims in Asia Minor, and all this had been achieved without major military effort.

3. THE SUCCESSION: GAIUS AND TIBERIUS GEMELLUS

The elimination of Drusus in 33 had left only Gaius and Tiberius Gemellus as potential successors to Tiberius' power, and Gaius always appeared the more likely contender. The fate of his mother and brothers had left him unscathed and apparently unmoved while he exercised considerable skill in keeping on the right side of Tiberius and winning the support of Macro, though Tiberius is said to have been well aware of the vices that Gaius was already unable to conceal.[3] In 33, the year of his quaestorship,[4] Gaius was married at Antium to Junia Claudilla, daughter of Tiberius' friend M. Silanus.[5] It was then proposed that he should succeed Drusus as augur, but instead he was granted a pontificate.[6] The marriage to Junia was shortlived: she died

---

[1] Tac. *Ann.* 6.44.
[2] Suet. *Cal.* 14.3, *Vit.* 2.4, Dio 59.27.3, Jos. *AJ* 18.101.
[3] Tac. *Ann.* 6.20, Suet. *Cal.* 10.2–11, Philo *Leg.* 33–40, *Flacc.* 12.
[4] Dio 58.23.1.
[5] Tac. *Ann.* 6.20, Suet. *Cal.* 12.1, Dio 58.25.2 (dating the marriage to 35).
[6] Suet. *Cal.* 12.1.

in childbirth and in consequence the bond between Gaius and Macro was strengthened by a liaison, in which Macro at least acquiesced, between the prince and the prefect's wife Ennia Thrasylla.[1]

As always Tiberius was reluctant to make a decision, and he may well have expressed his envy of Priam, who outlived all his descendants.[2] The ties of blood and affection inclined him to Gemellus, but Gemellus was too young. Gaius he disliked in spite of his sedulous flattery – as Germanicus' son the prince was popular with the masses, but this did nothing to recommend him to his grandfather. Claudius he rejected as mentally unfit, despite his maturity and love of intellectual pursuits. To look outside the family for a successor would make a mockery of the memory of Augustus and the very name Caesar. These considerations seem to have led him to see the succession of Gaius as a necessary evil. Ironically he complimented Macro on his timely adherence to the rising sun, and he is said, when Gaius one day spoke slightingly of Sulla, to have told him that he would display all Sulla's vices and none of his virtues. About Gemellus' future too he was lucidly fatalistic, saying to Gaius: 'You will kill him and another will kill you.'

4. TIBERIUS' DEATH

In March 37, returning to Capreae from the neighbourhood of Rome, Tiberius fell ill at Astura in Campania. A temporary recovery enabled him to reach Cerceii, but there he suffered a relapse. Finally he came to Misenum and settled in a villa that had once belonged to L. Lucullus.[3] Despite his valiant efforts to keep up appearances he did not deceive the doctor Charicles. Tiberius had always refused to consult the profession,[4] but Charicles, by clasping his hand as he left a banquet,

[1] Tac. *Ann.* 6.45, Suet. *Cal.* 12.2, Dio 58.28.4, Philo *Leg.* 39f., 61. Tacitus and Dio interpret the affair as a scheme of Macro's to strengthen his hold over Gaius, but Suetonius claims that Gaius seduced Ennia with the promise of marriage if he secured the principate, while Philo makes Ennia herself the prime mover. The first view is perhaps the most plausible. Ennia may have been the granddaughter of the astrologer Thrasyllus; cf. Cichorius, *Römische Studien*, 391ff.

[2] Tac. *Ann.* 6.46, Suet. *Tib.* 62.3, *Cal.* 19.3, Dio 58.23.4 (with a different explanation of the Priam story), 28.4, Jos. *AJ* 18.205–223.

[3] Tac. *Ann.* 6.50, Suet. *Tib.* 72f., *Cal.* 12.2f., Dio 58.28.

[4] Cf. Tac. *Ann.* 6.46, Suet. *Tib.* 68.4.

succeeded in taking his pulse and guaranteed to the impatient Macro that Tiberius had at most two days to live.

On 16 March Tiberius died.[1] The manner of his death is obscured by legend.[2] Tacitus claims that he fell into a coma and was presumed to be dead. But as Gaius was receiving congratulations, word came that Tiberius was conscious and asking for food. The panic-stricken flatterers melted away, leaving Gaius thunderstruck, but the dependable Macro kept his head and gave orders for Tiberius to be smothered with his own bedclothes. Dio tells a somewhat similar story: according to him it was Gaius who refused Tiberius' request for food and, assisted by Macro, smothered him with bedclothes on the pretext of keeping him warm. Suetonius records a number of accounts without committing himself: first, that Tiberius was given a slow poison by Gaius; second, that he was starved to death although he asked for food; third, that his ring was removed while he was in a coma and that when he regained consciousness and asked for it he was smothered with a pillow. Of these the second and third appear to be elements of a version of the story found in Tacitus and Dio. Suetonius also ascribes to Seneca another account of Tiberius' death, according to which Tiberius himself took off his ring, as if to hand it on to a successor, but after a while put it back on his finger and clenched his fist. For a long time he lay motionless, then suddenly he called for his attendants and when no one answered rose from the bed, collapsed beside it and died.

This story may well be close to the truth, for it is easy to see how the other details might develop. Tiberius' long silence could lead to the story of Gaius' and Macro's assumption that he was dead, his summoning of his servants could grow into the tale that Gaius had refused him food, and his momentary recovery would invite the malicious suggestion that in fact Gaius and Macro had had to give nature some assistance.

When the news of Tiberius' death reached Rome it was greeted with wild rejoicing.[3] The cry of 'Tiberius in the Tiber!' was raised, prayers

---

[1] Tac. *Ann.* 6.50, Suet. *Tib.* 73.1, confirmed by *F. Ost.* (*EJ* p. 43); Dio 58.28.5 gives 26 March in error. His epitaph: *ILS* 164.

[2] Tac. *Ann.* 6.50, Suet. *Tib.* 73, *Cal.* 12.2, Dio 58.28.3.

[3] Suet. *Tib.* 75.1f.

were offered to ensure that his soul went to hell, and threats to expose his body on the Gemoniae were uttered. Public opinion had been exacerbated by the execution and exposure on that very day of some prisoners. When they heard that Tiberius was dead they had begged for a delay, but in Gaius' absence there was no authority to which appeal could be made, and so the guards had carried out their orders.

Tiberius' body was brought from Misenum to Rome with a military escort.[1] Gaius, in full mourning, accompanied the procession, which entered the city on 29 March.[2] The princeps' will was read in the senate by Macro.[3] Tiberius instituted Gaius and Gemellus as joint heirs; he also commended Claudius by name to the senate, people and armies. Legacies to the armies and the people followed the Augustan model. The praetorians received 1,000 sesterces each, the men of the urban cohorts 500, the *uigiles* and the troops at large 300. The legacy to the people was of 45,000,000 sesterces. The Vestals and the *magistri uicorum* were also specially remembered. The consuls then, as had been prearranged, proposed that the will be declared null and void, on the ground that Tiberius had been of unsound mind. The senate and the mob that had broken into the building enthusiastically agreed. Nevertheless all the legacies were paid. Only the unfortunate Gemellus was deprived of his share: he was to die, as Tiberius had predicted, before the year was out.

Gaius then shocked the senate into resistance by demanding deification for Tiberius, as well as all the other honours that had once been granted to Augustus.[4] But eventually he contented himself with securing a state funeral. So on 3 April Tiberius' body was cremated, after Gaius himself had delivered the funeral oration.[5]

---

[1] Suet. *Tib.* 75.3, *Cal.* 13.
[2] Date in *F. Ost.* (*EJ* p. 43).
[3] Suet. *Tib.* 76, *Cal.* 14.1, *Claud.* 6.2, Dio 59.1f. Dio's suggestion that Tiberius bequeathed the principate jointly to Gaius and Gemellus is of course absurd.
[4] Dio 59.3.7.
[5] Suet. *Tib.* 75.3, *Cal.* 15.1, Dio 58.28.5, 59.3.8; for the date, cf. *F. Ost.* (*EJ* p. 43).

CONCLUSION

The twenty-two years of Tiberius' principate are a period of transition as well as of consolidation. The fortunes of the governing class were mixed. Tiberius always showed himself ready to advance men who like himself belonged to the nobility of the old republic, as he did the sons of newer consular families whose rise had been contemporaneous with that of Augustus.[1] Yet his fears for his own security and the readiness of unscrupulous opportunists to exploit his suspicions made high birth a perilous distinction, as Tacitus delights in pointing out.[2] However exaggerated the historian's claims may be, consulships and governorships must have seemed small compensation to those of the nobility whose talents and temper matched their birth. Only by accepting the major restraints that the principate imposed on independent action could they preserve some semblance of dignity.[3] Greater freedom Tiberius the republican was powerless to grant. Those who understood, like M. Lepidus, might flourish within limits – others, like Cn. Piso, learned the hard way. But worse than the curbs on individual achievement and glory was the insecurity to which Arruntius bore witness.[4] Thus, despite Tiberius' ingrained respect for birth and ability and his overall traditionalism, the effects of certain traits in his character combined with the very nature of the principate to weaken and demoralize the governing class and so to prepare the way not only for the undisguised despotism of Gaius but also for the bureaucracy of Claudius.

[1] Cf. Tac. *Ann.* 4.6; above, p. 126.
[2] Cf. Tac. *Ann.* 3.55, 4.66, 6.10, 14.47; below, p. 259.
[3] Cf. Tac. *Ann.* 4.20, 6.10; below, p. 260.
[4] Cf. Tac. *Ann.* 6.48; above, p. 239.

The same paradox marks the position of the magistrates and the senate. Tiberius made repeated efforts in the early years of his reign to force the senate to assume its responsibilities, and his sincerity cannot be doubted.[1] The principal reason for his failure was that he was too late. Augustus had already irrevocably undermined the senate's capacity for independent action. Unlike Tiberius, he had had no respect for the traditions of senatorial government. But open contempt for the authority of the senate had caused the downfall of Julius Caesar, and so he had thought it prudent to shelter behind an elaborate pretence of republicanism. During the long years of his reign the senate and magistrates had learned to be content with this outward show, to be satisfied with the trappings of importance without the realities of power. By the time that Tiberius offered them power once again, they had grown so used to dignified impotence that the chance to govern reduced them to quaking confusion. Yet Tiberius must bear some of the blame, even during the 'good years' – Capito's odious hypocrisy must not be allowed to conceal the fact that in a sense he was right.[2] Whenever Tiberius intervened to force his wishes on the senate, even if his object was to check adulation or to prevent the condemnation of an innocent man, he was depriving the senate of that power of decision it was already only too reluctant to use and encouraging it in its lamentable habit of decreeing only what it thought would be pleasing to the princeps. Any such exertions of his authority, even in a good cause, were inevitably detrimental to the republican freedom that Tiberius professed and honestly desired to encourage.[3] The final blow to senatorial government was delivered by his withdrawal to Capreae.[4] Had the senate not been so cowed already, it might have seized this chance to recover its independence, but instead its initiative became totally extinct, as it found itself reduced to ratifying decisions taken miles away by the princeps and a handful of advisers. Again the ultimate result was ironically to leave the way clear for open autocracy.

There is little sign that Tiberius' principate had profound effects on

---

[1] Cf. above, p. 129.
[2] Cf. Tac. *Ann.* 3.70; above, p. 161.
[3] Cf. Tac. *Ann.* 1.75 on his judicial activities; above, p. 151.
[4] Cf. above, p. 205.

other strata of society. It may be presumed that the power of the equestrian order in the army and the imperial civil service continued to grow in preparation for its flowering under Claudius, but apart from outstanding individuals in the highest posts – Seianus and Macro of course above all – there are few indications of equestrian influence. The imperial freedmen, who similarly come to open prominence in the time of Claudius, are even less in evidence: only a hint in Fulcinius Trio's will.[1] But again the increasing demoralization of the upper ranks of the senatorial order and the development in the last years of government by cabal will have produced a climate that fostered the changes to come. Of the masses there is almost nothing to say. They disliked Tiberius because he made no secret of the fact that he did not value their affection, and they grumbled about the price of bread and the lack of circuses.[2] But their absence of interest in political developments is shown by their ready acceptance of the transference of elections to the senate.[3] They sometimes manifest certain basic tendencies – love of lords, hatred of upstarts and loyalty to the Caesars – but they may fairly be said to have influenced nothing except on occasion Tiberius' suspicions.[4]

It is Tiberius' character that provides the key to the paradoxical appearance of his reign. Ancient theories of a stage-by-stage decline are nonsense, and his notorious dissimulation is largely a red herring. But his fear for his own security and his reluctance to make decisions are at the root of the outstanding evils of the reign and the failure of his republican good intentions. For years he had been the instrument of another man's will, and his career and even his life had been in danger. His submission to Augustus in accepting the principate at all brought a first measure of unreality to his efforts to put republican principles into practice, for his love of freedom was in constant friction with the awkward awareness that his safety depended on his status as princeps, as Augustus' chosen successor – yet if anyone was in a position to know that the republican exterior of the Augustan principate was a sham, it

[1] Tac. *Ann.* 6.38.
[2] Cf. above, p. 137.
[3] Tac. *Ann.* 1.15.
[4] Cf. Tac. *Ann.* 3.23, 29; 2.82, 3.4, 29, 5.4, 6.46.

was Tiberius. But it was fear that ultimately made his republicanism too completely hollow: the gnawing fear of conspiracy and assassination that rendered possible the abuse of the law of *maiestas*, despite the efforts of his reason to hold it in check, and, combined with his eagerness to shed responsibility, gave Seianus his chance. As a private citizen he would merely have been a lonely, suspicious, frightened old man. But because of the power that circumstances had forced on him, his suspicions and fears were transformed into lethal weapons, at first forged and skilfully directed by Seianus, then in the last years scattered at random by a warped and haunted mind. There is a kernel of truth in Arruntius' claim that Tiberius was changed and twisted by imperial power, for empire deprived his virtues of the only climate in which they could flourish freely and condemned them to a barren and stunted growth, while it nurtured his faults to an unnatural increase that yielded a grim harvest. Such suffering as Tiberius' principate brought upon Rome was but a sombre echo of the desolation that it wrought in Tiberius' own mind.

STEMMA
THE SOURCES
MAPS
BIBLIOGRAPHY
INDEX

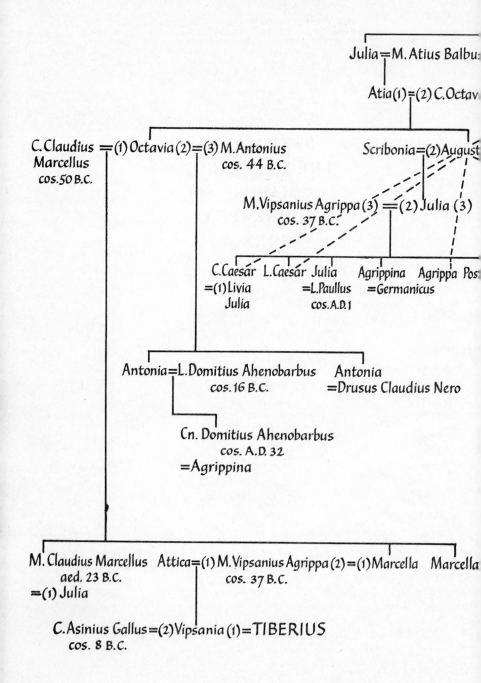

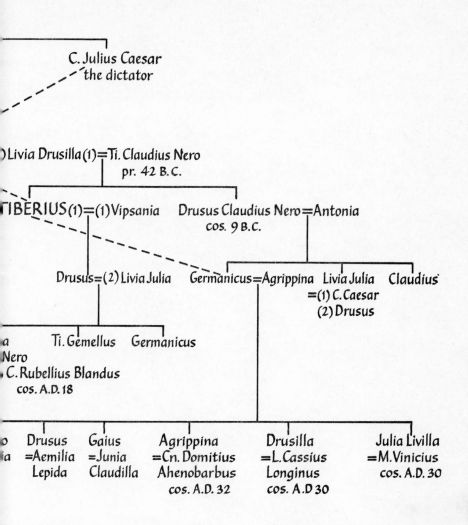

C. Julius Caesar
the dictator

) Livia Drusilla (1) = Ti. Claudius Nero
pr. 42 B.C.

TIBERIUS (1) = (1) Vipsania   Drusus Claudius Nero = Antonia
cos. 9 B.C.

Drusus = (2) Livia Julia   Germanicus = Agrippina   Livia Julia   Claudius
= (1) C. Caesar
(2) Drusus

a   Ti. Gemellus   Germanicus
Nero
C. Rubellius Blandus
cos. A.D. 18

o   Drusus   Gaius   Agrippina   Drusilla   Julia Livilla
ia   = Aemilia = Junia   = Cn. Domitius   = L. Cassius   = M. Vinicius
     Lepida   Claudilla Ahenobarbus   Longinus   cos. A.D. 30
                          cos. A.D. 32   cos. A.D 30

THE JULIO-CLAUDIANS IN THE REIGNS
OF AUGUSTUS AND TIBERIUS

THE SOURCES

Of the literary sources for the life of Tiberius, four deserve to be singled out: first and foremost the *Annals* of Cornelius Tacitus, unrivalled in literary merit and wealth of detail, then the *Roman History* of Cassius Dio, the works of the biographer Suetonius, who wrote lives of Augustus, Tiberius and Gaius, and the contemporary account of Velleius Paterculus, contained in his very brief history published in 30. For the principate of Augustus there also exists the first princeps' own short and carefully selected record of his achievements, the *Res Gestae*. Besides these, diverse writers in various genres offer valuable pieces of information: the elder and the younger Seneca, Valerius Maximus, the elder Pliny, the poets, especially Juvenal, the Jewish writers Philo and Josephus, and so on.

Inscriptions help to expand and consolidate our knowledge, recording the honours received throughout the empire by members of the ruling house and other men of distinction, the careers and occupations of senators, equestrian administrators, soldiers, freedmen and slaves, and the building and restoration of cities, temples, aqueducts and roads. The imperial coinage too sheds its own light, revealing the virtues that in the official view characterized the princeps and the régime, and the personalities, events and achievements on which it pleased the government that public attention should be focused.

TACITUS

The ancestry, birthplace and even the *praenomen* of Cornelius Tacitus are unknown.[1] In 77 he married the daughter of the famous governor of Britain, Cn. Julius Agricola, whose biography he published in 98. In 88 he reached the praetorship and more remarkably a priesthood, the quindecimvirate.[2] He was suffect consul in 97 and eventually governed the province of Asia, probably in 112-13. His first major work, the *Histories*, dealt with the turbulent year 69 and the rule of the Flavians. The *Annals*, begun perhaps about 115,[3] covered the reigns of Tiberius, Gaius, Claudius and Nero. The first six books were devoted to Tiberius; of these the greater part of the fifth and the beginning of the sixth are lost.

All Tacitus' historical writings are marked by a deep, though purely intellectual, distaste for the principate and a romantic admiration for the republic.[4] Thus he laments the unworthiness of his subject-matter by contrast with the stirring days of old.[5] Nevertheless he must have known that under the republic citizenship, not the consulate, would have been the limit of his aspirations, while in his practical dealings with the principate he was a realist: his early career, under the 'tyrant' Domitian, had been smooth, without interruption or hindrance.[6]

Despite an avowed moral purpose – to record for posterity conspicuous examples of virtue and wickedness in word and deed[7] – Tacitus claims to write without rancour or favourable bias.[8] But he is always at pains to show that he is not deceived by any façade of republicanism displayed by successive holders of the principate. Under Augustus, he pointedly remarks, the names of the magistracies were the same, but in fact the princeps had usurped the functions of all the vital elements in the republican constitution.[9] Before his accession Tiberius acted

[1] Cf. Syme, *Tacitus*, 611ff., who inclines towards Vasio as the historian's home town.

[2] On his career, cf. Syme, *Tacitus*, 59ff.

[3] Cf. Syme, *Tacitus*, 465ff.

[4] On Tacitus' attitude to the principate and his political opinions, cf. Syme, *Tacitus*, 364ff., 408ff., 547ff. Cf. also Münzer, *Klio* 1, 1902, 308ff., 312f., on the practice of dating by consular years; Pippidi, *Tibère*, 20.

[5] Tac. *Ann.* 4.32f.

[6] Cf. Syme, *Tacitus*, 540.

[7] Tac. *Ann.* 3.65.

[8] Tac. *Ann.* 1.1.

[9] Tac. *Ann.* 1.2f.

through the consuls, as if the old republic still existed.[1] His refusal to influence the course of senatorial debates is dismissed as a simulacrum of liberty, while his readiness to allow men not commended by himself to stand for the consulship is seen as equally specious, since such candidates would have no hope of success.[2] When Cn. Piso suggests that the senate should continue to meet in Tiberius' absence, Tacitus is quick to stress that even if he had carried the day he would have secured only the appearance of republican freedom.[3] Similarly he insists that Tiberius' refusal to assume long-term control of praetorian elections was democratic only in outward aspect and involved no sacrifice of real power.[4] What the senate's powers of decision were worth is made bitterly clear: when it debated with a great show of traditional prestige, it ordered matters of such vital importance as the right of provincial temples to grant asylum.[5] Such occasional echoes of the past merely serve to highlight the evils of the present. Thus the influence of Germanicus and Drusus in the senate was sufficient to set aside a law – in the way, says Tacitus, that laws were set aside in the days when they still had some force.[6] This obsession with penetrating the republican mask casts a shadow over Tacitus' famous appreciation of the 'good years' of Tiberius' reign.[7] All matters, he says, were discussed in the senate, the leading men were allowed to make speeches, consuls and praetors had their proper appearance. How hollow, in his opinion, all this was is shown a few pages later, when by way of illustration he records that the senate was empowered to vote a state funeral to an old friend of the princeps and was even, as a special treat, allowed to condemn one of his financial agents.[8] Not long after he seizes on an allusion by Tiberius to the old *senatus consultum ultimum*, which instructed the consuls to ensure that the republic came to no

---

[1] Tac. *Ann.* 1.7.
[2] Tac. *Ann.* 1.77, 81.
[3] Tac. *Ann.* 2.35.
[4] Tac. *Ann.* 2.36.
[5] Tac. *Ann.* 3.60.
[6] Tac. *Ann.* 2.52.
[7] Tac. *Ann.* 4.6.
[8] Tac. *Ann.* 4.15; note the deliberate echo of 4.6 in *patres . . . apud quos . . . tractabantur.*

harm – as if, he exclaims, this was a real consul or the constitution he was pretending to protect a republic![1]

As to the true nature of the principate, Tacitus is in no doubt. The concept as first devised by Augustus he dismisses as a cover for the reality of overwhelming military strength, strength that rested on control of the armies and the backing of the mass of the people and was reinforced by the foundation of a dynasty.[2] The justification of the principate was that it brought peace and security after the horrors of protracted civil war. Tacitus admits the fact, but does not find in it adequate compensation for all that had been lost.[3] For him the republic is synonymous with freedom, the principate with servitude.[4]

Adulation kept pace with autocracy: Tacitus alertly records notorious examples.[5] Thus the grant of tribunician power to Drusus gave the flatterers scope for shameful competition, in which Q. Haterius and M. Silanus excelled.[6] The end of the reign saw the rise of L. Vitellius, the supreme exponent of disgraceful adulation, albeit a scrupulous administrator in the provinces.[7] But even for the servile life could be difficult, as Tacitus gleefully observes: Tiberius feared freedom, but he hated flattery, and misconceived adulation might bring not only a rebuke but even exile.[8]

The sentimental republican views with sympathy the decline of the old republican nobility and the misfortunes, as he puts it, of illustrious houses.[9] Civil war and proscriptions had thinned the ranks of the nobles, and the principate put temptation in their path, since servility

---

[1] Tac. *Ann.* 4.19.
[2] Tac. *Ann.* 1.1–3. Cf. 1.8 on Augustus' legacies, the hostile necrology in 1.10, and the savage remark in 3.74 on the plurality of *imperatores* under the republic. On the dynasty, cf. 3.29, 4.3. His dislike of Augustus is also very apparent in 3.24. The dependence of the principate on military power underlies the account of the mutinies, with which the story of Tiberius' reign begins: cf. especially 1.28, 31, 38, and note also 6.30.
[3] Tac. *Ann.* 1.1f., 9f., 3.28.
[4] Tac. *Ann.* 1.1, 7, 46, 6.48.
[5] Cf. Tac. *Ann.* 1.1f., 4, 8, 3.35, 47, 69.
[6] Tac. *Ann.* 3.57.
[7] Tac. *Ann.* 6.32.
[8] Tac. *Ann.* 2.87, 3.65, 4.6, 17, 6.3.
[9] Tac. *Ann.* 3.24; cf. Münzer, *Klio* 1, 1902, 310ff.; Syme, *Tacitus*, 571ff.

might ensure high office and wealth or at least serve as some protection.[1]
For high birth could be dangerous, as Tacitus remarks more than once,
and he notes with feigned surprise that so distinguished a man as L.
Piso died a natural death.[2] Nevertheless he takes a grim pleasure in
chronicling the many occasions on which men of noble birth and other
prominent senators disgraced their station.[3] But whenever possible he
is eager to celebrate nobility and to find redeeming features.[4] Even
those who had dishonoured their ancestry in life, like Sempronius
Gracchus and the sinister Mam. Scaurus, might die in a manner worthy
of their names,[5] and Tacitus is willing to interpret ingratitude to the
princeps as a vestige of ancient nobility.[6] For parvenus, however
influential or innocuous they may be, Tacitus rarely has anything but
undisguised contempt.[7] Only occasionally do men of recent distinction
receive a measure of praise: such are Volusius Saturninus, Asinius
Agrippa, L. Lamia and Vibius Marsus.[8]

Tacitus is also on the alert for signs of the decline of society as a
whole. The rise of delation is symbolized by Romanius Hispo, the
archetypal informer.[9] Great orator himself, he always shows a lively
interest in the activities of the leading exponents of the art. [10] But a
skilful speaker might abuse his talents, like Scaurus, while under the
principate a new and unsavoury type of orator came to the fore, exem-
plified in Tiberius' reign by Fulcinius Trio and Domitius Afer.[11] It is
perhaps, however, the degradation and betrayal of friendship that
stand out above all else in Tacitus' narrative as a condemnation of
society, the senate and the principate.[12] After the fall of Seianus, when

[1] Tac. *Ann.* 1.1f., 3.65, 4.74; cf. 3.75 on the jurists Capito and Labeo.
[2] Tac. *Ann.* 3.55, 4.66, 14.47, and on Piso 6.10.
[3] As well as the examples of adulation cited above, cf. Tac. *Ann.* 1.8, 12f., 2.32,
3.17, 66, 5.3, 6.5, 7.
[4] Tac. *Ann.* 2.27, 3.22, 24, 32, 72, 75, 76, 4.21, 44, 75, 5.1, 6.27, 47.
[5] Tac. *Ann.* 1.53, 6.29.
[6] Tac. *Ann.* 2.37.
[7] Tac. *Ann.* 3.29, 48, 75, 4.3, 6.2, 15, 29; cf. Syme, *Tacitus*, 562f.
[8] Tac. *Ann.* 3.30, 4.61, 6.27, 47.
[9] Tac. *Ann.* 1.74.
[10] Cf. Tac. *Ann.* 3.24, 31, 34, 4.61.
[11] Tac. *Ann.* 6.29; 2.28, 4.52, 66.
[12] Tac. *Ann.* 2.27, 29, 3.11, 4.68.

friendship had become an excuse for prosecution, the speech of the *eques* M. Terentius is singled out as a defence of traditional values as well as an example of courage.[1] This theme too underlines the gulf between republic and principate, for now the withdrawal of the princeps' friendship could mean the end of a man's public career and even of his life.[2]

Talent too that might have flourished under the republic tended to be stifled by the principate. Tacitus observes the success of Poppaeus Sabinus, a man of modest origins who rose through the friendship of the Caesars because he had sufficient ability to be useful but not enough to be dangerous.[3] For true excellence there was no longer any scope, but Tacitus has no time for those who sought security in total inertia, like Haterius Agrippa.[4] Nor does ostentatious martyrdom win his approval; his highest praise is reserved for those who contrived to pursue the middle way between outright contumacy and gross obsequiousness and so achieved such greatness as was possible in the shadow of the princeps: M. Lepidus, L. Piso the *pontifex*, and Memmius Regulus.[5]

Despite his declaration of impartiality and his clear awareness of the bias of his sources,[6] his view of the principate as an institution made Tacitus inevitably hostile to Tiberius.[7] Tiberius constantly professed republican beliefs, yet during his reign the power of the monarchy was steadily consolidated, while the senate was reduced to new depths of degradation. Faced with this paradox, Tacitus could draw only one conclusion: Tiberius was a hypocrite. So the keynote of his character in Tacitus is dissimulation, alleged to be in his own eyes his greatest virtue, which did not desert him even on his deathbed.[8] The alternative possibility, that Tiberius' republicanism was sincere, but was fettered in its expression by his loyalty to Augustus' wishes, his fears for his

---

[1] Tac. *Ann.* 6.8, cf. 5.6.
[2] Tac. *Ann.* 3.24, 6.29.
[3] Tac. *Ann.* 6.39.
[4] Tac. *Ann.* 6.4.
[5] Tac. *Ann.* 4.20, cf. 6.34; 6.10; 14.47.
[6] Tac. *Ann.* 1.1, 4.11.
[7] Cf. Pippidi, *Tibère*, 73ff.; in general, Syme, *Tacitus*, 420ff.
[8] Tac. *Ann.* 1.4, 6, 7, 4.60, 71, 6.1, 45, 50.

own security, and the servile inclinations of the senate, was perhaps too painful for Tacitus to contemplate: if Tiberius' beliefs were genuine, his inability to realize them would be bitter proof of the futility of Tacitus' republican dream. Besides, Tacitus was utterly convinced that from the very origins of the principate any appearance of republicanism was a sham. This conviction, which applied to Augustus as much as to Tiberius, if not more, made it impossible for him ever to accept Tiberius' declarations at their face value.

Other traits recur: Tiberius is cruel,[1] vindictive,[2] arrogant,[3] suspicious,[4] ambiguous in speech,[5] hesitant in making decisions.[6] Apologists have been at pains to expose the techniques by which this image of the princeps is created and sustained and to claim that all the charges can be easily refuted.[7] But although it is indisputably true that Tacitus is unjust in his judgments on a number of occasions,[8] and that he is often inaccurate in presenting particular actions as examples of the characteristics listed above, the essential features of the portrait are correct. Tiberius could act with consummate hypocrisy, bore grudges and could be cruel to his enemies, was always suspicious, hated to be forced to make his meaning clear and was never eager to come to an irrevocable decision. If Tacitus' Tiberius is an oversimplified exaggeration, the Tiberius of the apologists is a ludicrous fiction.

Obsession with Tacitus' treatment of Tiberius' vices has prevented other aspects of the Tacitean picture from receiving the attention they deserve. Yet the historian records them clearly, doing greater justice to Tiberius' extremely complex nature than his critics will give him credit for. Tiberius is easily taken aback,[9] and despite his apparent unconcern for public opinion[10] and his reluctance to speak his mind, he is never-

[1] Tac. *Ann.* 1.4, 10, 74, 4.1.
[2] Tac. *Ann.* 1.12, 69.
[3] Tac. *Ann.* 1.4, 8, 10, 4.29.
[4] Tac. *Ann.* 1.13, 69, 4.67.
[5] Tac. *Ann.* 1.11, 3.51, 4.1, 30f., 5.3, 5, 13.3.
[6] Tac. *Ann.* 1.80, 2.65, 4.11, 57, 71, 6.46.
[7] Cf. especially the analysis of Pippidi, *Tibère*, 37ff., who is unfair to Tacitus in the matter of rumours.
[8] Notably at *Ann.* 1.13, 2.5, 30, 3.21.
[9] Tac. *Ann.* 1.12, 4.40.
[10] Cf. Tac. *Ann.* 6.38.

theless deeply upset when men judge him falsely,[1] and will sometimes go to great lengths to clarify his position.[2] Most striking of all is his extreme sensitivity, a sensitivity that could make him callously self-centred.[3]

The great flaw in Tacitus' presentation is his schematization of Tiberius' moral decline. The most elaborate passage of this kind serves as an obituary.[4] It divides Tiberius' life into five stages. Under Augustus his conduct and reputation were equally good, from 14 to 23 he was skilful in assuming the appearance of virtue, from 23 to 29 he was a mixture of good and bad, from 29 to 31 his cruelty was blatant but his lusts were still kept hidden, and finally, when his true nature was allowed complete freedom, his crimes and vices flourished with equal luxuriance. This crude and laborious attempt to invest the major events of Tiberius' reign with some psychological significance[5] deserves the contempt with which it has been treated; it is easy to point to its manifest inconsistencies.[6] But there is no justification for the common assumption that because the schema and the narrative are inconsistent, this provides a reason for rejecting both.

SUETONIUS

C. Suetonius Tranquillus, who may have come either from Pisaurum in Italy or Hippo Regius in Africa, was a protégé of Tacitus' friend the younger Pliny. He held three important imperial secretaryships: *a studiis, a bibliothecis* and *ab epistulis*. From the last of these he was dismissed by Hadrian in 121/2. His most important literary work, and the only one to survive almost complete, is his series of biographies of the first twelve Caesars.

[1] Note his loss of composure in such circumstances: Tac. *Ann.* 1.74, 4.42, 52, 6.13, 26.
[2] Note especially Tac. *Ann.* 6.38, which illuminates 6.24; a less extreme but equally futile attempt in 4.37.
[3] Tac. *Ann.* 1.12, 3.16, 4.40, 6.29.
[4] Tac. *Ann.* 6.51.
[5] Cf. Tac. *Ann.* 4.6f. on the death of Drusus and 5.3 on that of Livia.
[6] Contrast e.g. Tac. *Ann.* 4.7, which suggests that until 23 Tiberius' virtues were real, with the judgment on the same period in 6.51; cf. Pippidi, *Tibère*, 58ff., with some exaggeration.

The life of Tiberius falls roughly into three sections. The first of these covers his career under Augustus, and in it the arrangement of material is loosely chronological: family history, childhood, early career, retirement to Rhodes and finally the rise to power during the last decade of Augustus.[1] The second and largest segment of the work deals with Tiberius' principate and is subdivided in terms of virtues and vices.[2] The 'good years' are treated under the heading of moderation;[3] then, after an account of his withdrawal to Capreae,[4] Suetonius moves on with a melancholy relish to catalogue Tiberius' vices: lust, parsimony, avarice, cruelty to his relations and cruelty in general, and suspicion.[5] The short closing section comprises certain personal details – Tiberius' appearance, religious beliefs and education – and describes his death and the contents of his will.[6]

Insofar as they are treated at all, the major historical themes of Tiberius' reign are entirely subordinated to the moral schema. His relations with senate, magistrates and others, his judicial activities and his sumptuary, social and religious legislation are all brought, with more or less relevance, under the general rubric of moderation. All that Suetonius has to say about the vicissitudes of the dynasty is subsumed under Tiberius' hatred for his family. Public building and public expenditure come under the heading of parsimony, the law of *maiestas* appears under cruelty. Even the fall of Seianus is fitted in, being treated from the standpoint of Tiberius' suspicions and fears.

This arid, mechanical and tedious way of writing is in part explained by its origins. Biography as written by Suetonius is only a glorified epitaph. An epitaph recorded a man's filiation and listed his public offices and military successes; the oldest examples also catalogued his virtues, though later this would be the province of the funeral oration. All that Suetonius does is to clothe this traditional skeleton with a patchwork of dubious anecdotes and garbled examples. His Tiberius is never even a cardboard figure: under Augustus he is simply a name,

[1] Suet. *Tib.* 1–21.
[2] Cf. Suet. *Aug.* 9.9: *neque per tempora sed per species.*
[3] Suet. *Tib.* 26–36.
[4] Suet. *Tib.* 38–41.
[5] Suet. *Tib.* 42–67.
[6] Suet. *Tib.* 68–76.

while as princeps he is a label attached to a list of vices. No attempt is ever made to probe his motives or explain his actions. Indeed Suetonius is only once inspired to a rudimentary discussion, of Augustus' choice of Tiberius as his successor.[1]

In matters of chronology too Suetonius leaves everything to be desired. Even in the first, chronological section there are virtually no indications of date, while in the second chaos reigns: it is not even the case that all the examples cited to illustrate the moderation of the 'good years' actually come from that period. Nor is it only this chronological vacuum that diminishes the value of Suetonius' anecdotes. Their usefulness is further impaired by his habit of generalizing from unique instances, for instance the fates of Asinius Gallus and Junilla.[2]

Nevertheless Suetonius displays occasional traces of common sense, as when he follows the public records in the matter of the date and place of Tiberius' birth.[3] But his most valuable service to the historian is probably his preservation of a number of precious fragments of letters from Augustus to Tiberius, Augustus' will, and Tiberius' own letters and speeches.[4]

DIO

Cassius Dio Cocceianus, from Nicaea in Bithynia, was the son of Cassius Apronianus, who governed Cilicia and Dalmatia. He was suffect consul about 205 and held office for a second time in 229 as colleague of Alexander Severus.

Dio's own narrative is extant only for the opening and closing years of Tiberius' principate. From 17 to summer 31 we have only a series of fragments preserved by Xiphilinus and other excerptors: scraps for the years 17 to 19, longer pieces from 20 to 25, tiny fragments for 26 to 28, and then again portions of increasing size for 29 to 31. The text proper resumes in the summer of the latter year.[5]

The first major section of Dio's account deals with Tiberius' accept-

[1] Suet. *Tib.* 21.
[2] Suet. *Tib.* 61, cf. also 32.1.
[3] Suet. *Tib.* 5.
[4] Suet. *Tib.* 21.4ff., 23, 24.2, 61, 65.1, 67.
[5] At Dio 58.7.2.

ance of the principate, which according to him did not take place till after the suppression of the mutinies.[1] Then follows a description of the nature of Tiberius' rule in its initial phase, which for Dio lasted until the death of Germanicus.[2] Chronology receives little attention in these chapters, the overall structure and content of which are very reminiscent of Suetonius on Tiberius' moderation. Then comes a chronological record of what seemed to Dio the most important events of the reign; this continues until the text breaks off.[3] It is sketchy and full of trivialities, but significantly pays no attention at all to the German wars, to which Tacitus, yearning for glorious conquests to describe, devotes inordinate space. The portion which covers the years 31 to 37 has the same annalistic structure, but in content it resembles Tacitus much more closely. A few incidents not in Tacitus are mentioned, and there are several chronological blunders.

Dio begins with a character-sketch.[4] For him, as for Tacitus, the key to Tiberius' personality is dissimulation, but he couches the point more crudely than Tacitus in a rigid schema of rhetorical antitheses. Yet he shows some understanding of the difficulties that faced those who actually had to deal with Tiberius. It was dangerous, he says, to act in accordance with his words rather than with his real wishes, but even more dangerous to show that one had pierced his ambiguity, since he resented successful penetration of his thoughts. The safest thing was to fathom his intentions but not to advertise the fact. This analysis does not do justice to the complexities of Tiberius' character, but as a statement of the practical problem that perplexed his contemporaries it has much to commend it.

Dio exploits his conception of Tiberius' hypocrisy to explain various matters in the early part of the reign: his hesitation in accepting power at all, his distrust of Germanicus and his treatment of Libo Drusus.[5] He seems to have posited only one major change in Tiberius. This followed the death of Germanicus, and Dio canvasses two possible reasons: as long as he had a potential rival, Tiberius either deliberately

[1] Dio 57.2–7.
[2] Dio 57.7–13.
[3] Dio 57.14–17.
[4] Dio 57.1.
[5] Dio 57.2, 6, 15.4f.

clung to virtue or at least cherished the appearance of it, but with Germanicus dead he was free either to let himself go or to put off pretence, as the case might be.[1]

For the period after Germanicus' death what few indications survive suggest that Dio's Tiberius followed the by then standard pattern: avaricious, a prey to suspicion and fear, and immersed in cruelty and monstrous lusts.[2] Dio's final verdict is that Tiberius was a man with very many virtues and very many vices, and that first the good in his character predominated to the total exclusion of the bad, and then the bad as if the good had never existed.[3] This confirms that for him Germanicus' death was the one major turning-point in Tiberius' life. What responsibility, if any, he assigned to Seianus unfortunately cannot be determined.

VELLEIUS PATERCULUS

The one contemporary historian of Tiberius whose work survives, Velleius Paterculus (his *praenomen* too is unknown), is perhaps more interesting as a man than as a writer. His grandfather, C. Velleius, was a distinguished *eques*, who occupied the important post of *praefectus fabrum* under Pompey, M. Brutus and Tiberius' father, Ti. Claudius Nero.[4] Velleius understandably emphasizes his friendship with Nero. His father too followed an equestrian military career and served as *praefectus equitum* in Germany first under M. Vinicius, consul in 19 B.C., to whose grandson Velleius dedicated his work, then under Tiberius himself.[5]

Velleius maintained the connection with the Vinicii, serving as military tribune in Thrace and Macedonia under Marcus' son Publius, consul in A.D. 2, before accompanying Gaius Caesar on his eastern mission.[6] In A.D. 4 he succeeded his father as *praefectus equitum* under Tiberius, with whom he served until 12.[7] His senatorial career began

[1] Dio 57.13.6; for a less elaborate version of this opinion, cf. Suet. *Cal.* 6.2.
[2] Dio 58.16.1, 18, 22.
[3] Dio 58.28.5.
[4] Vell. 2.76.1; on the family in general, cf. Sumner, *HSCP* 74, 1970, 257ff.
[5] Vell. 2.104.3; cf. Sumner, *HSCP* 74, 1970, 265, and 288ff. on Vinicius.
[6] Vell. 2.101.
[7] Vell. 2.104.3.

in 6, when he was elected, no doubt with Tiberius' backing, as quaestor for the following year. But although he returned to Rome to take up office, he was immediately sent back to the Pannonian war with a special commission as a legate of Augustus.[1] Meanwhile his brother, Magius Celer Velleianus, won praise and decorations in Dalmatia.[2] Both men took part in Tiberius' triumph in 12,[3] and both attained the praetorship for 15, enjoying the posthumous commendation of Augustus reinforced by that of his successor.[4]

Velleius himself was to rise no higher, but both his sons eventually reached the consulship, Gaius in 60 and Lucius in 61.[5] The Velleii provide an excellent example of a family of modest origins advancing through equestrian military posts to senatorial rank and ultimately to the highest office. They enjoyed the favour of the imperial house, but earned it by loyal and competent service.

In 30 Velleius published a very brief historical work in two books, inscribed to M. Vinicius, consul in that year. Much of the earlier part is lost, but the chapters dealing with Augustus and Tiberius survive. For men like himself the principate afforded opportunities for honourable advancement far greater than any that had existed under the more rigid social structure of the republic; it is therefore hardly surprising that Velleius' enthusiasm for the régime is unbounded. Not only does he welcome the peace and stability that followed Augustus' victory; for him the restoration of the republic is a reality, not a cover for despotism.[6]

By concentrating on Augustus' foreign wars, especially those on the northern frontiers, he is able to devote more than half the space nominally allotted to Augustus to a narrative of Tiberius' early career. His account is a curious mixture of just appreciation and naïve exaggeration. Thus the importance of Tiberius' mission to Armenia is much overstated, but the Rhaetian and Vindelician campaigns are fairly treated, while the conquest of Pannonia is only mildly inflated.[7] The

[1] Vell. 2.111.2f.
[2] Vell. 2.115.1.
[3] Vell. 2.121.4.
[4] Vell. 2.124.
[5] Cf. Sumner, *HSCP* 74, 1970, 297.
[6] Vell. 2.89.
[7] Vell. 2.94–96.

grossest exaggeration is the claim that after the death of Drusus Tiberius reduced Germany almost to a tributary province.[1] But it must be remembered that this was Augustus' own opinion, on which his disastrous German policy was based. In his summary of Tiberius' position immediately before his retirement to Rhodes Velleius says no more than the truth.[2] Similarly his version of Tiberius' adoption, though full of flourishes, is based on the unquestionable fact that Augustus had to choose the one outstanding man available. Nor is there any reason to dispute his assertion that men rejoiced to see the continuity of the principate assured.[3] The enthusiasm of the troops when Tiberius returned to the Rhine is also entirely credible: Tiberius was known for his concern for the welfare of the army and his avoidance of unnecessary casualties,[4] and men whose lives might depend on a Lollius or a Varus had every reason to welcome the unexpected resurgence of a general they knew they could trust.[5] Velleius' considerable respect for Maroboduus echoes Tiberius' own judgment, and Tiberius' opinion is revealed again in the story of the Pannonian revolt, when Velleius comes close to stating bluntly that Augustus panicked and burdened Tiberius with far more troops than he needed.[6] The last campaigns in Germany, after the *clades Variana*, are treated soberly enough; the high-sounding phrase with which Velleius introduces them is no more than a rhetorical version of the truth.[7]

In all these chapters there are perhaps only two major instances of dishonesty: the claim that Tiberius' army was the first Roman force to reach the Elbe, and the attempt to suppress the link between the liquidation of Agrippa Postumus and Tiberius' accession.[8] In his praise and blame of individuals too there is little for which Velleius need be taken to task. He is very hostile to M. Lollius, Tiberius' enemy – but

[1] Vell. 2.97.4, cf. similarly 2.105ff. later.
[2] Vell. 2.99.
[3] Vell. 2.103.3; cf. Sumner, *HSCP* 74, 1970, 268f.
[4] Vell. 2.107.3, 114.
[5] Vell. 2.104.4f.; cf. Sumner, *HSCP* 74, 1970, 269f.
[6] Vell. 2.108, 113.2; cf. Sumner, *HSCP* 74, 1970, 272.
[7] Vell. 2.121.
[8] Vell. 2.106.2, 112.7.

Lollius was egregiously incompetent and almost certainly corrupt.[1] To Gaius Caesar on the other hand he is fair.[2] His criticisms of Caecina and Plautius Silvanus are just, as is his bitter attack on Varus, though the latter is blatantly inconsistent with his earlier claim that Tiberius had virtually pacified Germany.[3] The other commanders who win his approval were in the main friends and supporters of Tiberius, but there is no ground for supposing that they did not deserve his commendation.[4] He can hardly be blamed for lavishing praise on such men as L. Piso and M. Lepidus, who satisfied even the exigent Tacitus.[5]

The account of Tiberius' principate is paradoxically far more sketchy. Velleius' paean of praise naïvely repeats the points he has already made in favour of Augustus: why Tiberius should have had to do exactly the same things is not explained.[6] The successes of the reign are briefly listed, in a manner that stresses Tiberius' virtue and talents, and its outstanding villains castigated for their ingratitude.[7] The most interesting chapters are those in which Velleius defends Tiberius' reliance on Seianus, citing precedents where merit had compensated for the drawback of humble birth.[8] Despite his claim that the senate and people approved of Tiberius' choice, he is plainly on the defensive. Indeed his favourable picture of Tiberius' life as a whole takes on a deeper political significance when it is remembered that he was writing at a time when the unpopularity of Tiberius and Seianus, which had been increasing ever since the death of Drusus, had reached its height.[9]

---

[1] Vell. 2.97.1.
[2] Vell. 2.101f.
[3] Vell. 2.112.4ff., 117.
[4] Cf. Vell. 2.112, 116.
[5] Vell. 2.98.1, 115.2.
[6] Vell. 2.126, cf. 89.
[7] Vell. 2.129f.
[8] Vell. 2.127f.
[9] Cf. Sumner, *HSCP* 74, 1970, 270.

MAPS

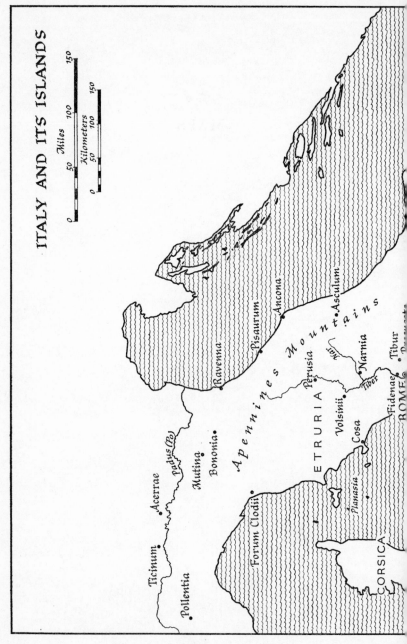

ITALY AND ITS ISLANDS

Miles

0   50   100   150

Kilometers

0   50   100   150

Ticinum
Acerrae
Padus (Po)
Mutina
Bononia
Ravenna
Pisaurium
Ancona
Apennines Mountains
Asculum
Pollentia
Forum Clodii
Planasia
Volsinii
Perusia
ETRURIA
Cosa
Fidenae
Nar
Tiber
Narnia
Tibur
ROME
Praeneste
CORSICA

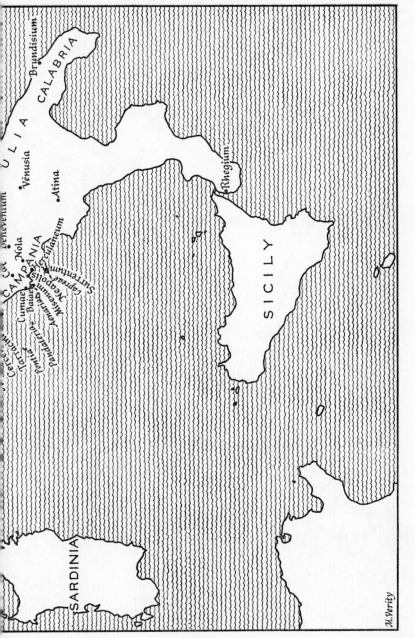

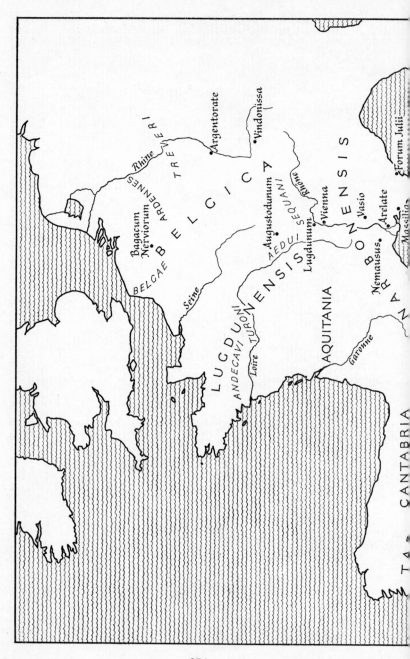

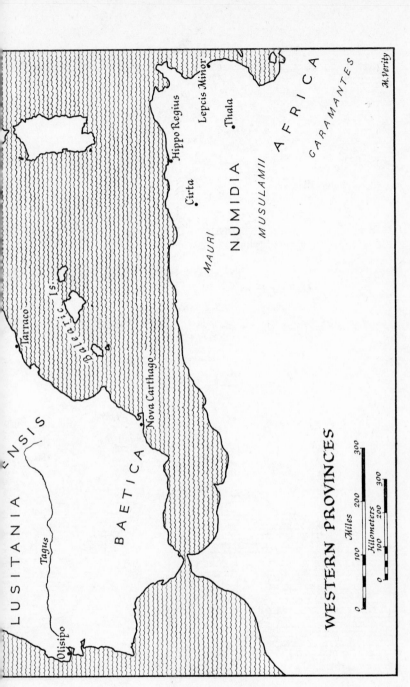

WESTERN PROVINCES

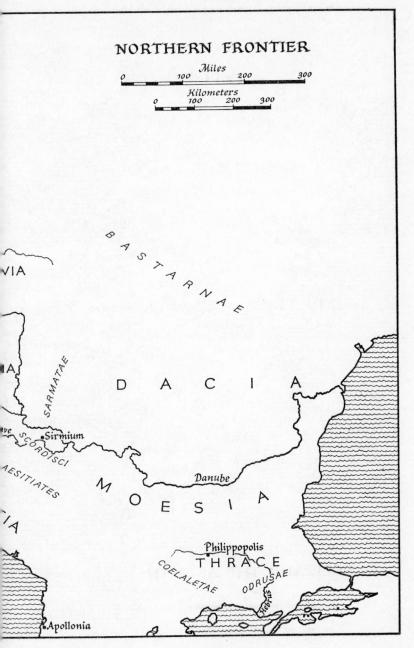

NORTHERN FRONTIER

Miles

0   100   200   300

Kilometers

0   100   200   300

BASTARNAE

VIA

SARMATAE

DACIA

SCORDISCI

•Sirmium

AESITIATES

Danube

MOESIA

Philippopolis

•
THRACE

COELALETAE

ODRUSAE

Hebrus

•Apollonia

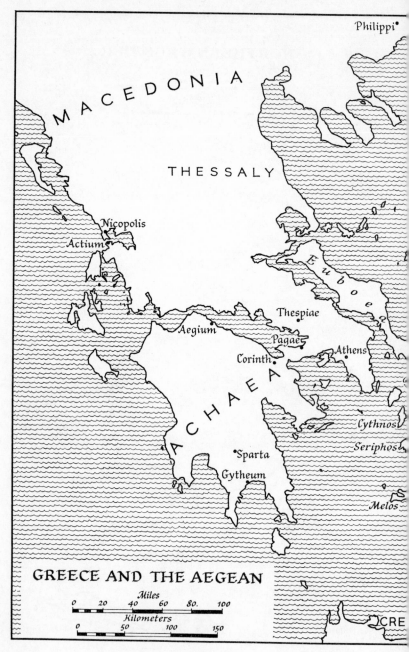

Philippi

MACEDONIA

THESSALY

Nicopolis
Actium

E u b o e a

Thespiae
Aegium
Pagae
Corinth
Athens

A C H A E A

Cythnos

Seriphos

Sparta
Gytheum

Melos

GREECE AND THE AEGEAN

Miles
0   20   40   60   80.   100

Kilometers
0   50   100   150

CRE

Samothrace

Nicaea

Cyzicus

Lampsacus

Troy

Lesbos

Pergamum

Mytilene

Thyatira

A S I A

Sardis

Chios

Smyrna

Colophon

Nysa

Ephesus

Tralles

Cibyra

Donusa

Amorgos

Cos

gandros

Thera

Rhodes

Lindos

M.Verity

279

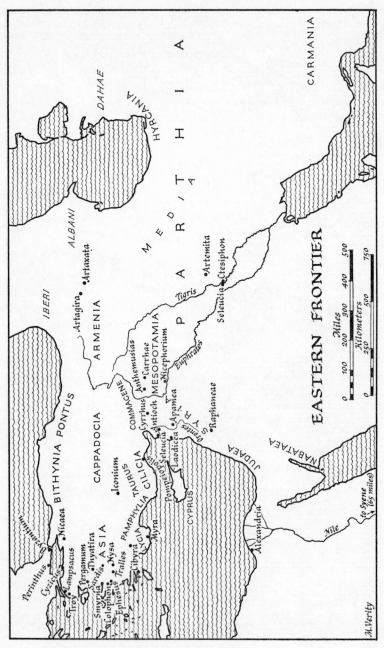

EASTERN FRONTIER

Miles
0 100 200 300 400 500

Kilometers
0   250   500   750

A. Verity

BIBLIOGRAPHY

AALDERS, G. J. D., Germanicus und Alexander der Grosse, *Historia* 10, 1961, 382–384.

ADAMS, F., The consular brothers of Sejanus, *AJP* 76, 1955, 70–76.

ALFÖLDY, G., La politique provinciale de Tibère, *Latomus* 24, 1965, 824–844.

ALLEN, W., The political atmosphere of the reign of Tiberius, *TAPA* 72, 1941, 1–25.

— The death of Agrippa Postumus, *TAPA* 78, 1947, 131–139.

ALLISON, J. E. and CLOUD, J. D., The Lex Julia maiestatis, *Latomus* 21, 1962, 711–731.

ASTIN, A. E., 'Nominare' in accounts of elections in the early principate, *Latomus* 28, 1969, 863–874.

BALSDON, J. P. V. D., The 'murder' of Drusus, son of Tiberius, *CR* 65, 1951, 75.

BAUMAN, R. A., *The crimen maiestatis in the Roman republic and Augustan principate*, Johannesburg, 1967.

— Tiberius and Murena, *Historia* 15, 1966, 420–431.

BÉRANGER, J., *Recherches sur l'aspect idéologique du principat*, Basel, 1953.

BICKEL, E., Das Denkmal der Varusschlacht in Bonn, *RhM* N.F. 95, 1952, 97–135.

BIRD, H. E., L. Aelius Seianus and his political significance, *Latomus* 28, 1969, 61–98.

BISHOP, J. D., Dating in Tacitus by moonless nights, *CP* 55, 1960, 164–170.

BODDINGTON, A., Sejanus. Whose conspiracy? *AJP* 84, 1963, 1–16.

BORZSÁK, S., Das Germanicusbild des Tacitus, *Latomus* 28, 1969, 558–600.

BRUNT, P. A., The lex Valeria Cornelia, *JRS* 51, 1961, 71–83.

— Charges of provincial maladministration under the early principate, *Historia* 10, 1961, 189–227.

CHARLESWORTH, M. P., The banishment of the elder Agrippina, *CP* 17, 1922, 260–261.

— Tiberius and the death of Augustus, *AJP* 44, 1923, 145–157.

— Livia and Tanaquil, *CR* 41, 1927, 55–57.

— The refusal of divine honours, an Augustan formula, *BSR* 15, 1939, 1–10.

CHILTON, C. W., The Roman law of treason under the early principate, *JRS* 45, 1955, 73–81.

CHRIST, K., Zum römischen Okkupation der Zentralalpen, *Historia* 6, 1957, 416–428.

CICHORIUS, C., *Römische Studien*, Berlin/Leipzig, 1922.

— Zur Familiengeschichte Seians, *Hermes* 39, 1904, 461–471.

DAITZ, S. G., Tacitus' technique of character portrayal, *AJP* 81, 1960, 30–52.

DEGRASSI, A., *I fasti consolari dell' impero Romano*, Roma, 1952.

DETWEILER, R., Historical perspectives on the death of Agrippa Postumus, *CJ* 65, 1970, 289–295.

DIECKMANN, H., Die effektive Mitregentschaft des Tiberius, *Klio* 15, 1917/18, 339–375.

DOBIÁŠ, J., King Maroboduus as a politician, *Klio* 38, 1960, 155–166.

DUPRAZ, L., Autour de l'association de Tibère au principat, *MH* 20, 1963, 172–185.

DURRY, M., *Les cohortes prétoriennes*, Paris, 1938.

EISENHUT, W., Der Tod des Tiberius-Sohnes Drusus, *MH* 7, 1950, 123–128.

FABIA, P., L'avènement officiel de Tibère, *Rev. Phil.* n.s. 33, 1909, 28–58.

FERRERO, L., La voce pubblica nel proemio degli Annali di Tacito, *Riv. Fil.* 74, 1946, 50–86.

FRANK, T., The financial crisis of 33 A.D., *AJP* 56, 1935, 336–341.

FREI-STOLBA, R., *Untersuchungen zu den Wahlen in der römischen Kaiserzeit*, Zürich, 1967.

FURNEAUX, H., *The Annals of Tacitus*, volume I: books I–VI², Oxford, 1896.

GAGÉ, J., La victoria Augusti et les auspices de Tibère, *Rev. Arch.* 32, 1930, 1–35.

GEIGER, J., M. Hortensius M. f. Q. n. Hortalus, *CR* 84, 1970, 132–134.

GELZER, M., *The Roman nobility*, Oxford, 1969.

GRANT, M., *Aspects of the principate of Tiberius*, New York, 1950.

GRENIER, A., Tibère et la Gaule, *REL* 14, 1936, 373–388.

GROAG, E., Studien zur Kaisergeschichte III: der Sturz der Iulia, *WS* 40, 1918, 150–167; 41, 1919, 74–88.

HARRER, G. A., Tacitus and Tiberius, *AJP* 41, 1920, 57–68.

HEIDEL, W. A., Why were the Jews banished from Italy in 19 A.D.?, *AJP* 41, 1920, 38–47.

HENDERSON, M. I., The establishment of the *equester ordo*, *JRS* 53, 1963, 61–72.

HOHL, E., Wann hat Tiberius das Prinzipat übernommen?, *Hermes* 68, 1933, 106–115.

— Primum facinus novi principatus, *Hermes* 70, 1935, 350–355.

— Zu den Testamenten des Augustus, *Klio* 30, 1937, 323–342.

INSTINSKY, H. U., Augustus und die Adoption des Tiberius, *Hermes* 94, 1966, 324–343.

JEROME, T. S., The Tacitean Tiberius, a study in historiographic method, *CP* 7, 1912, 265–292.

KAMPFF, G., Three senate meetings in the early principate, *Phoenix* 17, 1963, 25–58.

KIERDORF, W., Die Einleitung des Piso-Prozesses (Tac. ann. 3, 10), *Hermes* 97, 1969, 246–251.

KLINGNER, F., Tacitus über Augustus und Tiberius, Interpretationen zum Eingang der Annalen, *SB Bay. Akad. d. Wiss.*, Phil.-hist. Kl., 1953 Heft 7.

KOESTERMANN, E., *Cornelius Tacitus, Annalen*, Band I, Buch 1–3, Heidelberg, 1963; Band II, Buch 4–6, Heidelberg, 1965.

— Der pannonisch-dalmatinische Krieg 6–9 n. Chr., *Hermes* 81, 1953, 345–378.

— Die Majestätsprozesse unter Tiberius, *Historia* 4, 1955, 72–106.

— Der Sturz Seians, *Hermes* 83, 1955, 350–373.

— Die Feldzüge des Germanicus 14–16 n. Chr., *Historia* 6, 1957, 429–479.

— Die Mission des Germanicus im Orient, *Historia* 7, 1958, 331–375.

— Der Eingang der Annalen des Tacitus, *Historia* 10, 1961, 330–355.

KORNEMANN, E., *Tiberius*, Stuttgart, 1960.

— Der Prinzipat des Tiberius und der 'Genius Senatus', *SB Bay. Akad. d. Wiss.*, Phil.-hist. Kl., 1947 Heft 1.

LACEY, W. K., Nominatio and the elections under Tiberius, *Historia* 12, 1963, 167–176.

LEVICK, B. M., Drusus Caesar and the adoptions of A.D. 4, *Latomus* 25, 1966, 227–244.

— Imperial control of the elections under the early principate: commendatio, suffragatio and 'nominatio', *Historia* 16, 1967, 207–230.

LIEBENAM, W., Bemerkungen zur Tradition über Germanicus, *Fleckeisens Jahrbücher* 143, 1891, 717–736, 793–816, 865–888.

LIECHTENHAN, E., Das Ziel des Aufstandes der Rheinarmee, *MH* 4, 1947, 52–67.

MAGIE, D., *Roman rule in Asia Minor*, Princeton, 1950.

MARSH, F. B., *The reign of Tiberius*, Oxford, 1931.

— Tacitus and aristocratic tradition, *CP* 21, 1926, 289–310.

MEISE, E., *Untersuchungen zur Geschichte der Julisch–Claudischen Dynastie*, München, 1969.

MEISTER, K., Der Bericht des Tacitus über die Landung des Germanicus in der Emsmündung, *Hermes* 83, 1955, 92–106.

MERRILL, E. T., The expulsion of Jews from Rome under Tiberius, *CP* 14, 1919, 365–372.

MILTNER, F., Der Tacitusbericht über Idistaviso, *RhM* N.F. 59, 1952, 343–356.

MITFORD, T. B., A Cypriot oath of allegiance to Tiberius, *JRS* 50, 1960, 75–79.

MOGENET, J., La conjuration de Clemens, *AC* 23, 1954, 321–330.

MÜNZER, F., Die Entstehung der Historien des Tacitus, *Klio* 1, 1902, 300–330.

— Die Todesstrafe politischer Verbrecher in der späteren römischen Republik, *Hermes* 47, 1912, 161–182.

PAPPANO, A. E., Agrippa Postumus, *CP* 36, 1941, 30–45.

PARKER, H. M. D., *The Roman legions*, Oxford, 1928.

PIPPIDI, D. M., *Autour de Tibère*, Bucarest, 1944.

POLACCO, L., *Il volto di Tiberio*, Roma, 1955.

PREMERSTEIN, A. VON, Vom Werden und Wesen des Prinzipats, *Abh. Bay. Akad. d. Wiss.*, Phil.-hist. Abt., N.F. 15, 1937.

QUESTA, C., La morte di Augusto secondo Cassio Dione, *PdP* 14, 1959, 41–53.

ROGERS, R. S., *Criminal trials and criminal legislation under Tiberius*, Middletown, 1935.

— *Studies in the reign of Tiberius*, Baltimore, 1943.

— Lucius Arruntius, *CP* 26, 1931, 31–45.

— The date of the banishment of the astrologers, *CP* 26, 1931, 203–204.

— The conspiracy of Agrippina, *TAPA* 62, 1931, 141–168.

— Two criminal cases tried before Drusus Caesar, *CP* 27, 1932, 75–79.

— Der Prozess des Cotta Messallinus, *Hermes* 68, 1933, 121–123.

— Ignorance of the law in Tacitus and Dio: two instances from the history of Tiberius, *TAPA* 64, 1933, 18–27.

— Tiberius' reversal of an Augustan policy, *TAPA* 71, 1940, 532–536.

— Drusus Caesar's tribunician power, *AJP* 61, 1940, 457–459.

— A Tacitean pattern in narrating treason-trials, *TAPA* 83, 1952, 279–311.

— Treason in the early empire, *JRS* 49, 1959, 90–94.

ROSTOVTZEFF, M., L'empereur Tibère et le culte impérial, *Rev. Hist.* 163, 1930, 1–26.

ŠAŠEL, J., Drusus Ti. f. in Emona, *Historia* 19, 1970, 122–124.

SATTLER, P., *Studien aus dem Gebiet der alten Geschichte*, Wiesbaden, 1962.

SCHMITT, H. H., Der pannonische Aufstand des Jahres 14 n.Chr. und der Regierungsantritt des Tiberius, *Historia* 7, 1958, 378–383.

SCHMITTHENNER, W. (ed.), *Augustus*, Darmstadt, 1969.

SCOTT, K., Drusus, nicknamed 'Castor', *CP* 25, 1930, 155–161.

— Tiberius' refusal of the title 'Augustus', *CP* 27, 1932, 43–50.

— The *diritas* of Tiberius, *AJP* 53, 1932, 139–151.

— Ein Ausspruch des Tiberius an Galba, *Hermes* 67, 1932, 471–473.

SEALEY, R., The political attachments of L. Aelius Seianus, *Phoenix* 15, 1961, 97–114.

SEIBERT, J., Der Huldigungseid auf Kaiser Tiberius, *Historia* 19, 1970, 224–231.

SHOTTER, D. C. A., Elections under Tiberius, *CQ* 60, 1966, 321–332.

— Tiberius' part in the trial of Aemilia Lepida, *Historia* 15, 1966, 312–317.

— Tiberius and the spirit of Augustus, *GR*³ 13, 1966, 207–212.

— The trial of Gaius Silius (A.D. 24), *Latomus* 26, 1967, 712–716.

— Three notes on Tacitus *Annales* 1 and 2, *CP* 62, 1967, 116–118.

— Tacitus, Tiberius and Germanicus, *Historia* 17, 1968, 194–214.

— The case of Pomponius Labeo, *Latomus* 28, 1969, 654–656.

SMALLWOOD, E. M., Some notes on the Jews under Tiberius, *Latomus* 15, 1956, 314–329.

SPENGEL, A., Zur Geschichte des Kaisers Tiberius, *SB Bay. Akad. d. Wiss.*, Philos.-philol.-hist. Kl., 1903 Heft 1, 3–63.

STEIN, A., Drusus Castor, *Hermes* 53, 1918, 217–220.

STEWART, Z., Sejanus, Gaetulicus and Seneca, *AJP* 74, 1953, 70–85.

SUMNER, G. V., The family connections of L. Aelius Seianus, *Phoenix* 19, 1965, 134–145.

— Germanicus and Drusus Caesar, *Latomus* 26, 1967, 413–435.

— The truth about Velleius Paterculus: prolegomena, *HSCP* 74, 1970, 257–297.

SUTHERLAND, C. H. V., *Coinage in Roman imperial policy 31 B.C.–A.D. 68*, London, 1951.

— Two 'virtues' of Tiberius: a numismatic contribution to the history of his reign, *JRS* 28, 1938, 129–140.

SYME, R., *The Roman revolution*, Oxford, 1939.

— *Tacitus*, Oxford, 1958.

— *Ten studies in Tacitus*, Oxford, 1970.

— Seianus on the Aventine, *Hermes* 84, 1956/7, 257–266.

TAYLOR, L. R., *The divinity of the Roman emperor*, Middletown, 1931.

— Tiberius' refusals of divine honours, *TAPA* 60, 1929, 87–101.

— Tiberius' *ovatio* and the *ara numinis Augusti*, *AJP* 58, 1937, 185–193.

THIEL, J. H., Kaiser Tiberius (ein Beitrag zum Verständnis seiner Persönlichkeit), *Mnemosyne*[3] 2, 1935, 245–270; 3, 1935/6, 177–218; 4, 1936/7, 17–42.

TIBILETTI, G., *Principe e magistrati repubblicani*, Roma, 1953.

TIMPE, D., *Untersuchungen zur Kontinuität des frühen Prinzipats*, Wiesbaden, 1962.

— *Der Triumph des Germanicus*, Bonn, 1968.

TOWNEND, G. B., The trial of Aemilia Lepida in A.D. 20, *Latomus* 21, 1962, 484–493.

VILLERS, R., La dévolution du principat dans la famille d'Auguste, *REL* 28, 1950, 235–251.

WALSER, G., *Rom, das Reich und die fremden Völker in der Geschichtsschreibung der frühen Kaiserzeit*, Baden-Baden, 1951.

WELLER, J. A., Tacitus and Tiberius' Rhodian exile, *Phoenix* 12, 1958, 31–35.

WELLESLEY, K., The dies imperii of Tiberius, *JRS* 57, 1967, 23–30.

WILCKEN, U., Zum Germanicus-Papyrus, *Hermes* 63, 1928, 48–65.

WISEMAN, T. P., Pulcher Claudius, *HSCP* 74, 1970, 207–221.

YAVETZ, Z., *Plebs and princeps*, Oxford, 1969.

INDEX

Abdagaeses: 241ff.
Abdus: 240
Abudius Ruso: 236f.
Acerrae: 33
Acerronia: 127
Cn. Acerronius Proculus, cos. 37: 127
Achaea: 165, 172ff., 222
Acilius Aviola: 166
Actium: 11, 17, 19, 99
Acutia: 238
Adgandestrius: 95
Aedui: 165ff.
Aegium: 173
Sex. Aelius Catus, cos. 4: 179
Aelius Gallus: 222
L. Aelius Lamia, cos. 3: 43, 169, 229, 235, 259
L. Aelius Seianus, cos. 31: 58, 60, 73, 80, 119, 127ff., 131, 147f., 168, 178ff., 187ff., 193ff., 206ff., 227, 229f., 232ff., 236f., 239, 249f., 259, 263, 266, 269
Aelius Strabo: 218, 222
Q. Aelius Tubero, cos. 11 B.C.: 179
Aemilia Lepida, wife of Drusus son of Germanicus: 213, 238
Aemilia Lepida, wife of Mam. Scaurus: 155ff.
Aemilia Musa: 136
Aemilius: 199f.
M. Aemilius Lepidus, cos. 46 B.C.: 8

M. Aemilius Lepidus, cos. 6: 42f., 114, 131f., 136, 159, 179, 190, 226, 238, 247, 260, 269
M'. Aemilius Lepidus, cos. 11: 131, 156
Aemilius Rectus: 170f., 173
Mam. Aemilius Scaurus, cos. 21: 53, 55, 120, 128, 157, 159, 228, 236, 240, 259
Aenaria: 206
Africa: 46, 112, 131, 133, 145, 163, 167ff., 179, 191, 238
Agrippa Postumus: 37, 46, 48ff., 93, 176, 268
Agrippina, wife of Germanicus: 36, 46, 65, 68f., 80, 93, 99f., 102, 104, 106ff., 117, 120f., 130, 145, 176, 180, 182f., 187ff., 196ff., 204, 206ff., 223, 233f.
Agrippina, daughter of Germanicus: 127, 208
Albani: 241
Q. Albinovanus Pedo: 77
Albucilla: 238f.
Alexander Severus: 264
Alexandria: 103f., 164
Aliso: 83
Almus, Mons: 41
Ammochostus: 145f.
Amorgos: 171, 193
Ancharius Priscus: 157
Ancona: 112